PRACTICAL
MOVIEMAKING

PRACTICAL MOVIEMAKING

A Handbook for the Real World

Joe Wallenstein

FOREWORD BY DAVID JACOBS

McFarland & Company, Inc., Publishers

Jefferson, North Carolina, and London

LIBRARY OF CONGRESS CATALOGUING-IN-PUBLICATION DATA

Wallenstein, Joseph B.
    Practical moviemaking : a handbook for the real world /
Joe Wallenstein ; foreword by David Jacobs.
        p.   cm.
    Includes index.

    ISBN 978-0-7864-6675-7
    softcover : 50# alkaline paper ∞

    1. Motion pictures — Production and direction — Handbooks,
manuals, etc.   I. Title.
    PN1995.9.P7W3445 2012
    791.4302'32 — dc23   2011036829

BRITISH LIBRARY CATALOGUING DATA ARE AVAILABLE

Front cover images © 2012 Shutterstock

Manufactured in the United States of America

McFarland & Company, Inc., Publishers
    Box 611, Jefferson, North Carolina 28640
        www.mcfarlandpub.com

To my wife Peggy, our daughter Jennifer and our son Matt
who support me and lift my spirits, and for their unconditional love.

To Denis McCallion and Rick Marcelli
who insisted I do this book.

To Reed who refused to let me not do this book.

To my sister Sue and my brother-in-law Stan
for their constant encouragement and emotional support.

To my neice Robin and nephew Chris
for their love and friendship

To Carla and Jon Sanger for a long friendship
and even longer nights discussing film and filmmaking.

To Michael Filerman, an outstanding executive producer,
man of his word and a good friend.

And the late Eddie Denault who in one word
transformed me into a primetime producer.

Table of Contents

Foreword: Practical Magic

by David Jacobs

In the mid–1980s I wrote a three-hour television movie called: *Dallas: The Early Years*, a prequel to the television series *Dallas*, which I'd created some years earlier and which was still going strong. It was a big movie. Set in Texas, it was not merely a period piece; it was a *two*-period piece—1952 intercut with the Depression 30s. It had two huge Texas barbecues (one in each period) with hordes of guests. It had ranches, cowboys, horses, cattle, old cars and trucks, trains on the move, gambling, saloons and two or three brawls. It had the Klu Klux Klan. But mainly it had oil. It had an oil well gushing black oil into the sky and raining down on a field filled with wild-catters, local workers, sharecroppers, lawmen, and their vehicles and equipment. It had oil boom towns built on unpaved streets made of the glue-like mud found only in Texas. And it had a huge oil field fire, a conflagration burning down wells as far as the eye could see.

Based on my script, the studio estimated that the film would cost $6.5 million. This in a day when a million dollars was, well, a million dollars. This was also a day when the most the network would pay for a three-hour movie was $4.5 million. So the word came down that I had to rewrite the script to get a mere $2 million out. Almost one third!

Enter Joe Wallenstein, who said, in effect, "Not so fast. Don't rewrite just yet."

Joe and I had worked together often since we came out to Hollywood from New York in 1976. We meet on our first jobs. He taught me all he knew about production. Well, that's not really true: What he taught me was to trust him to give me the right advice to get as much of the budget on the screen as possible without hurting the script.

It happens that I figured out how he did it right at the start. *Magic!* He waved certain wands, said certain words, and before I knew it we were coming in on-time and on-budget, with the script shot and the production values better than I dreamed possible.

The upshot of this story is that Joe Wallenstein, aboard as producer, went to work on *Dallas: The Early Years* and came up with a budget of $4.5 million without requiring substantial rewrites.

The budget was not widely believed. My co-executive producer, Malcolm Stuart, a veteran filmmaker with 25 years of production experience, complimented Joe on the budget; even he was unable to identify how Joe aligned the numbers so they worked.

The studio production office watched us like a hawk.

I, however, had confidence; I knew how Joe was going to accomplish this. *Magic!*

And the *magic* worked: We shot the movie for $4.5 million without a rewrite. It was terrific.

Now, 25 years later, I've found out it *wasn't magic*. It was Joe Wallenstein's savvy — his thorough knowledge of every aspect of film production, applied creatively — that brought that movie in on-budget. And what a movie! It looked like millions more.

How did I find out how he did it?

It's all in this book.

Between 1978 and 2000 David Jacobs created and produced more than 700 hours of television. The best known series were Dallas *and* Knots Landing. *He retired from the industry in 2000 and teaches courses in film and culture in a Los Angeles high school and a film college. Everything he learned about production, he says, he learned from the author of this book.*

Introduction

Why this book? Why now? Why you? All reasonable questions.

As a former film student myself, I empathize with young people wishing to set sail on some of the world's most choppy waters — professional filmmaking. No other art form requires the coordinated talents, focus and collaboration that film demands. Painters paint alone, writers write in seclusion, sculptors shape in isolation. But filmmakers!

Film alone requires the talents, skills and focus of scores of individual craftsmen, engineers and artists. Organizing, equipping and forging them into a single smooth-running team is the fundamental obligation of professional filmmaking. Without it there is no film, just lots and lots of unpaid bills.

Every year young people (and some not so young) emerge from film schools around the world, ready to face the challenges their goals have created. Most will experience that moment of "Yikes, now what?" This book is that "now what."

It is the neophyte's guide to a happy production experience. The way that lemmings rush to the sea and human beings wave to the camera, the urge to make films is built into your biology. If you understand, I needn't say any more.

Flip phones and the Internet have fueled the fantasy that everybody can make a movie. And guess what? It's not just a fantasy. Filmmaking is not so difficult that only a handful of the especially gifted can do it. Otherwise there would be no way to explain my ascent in the film business.

When I graduated from New York University in 1967 I had no relatives in the film business and even less support from my peers. What I did have was desire! Coaches will tell you, "You can't teach speed." What I tell you is, "You *can* make it on desire." Incredible talent helps. So does being well-connected and filthy rich. I was none of those.

Every professional who has gone before me will have an opinion or a point of view on our subject. That's okay. Filmmaking is a subjective operation. One thing holds true — whether it is a small personal film or a big-budget blow-out, the process of making it right is the same. Only the size of the cast and crew, their salaries, the amount of equipment and the size of the egos will be different.

A good script, a fabulous cast, a dedicated crew, filmic locations, film permits, post-production facilities and personnel are all part of the ability to realize a film, regardless of its length or origination. Film is collaborative. Choose your fellow journeymen wisely.

After more than thirty years in the business, and now as Head of Physical Production at the prestigious USC School of Cinematic Arts, I find myself in the unique position of having seen it all: the clamoring youth wanting to get into the business, the aspiring film student looking for his big break and the polished professional making art and money.

Learning the craft is vastly different from exercising the craft. This book hopes to bridge the gap, the enormous gap. Making a small student film, say five minutes long, and being responsible for some investors' millions is vastly different. The expectations are different, the delivery requirements are different and the ensuing stress is different ... it's enormous.

I will never forget my very first faculty meeting at USC. Looking over the curriculum, I raised my hand and naively asked why we didn't teach the disciplines of location management, assistant directing and script supervision, to name a few. One of the more erudite professors responded, disdainfully, "Because we are not a trade school." I am a more practical man. I work practically, I teach practically, and I write practically. I figure, if you *want* to make films you must know *how* to make films. I have written this book in a friendly, practical style — like you were sitting here in my office at USC, bushy-tailed, bright-eyed and slightly scared to death at the coming prospects. I have to say that we've come around to my way of thinking here at USC. As a school, we are better for it. I'd like to think that I helped make some of the difference.

In my career I have been a Production Assistant (lovingly and not-so-lovingly referred to as a Go-fer), a Second Assistant Director, a First Assistant Director, a Unit Production Manager, a Production Manager, an Associate Producer, a Producer (for 22 years), a Director member of the Director's Guild of America, and a member of the Writer's Guild of America. I know first-hand what you, the reader, will experience.

On many occasions I have been called by students shooting on-location. They ask, "I have run into such-and-such situation. What would you do?" It is a source of great satisfaction that I am able to advise them. Happily, most come back with, "Thanks, Joe. It worked." I hope you will say the same.

Now a word to the aspiring filmmakers who will never get into film school, for whatever reason. Or the late bloomers, like me, who have no idea until right now that they want to pursue film. This book will be your guide, your friend, your easy-to-read resource. Carry it with you, read it on the bus or at the beach. I hope you will learn a lot.

There is one other thing you will learn in this book. During my time at USC we have made more than 14,000 films of various length and sophistication. We have done so without one fatality, one injury or one serious accident. The USC School of Cinematic Arts has a 100 percent safety record. This is not an accident (pun intended). It is the result of diligence on the part of the professors, unwavering support of the administration and the relentless focus on safety in filming by myself and my office. We pay attention to detail ... every detail. You have to have lived through this stuff to be able to pass it on.

My accumulated experience and the journey to writing this book took years; writing it took many months. However, unlike my travels along the road to filmmaker that had rest stops, road signs, travel lodges, platforms, plateaus and peaks, my odyssey to author was filled with cyclops, sirens and demoralizing whirlpools.

Reed Simonsen was my Virgil, guiding me through all the circles of writing hell. His patience, acumen and relentless optimism strengthened my resolve, kept me focused (and sane) and upgraded the quality of my work. He knew stuff. He knew publishers, editing and query letters. He encouraged me when I grew weary, laughed at my dumb jokes, written and spoken, and helped me develop a sense of what the readers would appreciate, learn from or find amusing.

Reed, a talented filmmaker in his own right, was extremely generous with his time and information. On many a Saturday morning he would knock on my office door, his hair still wet from his run around the track, to be sure I was at my computer writing.

Reed is also an experienced editor. That was not a small thing for me. While I am extremely organized as a Producer or Film Executive, the same cannot be said for my writing style. Reed taught me to embrace the "brain dump," the endless flood of thoughts and images that began to tumble from my memory. "Just write it down" was his never-ending mantra.

My wife Peggy, my daughter Jennifer and my son Matt were all relentless supporters of this book and everything I do. Trying to always be their hero is the driving force in my life. They encourage me, understand me and give me space when they can see the storm clouds brewing. Always curious about my film life, career and writing, their inspiration is what made me want to share my experiences. Peg, in particular, has the patience of a saint, is my cherished partner and a strong supporter of all my goals.

I thank David Jacobs, creator of *Dallas*, *Knots Landing* and *Dallas: The Early Years*, for his friendship, support and information. Cheerful and generous in both spirit and wisdom, I learned a great deal from him. In a line of work that can be torturous, David made producing fun.

Also deserving of thanks is Denis McCallion, the first person I met in California and who remains my best friend to this day, for constantly pushing me to commit what I know to paper. As a former Location Manager and Disney Executive, his viewpoints on various aspects of the book were invaluable. And thanks to Rick Marcelli, Manager extraordinaire, who constantly refers me as a "genius" because I actually have a job in Hollywood.

In closing, I wish to give a special thank you to USC, its students, faculty and staff. Here I get to rub shoulders with world-class filmmakers in a world-class institution. A special thanks to Dean Elizabeth Daley, who relentlessly sets a high standard and continues to push us in the tradition of a forward-leaning institution. We have the most modern and beautiful state-of-the-art facilities and equipment imaginable. We have global reach, alumni that populate the film industry and, most of all, a passion for professionalism. Filmmaking is collaboration. Come and collaborate a little with me.

Your journey to professionalism awaits you on the following pages, so let's begin your journey.

Producers

Who are they? What do they do? Why are there so many of them?
When asked these questions, most people not in *the business* will say: "The Producer is the guy who gets the money." In many instances, they will be correct. But that is not the only job of a producer. Producers are many things.

I am sure you have all seen the credits on a movie that list producer after producer. I once counted as many as nineteen on one film. Who are all these people, anyway?

Well, there are *Gap Producers* who supply *gap* money. There are *Bridge Producers* who supply *bridge* money. There are producers who supply *seed* money, *completion* money and *insurance* money. These are all terms for "start up" money. There are producers who supplied their management clients to the project and people who owned that all-important vintage car. All can be *producers*. Some may have owned the underlying rights to the script or developed the screenplay with personal money. Some may have controlled the location or were present when the project was first pitched. But, when most people think of a *Producer*, they think in the classical sense.

Basically, *the* Producer has the overview of the material. He may hire the Director. He is responsible for the preliminary shooting schedule, the day-out-of-days and the tentative budget. In conjunction with the Director, the Producer sets locations, participates in casting sessions and hires the crew.

The Producer stays ahead of the shooting company, making sure that the locations are secured and the sets are built and dressed according to discussions between the Production Designer and the Director.

The Producer oversees and facilitates all aspects of production — from working with the Production Manager to seeing that the show stays within its approved budget to arranging for the best and most cost-effective caterer.

The Producer is a "trouble-shooter" of sorts working out the details, eliminating the problems that could hamper shooting before they occur, and solving those problems that do arise.

In most instances, the Producer is the contact point between the production entity (studio, network, production company) and the shooting company.

A Producer's most important — and least understood — obligation is the creation of a nurturing, secure environment in which all parties, actors and crew alike, can do their best work the Producer fosters positive communication among all parties. The final say on safety or budget resides with the Producer.

Many producers will also find or create the project. In *biz lingo*, they "put in place the package." This means they find the actors and director who will make the movie, line up distribution, and locate and arrange for a completion bond.

Also, there are guys and gals like me; I was a *Producer-for-Hire*. As a freelance Producer, jobs came to me based on my track record, past relationships, and reputation for honesty and solid knowledge. I had good people skills, a healthy sense of humor and a great tolerance for pain, both physical and psychic.

As you might suspect, having so many different kinds of Producers can lead to chaos. There are two basic problems with crediting so many people as *Producers*. First, some will really think they have lots of power on the project. Second, if by some unhappy circumstance they should all end up in the same room together, the old adage will hold true: *When all is said and done, there will be a great deal more said than done.*

The truth is, the person who gets his hands dirty in production is the one credited with: *PRODUCED BY.* That is a signal to the industry that someone actually did the heavy lifting of physical production.

That is not to say that many of Hollywood's big-name producers don't know how to make their films. They do. They just prefer to spend their time and energy hobnobbing with studio executives and schmoozing the "A-list" movie stars. In this endeavor they are quite correct, since big-name stars, coupled with a producer's access to high-level studio executives, is the film business version of "one-stop-shopping."

So, who actually *produces* the project?

The task of actually overseeing, or producing, the film falls to the *Line Producer*. The term *Line Producer* began to appear in the early-to-mid-eighties when most of the movies-for-television were going to Canada to take advantage of the favorable exchange rate. Someone figured out that if they took a production manager and simply called him or her the *Line Producer*, they could save the expense of another salary. In their expedient shortsightedness they simply failed to acknowledge the difference between *producing* and *production managing*, and its impact on the Director.

Why do Directors need and want good Producers?

The set belongs to the Director and the Actor, meaning the Director's undivided attention must be on his actors. What does it mean that the set belongs to the Director and the Actors? Are not the Cinematographer, the crew, and the production design team equally important? They absolutely are. However, once their work for the scene is done — it has been rehearsed, lit and dressed — the actors must be allowed to work without distraction. That means the crew falls silent and stops moving. Generally speaking, actors don't like people not in the scene moving around in their eye-line or line of sight. It distracts them from their work. At that moment the real world is far away, and they and the Director are in a sort of cocoon of performance.

The Director works in a *bubble of purity,* free from all other distractions. The person who creates that bubble is the Producer.

Producing is two things. It is putting the director's vision (or sometimes the network's or studio's vision) on the screen. And it is making that film at an agreed upon price. The painful metaphor for that sometimes thorny conflict is called *sliding down the razor blade of life.*

Here's another version of the Razor Blade of Life:

I had a friend who worked at Disney (he's still my friend). When asked how his day went, he would reply: "SSDD, same shit, different day." Roseanne Roseannadanna on *Saturday Night Live* once famously asserted, "It's always somethin'." Here is what I mean.

While working on *Dallas: The Early Years,* I had the misfortune to inherit a high-strung, violence-prone, ego-driven actor who, while not the star of the show, was crucial to its completion. He was terribly insecure, and, as I would discover to some dismay, idle time did not serve him well. He would drink. And when drunk he became pugnacious. He crashed an executive's party at the Marriot. He knocked over and smashed a large, expensive ice sculpture; and when asked to leave, he punched one of the executives. Many letters of apology, bottles of champagne and vases of flowers later, we were allowed to continue to stay in the hotel.

This actor would sit in his room and brood. He felt he was not treated with sufficient respect by his fellow actors and worried that the crew didn't like him. Then one day he just went home ... to Los Angeles.

I found out about it when the Second Assistant Director went to put his call sheet under his door. There were two other un-retrieved call sheets laying on the floor. She called me, and I called Debra, the hotel manager. When we gained access to his room it became clear he had left. There was not one article of clothing or piece of personal effects.

I called back up to L.A., to the head of Lorimar's casting department, who called the actor's agent. Word came back: "He's home and he ain't coming back."

This was not a small problem. It was made worse by the fact that at that moment I was physically separated from Larry, our Director, and the elements for the following day were rolling into place.

I called our casting department. I begged and cajoled them into giving me his home number, something that at first they were reluctant to do. I may, in my angst, have also threatened bodily harm because I remember Barbra, the head casting honcho, being upset with me.

I called him.

Here this story takes a major abstract turn.

I grew up in a large three-storey house in Brooklyn. We had a parrot. It was a beautiful creature, green with a red and yellow crest. Never mind that it was fluent in Polish and German, it had a deep hatred for our German Shepherd. If she ever dared enter the kitchen, the bird would shriek "SCHWEINHUNDT" at the top of her lungs and scare the living daylights out of the poor animal.

One day my mother was in the basement tending to the laundry, my grandmother was in the living room dusting and cleaning, and my Dad was upstairs in his office. Suddenly the house was wracked with the urgent shriek of the parrot, "Help! Help! Help!" Everyone came running — my mother from the basement, Grandma from the living room and my father from his office. They all assembled in front of the bird's cage, expecting the absolute worst, at which point the bird said: "Helllloooo."

That's right. It just needed attention. Not unlike my actor friend whose story shall now continue.

"Jimmy (not his real name)," I said when he picked up the phone. "What's up?"

"I'm not coming back."

"Look, I don't know what's got you so upset, but if it's something I did or said, I'm sorry."

"It has nothing to do with you."

"Unfortunately, Jimmy, it has everything to do with me. If you aren't here to shoot tomorrow you'll just be another out-of-work actor, but it will be the end of my career."

"Why?"

"Because if you're not here and we don't go forward, the company will be out millions of dollars and you'll probably not work again. In time, they'll forget your name. But me? Me they will never forget or forgive."

He was silent.

"There's a ten-thirty flight out of Burbank that will get you here by two A.M. I'll send a car for you."

He continued to stay silent, during which time I could feel my lunch working its way back up my esophagus.

Finally, after what felt like an eternity, he said, "Okay."

I got him the very last seat on the plane; he had to, by contract, fly first-class anyway. I had him picked up by a teamster, who was, by 2:00 A.M., on platinum time, and deposited at the hotel by three.

We picked him up on time the next morning and got him to the set.

Larry never knew how close we had come to not having our actor.

When I ran into Larry later that day he looked at me and said, "You look like shit. Don't you ever sleep?"

The moral of this story is that if you're going to be a Producer, you must have patience, good instincts, a feeling for the psychological and, most importantly ... a Panamanian parrot.

Being able to juggle opposing agendas requires judgment, experience, skill and, more often than not, a healthy dose of blind, dumb luck.

Television is its own universe.

The reason they could downplay the role of Producer for television movies was they were of short duration and limited in scope. For a television series or motion picture, the Line Producer/Director relationship is decidedly different. Any experienced director worth his salt will want the steady hand and solid shoulders of a good Producer.

The production management function is slightly different. In addition to finding and hiring the best possible below-the-line crew, the Production Manager is directly responsible for how the money is spent. In other words, the budget is the priority for most Production Managers.

Let me just stop here and clarify a term I just used: *below-the-line*. Budgets are divided among *above-the-line, below-the-line, post* and *other* or *contingency*. *Above-the-line* consists of the story rights, the Writer's salary, the Producer's salary, the cost of the Director, cast, stunts and sometimes music. *Below-the-line* consists of all the rest, UPM, A.D.s, Cinematographer, electric, grip, prop, sound and so on. I will discuss this in more detail in the chapter on budgeting.

In terms of producing and production managing, think of a crowd of people. Clearly your perspective varies depending on whether you are viewing events from the middle or looking at it from the height of a viewing platform. In other words, are you seeing the overview or the eye of the storm. The Producer must have the overview from his viewing platform. The Production Manager can battle on from the middle of the melee.

The eternal conflict of the Production Manager-Line Producer: The first time he or she makes a decision based strictly on money, s/he is likely to lose the confidence of her Director.

Why?

Directors understand and respect money, but by and large they don't want their vision impeded, impaired or interrupted by it. Therefore, Directors tend to look to their Producers for support, collaboration and problem-solving. They understand that Production Managers answer to the money element, i.e., studio, network, production company.

There are exceptions, of course.

Director Sidney Lumet was famous not only as a great Director but for his consistency in bringing his films in on time and on, or under, budget. Every Assistant Director in New York yearned to work for him. He liked, understood and respected production. He saw it not as an obstacle but as a supportive process to be embraced.

Dog Day Afternoon was partially shot in my neighborhood. I would go and watch every day. I fantasized that one day I would have a working relationship with such a marvelously prepared, production savvy talent as Sidney Lumet. Larry Elikann, quirks and all, was the closest I got. Larry's preparation techniques might have been questionable, but his talent and vision were indisputable. He was a handful, but also someone from whom I learned a great deal about directing. He had cut his teeth in live television, and staging came naturally to him.

There is another route to Line Producing. It is the creative producer who knows physical production. Let me give an example from my own work experience. I was working as a creative producer when I was hired to be the sole Producer for the long-running hit television series *Knots Landing*.

David Jacobs, the creator, and Michael Filerman were the Executive Producers. They were brilliant at what they did, but neither pretended to know much about physical production. So, in consultation with them, and with their knowledge and permission, I hired all the directors, editors and production personnel. I was even involved in color schemes, wardrobe selection and fabrics for furniture. I attended every single casting session.

When I left, I went to work for Aaron Spelling. The first series to which I was assigned was *Hotel*. Before production commenced, I went to dinner with the two show-runners, a husband and wife team named Bill and Jo La Mond. At that dinner Jo said to me: "You realize that you will never be the sole producer of a television series again." She was right.

Television, too, has its share of producer titles. There are Executive Producers, Co-Executive Producers, Supervising Producers, Coordinating Producers, Consulting Producers, and on and on. Why, you ask. The fact is that the "Producer" credit is a form of currency in Hollywood. It goes on your resume, makes it onto IMDB and sounds good at parties. However, knowing "good money" from "bad money," and knowing how to handle directors, is the real mark of a creative producer who understands physical production. More on this soon.

Allow me to start at the beginning.

I joined the Director's Guild of America in 1968. I was fresh out of NYU and eager to start my career. The DGA's business agent called me one day and said I should come up to the office. There was a man from MGM coming to town to interview potential Production Assistants for a film called *Mister Buddwing*, starring James Garner.

I sat in the outer office of the Guild, one leg dangling over the other, awaiting my chance. A big man in a business suit, his hair cut militarily short, entered and approached me. He took my right ankle in his hand and looked at his wristwatch, as if checking for a pulse. After a second he looked at me and said, "You're hired."

That was how I got my first job. The man's name was Roger Vreeland, and he was an old-fashioned, big-time MGM Production Manager. I learned many lessons from Roger but none more important than that you never say "no" to your Director. As Roger put it:

> If at eight o'clock in the morning the Director comes up to you and says he wants the Empire State building moved across the street, you say, "Yes Sir, I'll get on that right away." At three o'clock, after several hours of filming, after the Director has had lunch and low blood sugar is no longer an issue, you come back and say you were all set to move the building when the city intervened and prohibited it. After declaring how difficult it is to shoot in New York and swearing profusely to show he means business, your Director will go back to the task of completing the day's work.

Truer words were never spoken.

Many years later, with many miles of hard road under my belt, I produced the aforementioned CBS mini-series called *Dallas: The Early Years*. The Director was the aforementioned curmudgeon of a guy named Larry Elikann, may he rest in peace. In fact, if you looked up the word *curmudgeon* in the dictionary, you would find Larry's picture there. He was the original *Grumpy Old Man*. But he was a terrific Director, and we had a great love/hate relationship. In truth, I really loved and admired him. One thing I knew about working with Larry was that no matter the trials or tribulations, we would make a good film.

We were filming on the East Palestine Railroad one day when Larry decided that we should create a field of mud on either side of the tracks. To do so would require a significant amount of digging and clawing equipment, and several water trucks. It would have been an expensive and time-consuming ordeal and was a particularly bad idea, given our schedule.

I did what any good Producer would do and said, "Sure, Chief, great idea." And I went about my business. An hour later I went up to Larry and told him that we had stopped working on the next location, a Western town set called "Cow Town," and that all the equipment was on the way to us to prepare his muddy tracks. I added, "We will probably have to push the Cow Town location back a couple of days because we have diverted all our resources to our current location." He thought about that for a second and bellowed, "No. We're not pushing back. Who's idea was that? No. No. Send the trucks back. Keep working on Cow Town. That's a terrible idea."

"Yes sir," I said, trying to sound as contrite as possible.

Larry walked a few steps, then turned back, and with his voice lowered, a slight twinkle in his eye, he murmured, "You'll pay for that."

What Larry meant I never knew for sure, but always suspected — was that I had never made the call to stop work in Cow Town in the first place.

I stayed behind to direct second unit when the main body of the crew moved on to Cow Town. Two days later Larry stood in the middle of the Cow Town set complaining about the mud not being muddy enough. He blurted, "This would never have happened if Joe was here." It was an expression of my metaphor "overview versus eye-of-the-storm." It was also the closest he would ever come to admitting how much he relied on me and how much he secretly liked me. Roger Vreeland was right — never say "no" to your director.

There are other Larry Elikann stories I will tell in later chapters. But for now the point is simply this: The Producer/Director relationship, when correctly formed, can and will have an enormous impact on the outcome of a project.

There is a common saying in Hollywood that "Dying is easy, comedy is hard." My version of this adage is: "Making movies is easy, people are hard."

If one takes the arrogance, egos and excess out of the production's equation, the work of making a movie is relatively simple. A very experienced Producer once observed, "Give me a telephone, a yellow pad, a pencil and the yellow pages, and I can make any movie in the world." That may be oversimplifying it, but not by much. The process of visual storytelling is not so magical, so remote, that only a handful of especially gifted aliens dropped here from outer space can accomplish it. It takes common sense and the ability to pay attention to details; for, as a wise man once said, "The devil is in the details."

Or perhaps a more descriptive way to put it might be: "You must learn how to pick pepper out of fly shit."

Well, you have just taken the first step to that end. You have purchased, borrowed (or stolen) this book. Now you need a project, something to produce.

Here I offer a word of solace to all you young filmmakers out there. It is a quote from Chairman Joe, so hear it well: "It is easier to shoot than to prep." And "Prep is everything."

Once you have your precious project, I will give you the most important two words any producer can know. Two words that when correctly understood and ingrained in your consciousness will help you break the backbone of production. They are as simple as they sound, but they can take a lifetime to master. They are *anticipation* and *communication*.

Anticipation and Communication

It's Time to Produce!

Anticipation and communication. At first glance this seems simple enough. After all, who hasn't anticipated a good meal, a hot date, a fabulous vacation. And what is so difficult about communication in the world of the cell phone, the iPod and the Internet? What could be simpler?

Uhhh, not so fast.

In the context of filmmaking, *anticipation,* which sounds like such a simple word, is really much more complex in practice. I say complex because in order to really anticipate, you must know the script better than the person who wrote it. I will discuss this in greater detail in the chapter about "the Board." Likewise, *communication* in filmmaking is crucial, but remember that timing is everything. I will go into greater depth on this subject as well.

You have heard of Murphy's Law, I presume. Well, Murphy was a filmmaker. His law states: "Anything that can go wrong will go wrong." As a physical production filmmaker you will spend most of your waking life fighting to keep "Murphy" at bay. In order to do this you must anticipate him. You must look at every scene of your movie for what could possibly go wrong. This is a negative way to look at things, true. It will not make you the life of the party. But what it will do is make you a Producer who can handle any of the many variables that come flying at you, and at the end of the production it will make you the hero.

I like to think of production as the still waters of a clear lake, smooth as glass. But drop a pebble into that lake and the ripples, small at first, will go out and become wider and larger.

Small things can have big consequences.

The inexperienced Producer says to himself, "I have my cast, I have my crew, I have my location and I have the funding. I'm all set. After all, what could possibly go wrong?"

Were that Producer to look up, he would catch a glimpse of "Murphy" running along the roof of a sound stage somewhere, jumping for joy and screaming with glee.

In filmmaking, something always goes wrong.

It's important to remember that basically there are two kinds of producers. There is the producer who, either by laziness or lack of experience, will wait until there is a significant problem, then run around like "Chicken Little" proclaiming "The sky is falling! The sky is falling!" then fix the problem so everyone will say he "saved the day." This is a poorest form of problem solving.

Then there is my kind of Producer, the one who stays ahead of the company, anticipating glitches in the roadbed and fixing them before they become the Director's problem. Remember the *bubble of purity?* That kind of producing calls less attention to the work, but that's okay.

I am not the star or the centerpiece of the show. I am more. I am Atlas holding the world on my shoulders.

By "looking ahead and fixing the problem," I am expressing the concept of "anticipation." Just like music, cinematography or production design should not be so apparent that they detract from the tapestry of the film, so, too, should producing be seamless and invisible.

There is rarely, although they do occur, such a thing as a "good" surprise in production. Most of the "good" surprises occur in post-production, when sitting in the dark with your editor you discover a "take" or a series of shots that enables you to change the tone, the direction or the intent of the scene. "Surprises" can be deadly for a Director and must be avoided at all cost, but problems do happen. Actors get sick; half your crew quits to take a job for higher pay in the middle of your shoot; a location you were sure you had locked up now wants more money than your budget can sustain; someone in payroll forgot that Monday was a holiday and failed to transfer sufficient funds to cover the checks you just wrote. Shall I go on?

Here is the magic bullet to the first law of *anticipation:* Always have a "Plan B."

Since actors do occasionally get sick, and crap really does hit the spinning blades (frequently), you need to have a Plan B ready. For instance, have in mind other scenes you can shoot when an actor is sick or late. Shutting down a show is not an option. If you lose your crew, have your anticipated second and third options — a Plan B and Plan C. Have you planned for Murphy?

There is a classic story of a major production going to upstate New York to film at a particular mansion. It was called *Funny Girl.* Perhaps you've heard of it. In those days, when a studio went on location they sent all their equipment in very large trucks rumbling cross the country. The deal was struck. Contracts were drawn and money was paid. The morning of the shoot the Production Manager showed up at the house. Behind him, lined up as far as the eye could see, were two dozen large trucks sent from California by the studio. The head of the household took one look at the entourage and said, "We've changed our minds."

"But, but ... you can't," stammered the Production Manager, "We have a contract."

"Did I ever mention, my wife and I have never been to Europe?" the land owner said.

I can feel for this Production Manager, as I'm sure his whole life flashed before his eyes.

The Production Manager could have waved the contract in the air and protested, "You have signed a contract!" To which the man would have said, "So, sue me." And they might actually have sued him. But the seven years it would have taken to go to court would not have helped his current situation.

The unhappy Production manager looked back over his shoulder at the great rolling circus lumbering toward the mansion and thought about having to explain to his bosses why they never got the shots they needed.

"Which would you prefer," he asked the Lord of the Manor, "a night flight or a day one?"

You must learn to anticipate, and sometimes think on your feet.

You can never assume. Remember the adage: Ass-u-me makes an *ass* out of *u* and *me*. In other words, just because you think you have the location "locked up" doesn't mean you have the location "locked up."

Here's another true story.

Enter "Thuglet." Thuglet was actually a very pretty, very sweet young woman named Lisa. She was one of the first females taken into the 399 Teamsters union when Location Managers were spurned (unfortunately and foolishly, in my opinion) by the Directors Guild of America. She was, for the most part, very upbeat and bubbly, and she could charm a cobra out of its basket.

She also had all the traits of her brother teamsters.

I would find her asleep in the van with her feet up on the window ledge, cigarette ashes covering her jacket, cups of half-drunk, cold coffee strewn about the van. And she could swear like a sailor. I would find her with the grips and electricians playing liars poker or kicking a soccer ball with the drivers. I teasingly nicknamed her "Thuglet."

All the guys on the show were acutely aware of her and would try to flirt. They would soon find out that you only got into Thuglet's "space" when you were invited in.

I got a big kick out of her.

However, "Thuglet" did not like to be the bearer of bad news. Hence the following story.

I had the honor of doing a made-for-television movie with Jessica Tandy. Miss Tandy had just won an Oscar for her work on *Driving Miss Daisy*. This was her first film after her momentous win.

We were filming in downtown Los Angeles at a warehouse that we thought we had secured for as long as we needed it. We shot all week and were nearing the end when Lisa/Thuglet approached me, looking ashen. She informed me that we would be losing the location in two hours.

"Why didn't you say something sooner?" I asked, trying to stifle my urge to strangle her.

"I thought we would be done, and I didn't want anybody to get upset with me for not making a better deal," was her insufficient reply.

She had handed me a significant dilemma. I could go to the Director, a man only slightly less curmudgeonly than Larry Elikann, and tell him we were about to lose the location, or I could try to locate the warehouse owner and beg for more time.

At that very moment one of the Assistant Directors approached me and said, "Joe, Miss Tandy would like a word with you." I went to her immediately.

"Joe, Dear," she said sweetly, as I reached her side, "sit down a moment if you will." I sat. She leaned in toward me and, in a tone that seemed rife with embarrassment, asked, "Would you know where I can find a dentist?"

"You mean for next week?" I asked stupidly.

"Well," she said, "I was hoping for sooner. You see I have had an abscessed tooth and the pain is getting overwhelming."

"How long has it been bothering you?" I inquired.

"It started around six this morning when I came in for make up."

I was dumbstruck. This incredible talent and unbelievably professional woman had worked for almost twelve hours enduring the pain of an infected tooth.

I immediately called my own dentist. He was only too happy to wait for her. We put Miss Tandy in a car and drove her to him. The Director was completely sympathetic at that point when we wrapped for the day. Over the weekend the script underwent a rewrite and the scene we would have shot at the warehouse was eliminated. The Location Manager got to live, and I got a tremendous lesson in grace under pressure. Luck be a classy lady, like Jessica Tandy.

Married to *anticipation* is the next great secret—*communication!*

Had my Location Manager communicated to me the true terms of her deal with the warehouse owner, we might have been spared considerable angst. Luck, as it turns out, can sometimes trump poor decision-making, but you can't always count on luck to "save your bacon." The moral of the story is. Anticipation without communication is a recipe for trouble.

I am currently the Head of Physical Production at the USC School of Cinematic Arts. Every year, in every production class at school, I continuously repeat the mantra "anticipation and communication." Mostly I get back blank stares. If I am lucky, I will get the occasional "what-is-this-idiot-talking-about" look of condescension, I know to them it sounds like what you talking to your dog must sound like to her. "Blah, blah, blah, Misty. Blah, blah, blah, Misty." Young film students, focused and intense, quickly loose sight of the fact that there is a world out there, the real world. It does not stop or change to accommodate their filmic visions.

I was sitting in the back of a class one day while two students where mapping out their elaborate plans for a shoot two weekends in the future. A girl, not on their team, raised her hand and warned, "That Saturday there is a football game on campus." I sat up in my seat. The other kids began to murmur, then to postulate Plan B alternatives. I jumped up, threw my arms into the air like Rocky Balboa on the top steps of city Hall, and yelled, "Yes ... Yes ... anticipation and communication."

It is so important to think beyond the moment and communicate with those who have not thought about the larger situation. This is real producing!

In the olden days, meaning the fifties, sixties and seventies, crews might have responded to that seeming intrusion into their project with, "Hey, Moe, stay in your own department." In the old days, when crossing union boundaries was frowned upon, that input might have been viewed negatively. In today's world of all-communication-all-the-time, such help is a welcome addition. Remember, you are trying to forge a team. No one should feel that information being offered from outside a specific department is meant to embarrass or humiliate them. You are a team with a common purpose, and a good idea or helpful information can and should be able to come from anywhere.

One of the young guys at school, a particularly gifted young man whose films I am certain we will see in the future, had the reputation for being particularly welcoming to the ideas of others. Consequently, all the other kids wanted to be part of his team, a place where their input would be welcomed, not rebuffed. The young student didn't automatically accept those ideas or alter his plans, but he considered each of them thoroughly.

That is the kind of filmmakers I sincerely hope you will become.

And while we're at it, how *did* I get to be the Head of Physical Production at the USC School of Cinematic Arts, the number one school of its kind in the world? It would be swell if I could honestly say it was because they scanned the entire spectrum of the entertainment industry for the one person of such talent, experience and profile that to have anyone else was unthinkable, and then they begged me to do it. Uh, but...

What really happened?

So ... one day I was standing in the paddock of Santa Anita Racetrack waiting for the start of the first race when my cell phone went off. It was Michael Filerman, my friend and fellow Producer of several projects.

"You have any desire to run the Production Department of the USC film school," he inquired?

I just looked at my phone stupidly.

"What does that even mean," I asked?

"I don't know, but Barbara Corday is looking for someone to run the department and I mentioned your name."

Barbara had been an executive at CBS for whom Michael and I produced a remake of the movie *Three Coins in the Fountain* in Rome and Luxembourg. I liked Barbara. She had been a good executive.

"What did she say?"

"She said she thought it was a good idea."

I hesitated for just a moment. My horse was starting to make his way out of the paddock and into the tunnel to the main track.

"By the way," I restarted, "would this be a paying job?"

"Why, yes," said Michael, "I believe it would be."

"Then I'm interested," I said.

"Great. Call her right away. She's expecting your call."

He gave me Barbara's number.

Now, I should say that in this business when you are up for a job and you are the number one (or only) choice, you still only have a narrow window before they move on to the next candidate. Still, I waited until the first race went off. Of course I lost. As a dear friend of mine would have said, "It's a good thing there were only eight horses in that race or your horse would have finished ninth."

I called Barbara.

We had a lovely meeting, during which I asked her, "What are depths of my responsibility and the heights of my authority?"

I do love and admire Barbara. I respect her as an executive and a wonderful Chairman of the Film Department. However, after eight years I still don't have a definitive answer. All I know is that if I were paid by aggravation, I would be one of the wealthiest guys in Hollywood.

The truth, however, is that as hard as it can be molding, bridling, and educating the world's next filmmakers, I do love it. It's exhilarating to be working with so many young, bright, talented, idealistic future filmmakers. If only they didn't insist on filming over cliffs, in the ocean, far off into the desert, on the tops of buildings, or in the middle of downtown L.A. during rush hour.

Back to business.

The hardest, most difficult thing to define that a Producer does is create the environment in which all the creative elements can flourish. (Yeah, yeah, yeah, that's right — *bubble of purity*.) It means getting people to *communicate* with each other. And, by the way, not all communication is verbal. It means caring about people's wellbeing. It is rain gear in the rain for a soggy crew and space heaters in the freezing cold for the hard-working teamsters. It is air conditioning on a scorching hot day and Gatorade in the desert. It is seeing that the cast and crew are well fed. It is trying to accommodate actresses' schedules if they are also soccer moms or have an ailing relative. It is keeping personnel friction away from the set. It is seeing to it that the next day's "call time" is published early enough so people can make personal plans. It is having the ability to listen to peoples' complaints and provide a shoulder to cry on. Most of all, it is ensuring that all the appropriate *need-to-know* entities have the same information at the same time. That is called "working off the same page," and it is crucial to production.

A Producer is part psychiatrist, part father, part mother, part confessor, but always a sympathetic ear and, yes, sometimes a hard-assed traffic cop. There are times when producing can mean taking a difficult position at a critical time.

One case in point: I once worked on a show with a leather queen for a gaffer. This particular individual wore silver chains, black leather garments and spiked wristbands. He made no secret of his dislike for me. The animosity stemmed from my having caught some of his men stealing and then firing them. Thereafter, every time one of his electricians saw me, if they were carrying a lamp, they would purposefully tilt it forward, causing an expensive filter (called a Macbeth) to fall to the ground and break. Each Macbeth was valued at a hundred and fifty dollars. They thought it was funny.

Finally, after watching the third filter hit the ground, I announced that the next man to break a Macbeth would be let go for incompetence. That infuriated the leather queen, who cornered me behind the trucks the next day and threatened me, using the most foul language.

What could I do?

I fired him.

Normally, when you replace a department head, the whole crew goes too. Cognizant of that tendency, and wishing to excise any more bad blood, I called the electric department together. I said, "Anyone who is uncomfortable with my decision can leave and there will be no hard feelings."

To their credit, everyone, to a man, stayed. Morale picked up, and things went smoothly from there on. It had been a tough decision. It could have gone badly for the show. However, everyone appreciated my clear communication and leadership. When people understand a situation, it raises their morale.

Communication is essential to morale.

It is impossible to overstate or overestimate the importance of cast and crew morale. One of the reasons I always arrived at a location with the first trucks was to show the crew that I would never ask them to work hours I wasn't willing to work. High crew morale results in a happy work environment and thus a better product.

I hate to deviate too much, but since we are on the subject of morale, I must state a simple truth: When it comes to set morale, never overlook the significance of food. I like to tell my students at USC that "the army travels on its stomach."

A well-fed crew is a happy crew. That is why productions routinely spend thousands of dollars on meals, craft services and production office edibles. The very first question crew members will ask on the first day of principal photography is: "Who's catering?" It's crazy, but it's true.

Nowhere in union contracts is it mandated that coffee and doughnuts be provided to the set every morning, but woe to the Producer who fails to supply them. I once worked, briefly, for an Executive Producer who thought he would save money by not buying coffee and doughnuts for the crew. The crew simply wandered off and found a doughnut shop. We lost an hour of morning filming that resulted in finishing the day's work on double-time pay. It cost that fool three times what the coffee and doughnuts would have. This is a perfect example of what I mean by "bad money"—money spent in a short-sighted way that results in higher costs later, and in a disgruntled crew. So much of that cost could have been anticipated and avoided.

When things go wrong, as they always do, a good Producer knows how to implement his Plan Bs and Cs without causing too much chaos or affecting the creative process. Here is a true story of what I mean:

I did a project for Disney some years ago. The Director was a first-timer. He was a terrific young guy named Peyton. He was bright, enthusiastic and very responsible. He understood that the way to a career was great work accomplished on-time and on-budget. He was eager but a little nervous as his first day approached.

Our first location was at a school on top of a hill. I was at the location an hour and a half before the first call, making sure everything was running smoothly. I stood on a bluff and watched the first trucks roll in — the production van, the honey wagon, the make-up trailer and the catering truck. A few minutes later the five-ton truck transporting the camera gear rolled in. The Assistant Cameraman opened the back door.

To everyone's shock and dismay, there was not one stick of equipment inside the vehicle. The driver had simply taken the wrong truck. I turned around and, sure enough, Peyton was headed my way. He was bright-eyed and bushy-tailed and excited about the first day. The last thing I needed was a neophyte Director to struggle under this disaster, compromise his creative process and start rushing into bad decisions.

I quickly instructed the driver to call the camera house and get the truck that actually had the gear on its way immediately. I welcomed Peyton and pulled him toward the coffee and doughnut wagon. Some of the other crew were already at the catering truck, so it didn't seem unusual to him. I delayed as long as I could, never mentioning that we had no equipment with which to shoot.

After a half hour I suggested we bring the actors in and start to rehearse. We did that for about ten minutes. I was running out of time. At any moment Peyton would realize there was no camera. I walked him back toward my car under the pretext of retrieving my script and asking him some questions. Down the hill, on the road leading up, I could see the second five-ton, the one that actually held our gear, lumbering up the sloping road toward us.

In the end, we only lost about fifteen minutes of shooting time. Peyton never knew about the first truck. He continued to be relaxed, upbeat and enthusiastic. We made the day and ended up making a good picture. Peyton was off to a good career. I had the satisfaction of protecting a fledgling talent from the stress and anxiety of getting off to a bad start that might have set the dominoes tumbling in a negative direction. I had not anticipated, necessarily, an empty camera truck, but I had trained myself to be calm, think on my toes and communicate effectively ... and I was there early!

Not all my stories are victories, but I do believe that each failure came down to forgetting those two all-important concepts.

The very next film I worked on I ran into an unusually peculiar situation. I was hired by a studio to produce a project. The Executive Producer called in the Director, the Assistant Director, the Production Designer, the Cinematographer and me. He made the introductions. When he introduced me to the Director as the Line Producer, the Director responded, "Oh, so you're the enemy."

I was taken aback, to say the least. Of all the things one could say about Line Producers, "enemy" is not one of them. It reflected a troubled past, and it forecast a turbulent future. I hoped that the comment was just an off-handed wisecrack, but it was not. Our relationship never jelled. He repeatedly lied to me, withheld information and instructed his Assistant Director not to speak to me. Predictably, the show struggled. In the end, we made it through, but it was much more difficult than it needed to be. This particular director continued to work, but he never rose above mediocrity. He was unable to communicate in a way that helped us anticipate needs together. I repeat: "Filmmaking is not hard ... people are hard."

Part of anticipating and communicating is also knowing when to sit back and listen. As a Producer I attended every casting session. I tended not to insert myself into their discussions unless my opinion was sought. I will, however, absolutely insert myself if something "bumps." For example: I was in a casting session where all three, the Writer, Director and the Casting Director, fell in love with a particular actor. In their fervor they completely missed the point that he would have no credibility in the part because he was a third the size of the actor he was supposed to be throwing around the room. When I said that, they agreed and were appreciative that I had kept them from making an embarrassing mistake.

Sometimes my opinion is sought because over the years I have amassed a great deal of knowledge about different actors and actresses from having worked with them on other projects. The important thing is that anticipation is always based on what is best for the show and the people for whom I work.

Communication can help avoid all kinds of problems. Here's a case in point: Some years ago I produced for the TV series *Hotel*. Aaron Spelling and Spelling Entertainment were famous for "stunt-casting"— that is, bringing in recognizable guest stars. They decided to hire Charlene Tilton, "Miss Lucy" on the series *Dallas*. She was to play opposite James Brolin. The only problem that was Brolin was well over six feet tall and Ms. Tilton was barely five feet. At best, she came up to his belly button. No one talked about it.

The Director decided to do a dolly shot, a walk-and-talk between Brolin and Charlene. We were in dailies when the shot came on. All you could see was James Brolin and the top of this blond head bobbing along beside him. The Executive Producer was outraged. "How did she get so short," he asked loudly? That was all it took for seriousness to go out the window. In the dark a voice said, "Maybe when they sent the wardrobe to the dry cleaners she was still inside and they shrunk them both." I remember laughing, but overall I kept quiet.

The lights came on. "What will we do?" the Executive asked, a slight panic in his voice?

"Maybe we could put her on an apple box," someone suggested.

At that point I did speak. "Yeah," I said, "we could strap her feet to the apple box and she could hop alongside him."

The Executive Producer glared as if he wanted to kill me. I realized I had not only shot myself in the foot but my stomach and my head as well. Fortunately, the Director saved the day. "I will re-shoot the shot as two moving singles, and the editors can cut it so the size difference is minimized."

"See," said the Executive Producer, stitching back the pieces of his credibility, "That's what I meant."

Speaking of Aaron Spelling, I adored him. He was easily the smartest man I ever met in the entertainment business. He could handle people better than the Pope. He was capable of schmoozing and cajoling someone at the very same time he was trying to fire them. But I want to tell this story anyway.

I was at the *People's Choice Awards* while on *Hotel*. I was at a table with the cast, and Aaron was at a table of his executives. At one point I got up to go to the restroom and ran smack dab into him. Aaron threw his arms around me and proclaimed, "Joe, you are the best producer we have ever had at Spelling Entertainment, you will have a job with us for the rest of your life." He kissed me on the cheek and moved on.

When I returned to my table I said to my wife, "I think I just got fired."

So there they are, the ups and downs, the highs and lows, of being a Producer and the two most important words I can teach you: anticipation and communication.

Obviously, you have to love it in order to continually subject yourself to the madness. You must be able to handle pressure, endure stress and live on adrenalin. You must be able to thrive on the rollercoaster of production. And when you are at your lowest ebb, you must be able to say to yourself, as the proverbial man who followed behind the elephants picking up elephant poop, "What ... and give up show business?"

The People with Whom You Work

Too Many Titles, So Little Clarity

We have already spoken at length about the roles, jobs and diversity of Producers. There are so many other personnel on a set that you will oversee or with whom you will have to interface that it's useful to know their responsibilities. It is important to know that all of these jobs grew out of a need discovered on-set. Here is a brief job description of these roles to get you started.

It is important to note that in almost all areas there is overlap of responsibilities.

THE DIRECTOR

The Director is responsible for carrying out his vision of the film. He or she is solely responsible for directing the actors. No one else (not even the writer) may discuss performance or script issues with the actors on the set.

The Director approves the recommendations of all the various departments necessary to creatively make the movie: the production design, cinematography, wardrobe, props and set dressings.

The Director works with his Assistant Director to finalize a realistic shooting schedule that takes into account the needs of both production and actor performance.

In most instances, the Director gets the first version (called an *edit* or a *cut*) of the film. In rare circumstances, the Director may also get the final cut.

As mentioned, there is some overlap. A Director may love a location that cannot be accessed safely or in a timely manner. Directors work with Location Managers and the production team to find something that satisfies the Director's vision and is affordable and accessible.

As a general rule, the Producer oversees the production, but the set belongs to the Director and the Actors.

THE ASSISTANT DIRECTOR

Per the DGA contract, the First Assistant Director assists the Director. But what does that mean? A First Assistant Director is to a Director what the First Mate of a ship is to the Captain. He or she executes the latter's instructions on or around the set. An "AD" sorts out the many bodies working on a set. In other words, he runs the set.

ADs are responsible for keeping the even flow of production by always looking to the next scene and being sure that all elements of a scene are nearby and ready. S/he generates (or oversees) call sheets and production reports, even though someone else usually roughs in those documents. The casting department usually gives the Actors their first call for work, but all subsequent call times are determined by the Assistant Director in consultation with the Director.

Sometimes called the "First," an AD should never be out of sight of the Director. This is why an AD must have a good Second Assistant Director.

The First may set background action as well.

THE SECOND ASSISTANT DIRECTOR

The Second AD assists the First AD. He or she makes the first pass at the paperwork; calls actors; stages background action; and is responsible for the distribution and collection of walkie-talkies.

The Second will distribute rewrite pages to actors, keep track of the actors between set-ups, and rounds them up for work and escorts them to the set at the request of the First.

Sometimes the Second may set background action but only when approved by the "First" and the Director.

It may seem humorous to an outsider, but a Second can have an assistant, which is called "The Second Second."

DIRECTOR OF PHOTOGRAPHY,
aka the Cinematographer

The DP works with the Director to establish the visual style and tone of the film. He works with the Production Designer on the color aspects, known as the color pallet.

He oversees the lighting of the sets and works with the Director on shot selection and coverage.

The Grip and Electrician are considered part of his crew in most instances, although they are technically in other departments and members of different unions.

PRODUCTION DESIGNER

As the name suggests, the Production Designer designs the production, from the type of architecture to the sets and set dressings, even down to the kinds and colors of vehicles used.

The Production Designer is part of the creative triangle comprised of Cinematographer, Wardrobe Designer and Art Department. Here is a real-world example of how this works: The Head of Wardrobe wants everyone dressed in black, the location has yellow walls, the Director wants a white Rolls Royce to pull up. Who sees the problems with all of this? Well, the Cinematographer hates the color white on cars because it bounces the light too much, and next to a yellow wall all this light tends to turn the actor's skin tone a pasty yellow. The Production Designer pulling all these pieces together must convince the Director to use a different colored car or a different location with better walls, and so on.

A Production Designer must be good at communication and constructive compromise.

LOCATION MANAGER

The Location Manager reports to the Production Designer. S/he is charged with finding and securing suitable locations.

Managing a location is vastly different from finding one. A good Location Manager will interface with neighborhood businesses and residents. More than simply finding the location, being able to return to it in the future is probably the most important part of location management. He or she must arrange for poster board to protect the floors of sensitive locales, and make sure a location is spotless, with all plants and furniture having been replaced in their proper spaces following a shoot. S/he must also follow up with a location to take care of any loss or damage.

A Location Manager must secure permits, provide insurance, work with the Transportation Captain for cast and crew parking, and arrange for a place for crew meals. S/he may have to order and help erect tents as places for rest or meals when the temperature warrants such.

GAFFER

This is a funny way of saying "lighting." The Gaffer works with the Cinematographer to achieve the correct light for any given shot, location or set. Usually, in television, he or she has a crew of four to twelve people working together. In features, the numbers can stretch far beyond that.

Gaffer is a British colloquialism for grandfather or boss.

ELECTRIC BEST BOY

The Best Boy is responsible for manpower and materials. He or she hires day-checkers; distributes and collects time-cards; and calls for and arranges pick-ups of additional equipment.

Depending on the size of the show, s/he may or may not stay with the electric truck managing and distributing equipment.

GRIP

Grips rig things for the camera. They push dollies and work in conjunction with electricians, placing cards, flags and scrims. They also gel windows.

GRIP BEST BOY

The Grip Best Boy is essentially the same as Electric Best Boy, but in terms of the needs of the grip department.

SCRIPT SUPERVISOR

A Script Supervisor is an Editor's best friend. He or she keeps continuity; times scenes; and is responsible for matching. S/he will create the editor's notes about which takes are preferred by the Director.

(And speaking of "matching," it is not solely the province of the Script Supervisor. Wardrobe, set dressing and make-up and hair should always take stills of each scene. If at a later date the scene needs to be reshot or pieces added they will be able to match the original.)

Identifying a
Potential Project

It's one thing to want to be a Producer, it's another thing to have something to produce and then make it actually happen.

I'll never forget Lee Rich, the legendary head of Lorimar Television, and his partner Merv Adelson. The Old Testament begins with the words: "In the beginning God created the heavens and the earth." Outside Lee's office there was a plaque on the wall which read: "In the beginning, there was the word." Knowing Lee's reverence for writers, I always believed he was saying that the writer creates the universe of the project. In other words, in some sense the Writer is God. This is a notion with which many writers would quarrel, since many of them believe they are treated like the Devil himself. So to amend Lee's adage, let us say: "In the beginning, there is the Project."

Happily, projects come in all shapes and sizes. A project may be the result of a book, a short story, a magazine article, a play, a fairy tale or a real-life story culled from the annals of your own sordid past.

Typically, a projects is one about which you feel passionate, the one on which you will stake your life-savings, hit your in-laws up for cash, and bore your dearest friends. This will either be a subject about which you feel strongly, a personal episode in your life, or a political statement which must be shared with the world. It doesn't matter what it is; the point is, it is not about the money. Some of the best little movies of the last ten years would not have seen the light of day at a studio. It takes tenacity. Someone wisely said "In order to be in *movie development* you must start when you are seven years old." Though an exaggeration, it's pretty close to the truth.

I once spent three years developing a project with Michael Filerman for NBC. We brought in three different writers. NBC paid out more than a hundred and fifty thousand dollars in writing fees. In the end, the head of development never read the script and it was never made.

Let's assume you want to use a story from your own life. A writer, whose name escapes me, once remarked that in order to be a good writer, "You have to have been married twice and spent time in jail." That doesn't mean you need to be an ex-felon. It does mean that if you're going to write from experience, you must have some experiences to write about.

Once you have decided on a project, you can either write it yourself or hire a writer to do it for you. It's easy to find a writer. Hollywood has as many writers as ambitious starlets.

Some wonderful writers passed through Lorimar while I was there: Bill Blinn, Earl Hamner, Sally Robison, Ann Marcus, Lindsey Harrison and David Jacobs, to name but a few.

I once asked David Jacobs what was special about writing an episodic show like *Dallas* or *Knots Landing.* He answered that the creator was like God. "He makes the world in which the characters exist. He makes the characters themselves. He sets up their hurdles and supplies their remedies. He supplies the words in their mouths and the villages in which they live. He controls when they fall in love and when they die."

So now you know the project you want to make. You may have even hired a writer or started writing. You may even have the script the way you want it. Now what? Unless you already have funding, you will now have to raise the money.

The easiest way to tell that you are not dealing with serious money people is the request for "just a top sheet," except you will even hear that today in Hollywood from people who should know better.

Hear this: "A top sheet without the back up is a fiction greater than your plot."

In other words, numbers on a budget top sheet are just numbers pulled out of thin air unless you can substantiate how they got there.

Why?

Think of the top sheet as the Table of Contents of a book — this one, for instance. Each department or item in the budget is like a chapter title. If in this book Chapter Six is eighty pages, item six on the budget top sheet might say: "one million, eight hundred thousand" (expressed as $1,800,000). The question then should be: How did someone arrive at that amount? In other words, if you can't back up the number on the top sheet with facts, the number has no real validity. It is just a number pulled from thin air.

Does this mean the people asking for the top sheet are charlatans? No. But it would get me to question how serious they really were about putting up money. People who are serious, even studios with large estimating departments, will pay anywhere from three to five thousand dollars to have some knowledgeable Production Manager or Producer do a production board, a day-out-of-days, and ultimately the budget. Then when the budget numbers are placed on the top sheet, anyone reading it will know the numbers are based on solid, supportable evidence.

Yes, I know, there are old dogs in Hollywood who will say, "I've been doing this so long, I can just look at a script and know what it costs." Maybe they can. But for most of us, we have to do the "heavy lifting" known as research.

There are two kinds of research when preparing a production. The first harkens back to the wise guy who said, "All I need to produce a film is a telephone, a Yellow Pages, a yellow pad and some pencils." (And in a not-too-distant chapter I will show you just how to do that.) Then there is the second way — the get-up-off-your-ass-and-go-out-and-see-it-with-your-own-two-eyes way. Both are important to learn.

While filming *Dallas: The Early Years,* David Jacobs told me that he had read a book he liked very much. He thought it would make a terrific movie. It was called *The English Lady.* It was written by a gentleman named William Harrington and told the story of a young English noble woman, Lady Nancy Brookeford, who was in line by marriage to become the Queen of England. Instead, she became a spy for her country. It had all the elements of a successful film — a heroic heroine, a coming-of-age story, romance, and a through-line of intrigue and danger. It was all set against the backdrop of Hitler's rise to power and the calamity of the Second World War. It was big. It was bold. It was practically un-producible. So, of course, David, his business manager at the time and I optioned the book. David wrote a terrific script, and we eventually bought the book outright.

The studios in those days said to us, "We're not doing World War II." There was also the problem of no female lead with enough clout to get the project made. And there was the question of how much the film would cost. How much? Nobody knew. And no "top sheet" could smooth that fact over. What to do?

We put up more money, known in the trade as "throwing-good-after-bad," and went to Europe. We were determined to find the money on the Continent and scout locations there while we came up with a realistic budget. For the next month and a half we wandered through England, Germany, Austria, Czechoslovakia, Hungary and Yugoslavia. We looked at sound stages, scouted airfields, and met with money managers and media moguls. We interviewed department heads, ate like we were going to the electric chair, and managed to come up with a sound, defensible budget. We even managed to stitch together the financing from Germany, France, Italy and England. We were good to go. Then it happened...

The Germans woke up one morning and said to themselves, "Ack, not another Nazis-are-assholes movie," and withdrew their funding. No sooner did they split than the French, the Italians and the Brits followed suit. Why? It was a film good enough to make the day before; why not now?

This phenomenon is so common that I would be doing you a disservice not to prepare you for it here. It is known in the business as "The Ugliest Gorilla." A strange term for certain, but it's a concept that could only have been birthed in Tinsel Town.

It's a concept that comes from the following wholly inappropriate story, and it goes like this:

> Two men are stranded on a deserted island in the middle of the Pacific Ocean. They have no food, no water, and, worst of all, no women. The lack of sustenance is difficult enough, but the absence of female flesh is unbearable.
>
> Late at night they can hear the sounds of feminine laughter wafting across the shark-infested waters from a distant and equally isolated island. Finally, the desire for romance overrides their fear of swimming with sharks. And so one moonless night they take the plunge.
>
> After a long and exhausting swim the men reach the far island. They claw their way up the hill to an overlook, and there, down below in the hollow, are about a dozen female gorillas. One man is crestfallen, but the other is by now so desperate that he rushes down the hill and throws himself upon the first gorilla he reaches. He is in the throws of carnal bliss when he notices the other gorillas laughing and slapping their knees in mirth. Distracted, he looks back at his buddy, who has just now reached the clearing, and asks, "What-the-hell's so funny?"
>
> His friend, who can hardly contain his laughter, replies: "You ... you're screwing the ugliest one."

I know that was a long way to go for a dumb joke. But the point of it is so important to understand that I don't want you to forget it: Nobody in Hollywood wants to be caught screwing the "Ugliest Gorilla." That is why when Germany pulled out of our project, France, Italy and England had second thoughts about it as well. They reasoned that if Germany was right to pull out, we should as well. We don't want to be the ones caught screwing the Ugliest Gorilla.

There is a version of this premise closer to home. It is called the difference between a New York Producer and a Hollywood Producer, and it goes like this:

> A New York Producer is walking down Forty-Fifth Street when he sees a wallet lying on the sidewalk. He reaches down, picks it up and realizes there is ten thousand dollars cash inside. The New York Producer looks around and says to himself, "I hope nobody saw me take this." On Rodeo drive, a Hollywood Producer comes across a wallet with ten thousand dollars, looks around and

says, "If this is really ten thousand dollars in here, how come nobody else picked it up?"

Have I made my point clear enough yet? Despite the Ugliest Gorilla phenomenon and the mindset of Executive Producers and studios in general, films do get made. Here is a story of the one that "didn't get away."

When David Jacobs wrote *Dallas: The Early Years,* Lorimar estimators published the original budget at 6.5 million dollars. The network said they would only pay 4.5 million.

Lee Rich was not about to make up the 2 million dollars. He told David to rewrite the script for the new numbers. David felt strongly that the script was exactly where it needed to be and he didn't want to tamper with it.

He called me.

Over lunch David gave me a vital piece of information. He told me that Larry Elikann had already been hired to direct on a "pay-or-play" contract. That meant that Larry would be paid his rate of one hundred and fifty thousand dollars whether the project got made or not. It was a lot of money to just throw away.

Fortunately for us, the Head of Production for Lorimar was a terrific guy named Eddie Denault. I went to see him and asked if he would be willing, given that they were already on the hook for Larry's salary, to send Larry, myself and the head of the art department to Texas for a few days. It would probably cost three or four thousand dollars. To his everlasting credit, he agreed.

Because they had never been to the proposed location, the estimators had budgeted the buildings of the set — namely, oil/rigs — at studio labor prices. In terms of actual price it meant that each oil/rig was budgeted at fifty-four thousand dollars. It took us half a day to find local roughnecks who could build our rigs for eleven thousand apiece.

Another thing happened on location in the field where we wanted to build our oil/rigs. As it turned out, the script called for the rigs to be set ablaze and burned to the ground. There were supposed to be oil/rigs as far as the eye could see. The head of the art department asked Larry where the action was going to take place. He said mainly in the middle foreground. "That means the rigs in the way back will be in soft focus," the artist replied. "Why not build those out of paper mache?" It was a brilliant idea.

We looked around and found cheaper lodging than what had been budgeted for, as well as some other items that were cheaper than expected. The long and the short of it was that by the end of the week we had taken 1.5 million dollars out of the budget. Another half million came out of casting. When Barbara Miller, Lorimar's VP of Casting, made the original budget, she assumed bigger name stars than who we actually used.

Lee Rich green lit the project at the new budget price. David never had to change a word, and the show garnered a thirty-six share in the ratings. It was a big success! The point is, sometimes you have to root around in the dirt to get the real numbers.

I can't close this chapter without talking a little more about studios. With that as a preface, there is actually another kind of project. We'll call it "All About the Benjamins."

There was a movie some time ago titled *All About the Benjamins*. It wasn't a reference to a family by that name but the fact that Benjamin Franklin's face appears on the hundred dollar bill. In other words, it is a reference to only being concerned with the money. Sure, all filmmakers and studios want to make money but some movies are so lacking in any redeeming value that the quest for "the Benjamins" is the only plausible way to explain how the picture got made. It is, after all, the studio's obligation to its shareholders to try and hit a homerun every time. That is why one hit movie begets a spin-off ... or two or three. In a perfect world your project will accomplish both; it will be a stunningly memorable film of great emotion, intelligence and profundity that breaks through at the box office. It is the one sure-fire way to get up to bat again.

By the way, just in case you think you must have all your ducks in a row when pitching to a studio executive, I offer this: A master of the one-sheet lobby poster sold *Aloha Bobby and Rose* on the following pitch: "Aloha means Hello and Good-bye. This is a story about the time in-between."

That's right, they bought it. Just as they did when he pitched *American Hot Wax,* the nostalgic take on disc jockey Alan Freed. His pitched "*Saturday Night Fever:* the explosion of the seventies. *American Hot Wax:* Let us show you who lit the fuse."

There is another reason a project might be bought: Castability. I knew the agent who represented the writers of *Flatliners*. He sent the script out to a dozen producers on Wednesday, and by Monday he had three of them begging for the project. This is every agent and Writer's wet dream. The excitement wasn't from the brilliance of the script but due to how many young, recognizable, up-and-coming actors would leap at the chance to be in it.

So however you come to it, by hook or by crook, remember there is no right or wrong way. As William Goldman so aptly put it, "When it comes to the picture business, nobody knows nothin.'"

I would modify Mr. Goldman a little. I have learned this: The higher the cost of your project the more difficult it will be to obtain money and retain control. If you are embarking on your first project, don't make it *Avatar*. The chances that anyone will turn you loose with a couple of hundred million dollars are slim-to-none. Be realistic. Don't bite off more than you can chew at first.

With big budgets come big stars and all that baggage as well. The crews will be bigger, the salaries higher and the egos more intrusive. Make your film, the one that really means something to you. If you are lucky it will touch the hearts and minds of others. At the very least your ability to break even or even realize a profit will be within reach. You can always go *up* from there!

Okay, you have your project. You are ready to dip your big toe into the murky waters of production. They say "The longest journey starts with the first step." That "first step" is what we call "critical assumptions."

Critical Assumptions

You are going to take a long-anticipated trip. You want to go north to Alaska. Your wife wants to head east, to her parents. You plan it out. You want to drive at night to avoid the traffic. She wants to travel by day to see the sights. You want to drive along the northern route of Interstate 80. She wants to take a more southerly route.

What is the outcome of the above hypothetical? You will end up taking the southern route during the day to see your in-laws.

Great. You have settled your travel plans and kept your marriage intact. But what else have you done? You have identified a game plan for producing your project.

You have made critical assumptions.

Planning a film is like that. It is a journey of decisions. In order to organize such a massive project like a motion picture, you must first break it down into all its little pieces or elements. The first step is to formulate your "travel plans." Once again, I am going to reference *The English Lady* as the perfect example. It has virtually every element you could possibly come across in making your film: multiple distant locations; it's a period piece; it has a large international cast and tons of background performers. It has trains, planes, automobiles and boats. It has guns of all stripe and explosions galore! It has minor-age children, animals and nudity. It has extensive stunt work and air-to-air combat. It has stage work and multiple locations. It has elements that will force your company to move to them rather than transporting the elements to your company.

The complete copy of the original 24 page can be found in Appendix A. In order to better understand how a script is broken down, you may want to pause here and read those pages. If not, here is what I mean by critical assumptions:

ENGLISH LADY CRITICAL ASSUMPTIONS

1. We would film in England and Germany.

2. Our stage work would be accomplished in England, probably at Shepperton Studios.

3. We would seek the "right actress" to portray Lady Nan, not necessarily the biggest star.

4. We would surround her with recognizable and seasoned names.

5. The Producers, the Director, the Production Designer and the Sound Mixer and Recordist would come from Los Angeles.

6. Some of our fighter planes would be leased in Czechoslovakia, flown to Germany and repainted to look like "Storches."

7. We would alternate five and six day shooting weeks to accommodate travel and crew rest.

8. Our film would be processed in London, a duplicate negative made and held, and our dailies, once viewed, would be flown to Los Angeles.

9. All postproduction would be accomplished in L.A. with the exception of the music that would be performed by the Czech National Orchestra and recorded in Prague.

10. Because of the magnitude of the production, an additional Producer would be hired to stay ahead of the company.

With all this massive amount of work, where does one possibly start? How does a filmmaker know he's on the right track? That person is you, and you must make some "critical assumptions." Assumptions are just that — speculations — but it is critical that you make them. It is not that you can't — or won't — deviate from your initial plans; it's just that going out the door you must know in what direction you're heading. It's *critical* you take that first step and assume some things. Assuming, in this context, is just one form of anticipation.

Critical assumptions provide another asset. They enable you to do more than one thing at a time. For example, I didn't need to know every detail of my project to know we would need vintage aircraft. I didn't need a final shooting schedule before contacting and hiring additional Producers. Critical assumptions allow a filmmaker to move along parallel but equally important paths.

Okay, so you have made several critical assumptions about your project. Now what?

You look to the script for the answer.

Now comes "the Board." But what is "the Board?"

The Board is a "thing." It may have anywhere from four to twelve panels, and it is home to dozens and dozens of little cardboard strips upon which great sums of information will be transcribed.

The next three chapters, "Breaking Down the Script," "Creating the Production Board" and "Scheduling," could, and probably should, be rolled into a single chapter. I have separated them because while they are all intertwined, they each have elements so fundamental that I want to concentrate on them individually.

By-the-way, "the Board" is often also referred to as the "Strip Board" because of the little cardboard strips of which it is comprised, or "the Production Board" because it is critical to the "production" function. Whatever it is called, it is the spine of your project. From "the Board" will come your shooting schedule, your travel plans and the time you employ your actors — all that will translate to significant portions of your budget. It is also the instrument that will "save the day" when things, as they always do, start to go wrong. "The Board" is your filmmaking lifeline.

Breaking Down the Script

You have your script. You are about to embark on the heady journey of production. What is the first thing you do? You read it.

"Geez, Joe, I have read it. I bought it, didn't I?"

"Yes, but now *really* read it."

Find a quiet place where no one will interrupt you. Read it as if you are seated in the theater watching it. Immerse yourself in it. See the characters, the locations. Hear the music. Marvel at the sets.

Now that you've read it ... you read it again — twice, three times, maybe more. You have to read it until you really see it.

Now gather up a yellow pad, some pencils, a pen and a twelve-inch ruler. You will also need a one, two or three inch, three-ring, loose-leaf notebook, as well as several fine-tipped markers of various colors such as red, black, blue, yellow, green, purple and orange.

It's time to number and line the script.

NUMBERING AND LINING THE SCRIPT

Often a script will be printed and distributed without scene numbers. You must supply them. Be aware that once you have attached numbers to the script, you have created the *Master Copy*. Any additions and omissions (called omits) from here on must be acknowledged as such. What you don't want to do is replace scene three by making scene four the new three. This will knock the board completely out of whack.

First, place the script into a loose-leaf notebook. In addition to numbering the scenes, you will be *lining* the script as well. *Lining* simply means taking a pen or pencil and drawing a line with the ruler at the end or bottom of each scene. Once you do that you are able to determine the length of a scene or how many pages it is in terms of *eighths of a page*. This is a little different concept if you're aren't used to it. Here's how it's done.

Script pages are broken down into eighths of a page. A little trick: Look at the middle ring in your three-ring binder. It is approximately half way down the page or ⅘ down. Using that as a starting point, if the scene ends between the middle and third ring it is ⅝ of a page. You will get pretty good at this with practice.

If a page is really full, it may appear as more than ⅝. Resist the temptation to credit the page as ⁹⁄₈ or 1⅛. Thus two and a half pages would be 2⁴⁄₈, and so on. For the purposes of scheduling, you must not credit any page as more than eight eighths. At the end of the process, the number of pages, no matter how full, should match the number of pages in the shooting schedule.

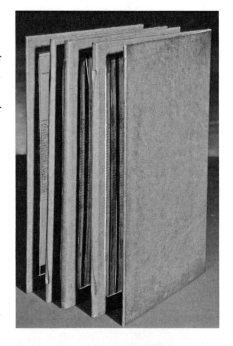

Once calculated, you should ascribe a number of eighths to the scene and write that number at the right margin at the top of the scene. In the aforementioned example, at the top margin of the start of the scene would be the 2⅛ designation.

Numbering and lining the script is time consuming. This is particularly

Top: Figure 1. The Board closed. *Bottom:* Figure 2. The Board Open: an example of what it takes to schedule a motion picture. Day strips are in yellow, night strips are in blue, and interior stage in white.

true if you do it right. You must now reread every word of the script you just read for its content.

Speed is not your objective, *accuracy* and *knowledge* is what you are after. Let me say that again: Accuracy, not speed or ease.

When I was in high school, my mother used to say to me, "The way to learn is to see it, say it, write it." Nearly forty years later I am saying the same thing to you. The whole point of *breaking down a script* is to reduce it to its most minuscule parts. You must literally know it better than the person who wrote it. By the time you begin to create the schedule you will have read the script at least 3 times in its entirety — once for content, a second time for numbering and lining, and a third for breaking down the scenes.

Today most people rely on the computer to do the heavy lifting of breaking down and scheduling. It is the modern, the cool, the hip way to do it. But when it comes to being responsible for other people's money, speed, hip and cool are not your objective. Your objective is precision and thorough absorption, accuracy and knowledge.

If you learn nothing else from this book, learn that. And if you do not at least once do it by hand, you will never really understand the significance of your foundation. Remember, a house without a strong foundation will not stand.

Is it correct to number scenes within a scene? The answer to this is *yes;* for example, close-ups or POVs. POV stands for *point of view* and refers to what a particular character sees. This is because you may not end up shooting that close-up or point-of-view at the same time or location where you shoot the rest of the scene. You may have to schedule them at another appropriate time.

From page one to the end, the process is the same. Find the end of a scene and, with your pencil and ruler, draw a line completely across the page. Now go back to the start of the scene and reread it. When you have approximated how many eighths of a page it is, write that number in the upper right margin of the page near the beginning of the scene.

If a scene takes up the whole page, take your pen and write a large "one" near the top right margin.

But what if the scene runs several pages; starts near, but not at, the top of one page; and ends somewhere in the middle of the last page? On each and every page that is completely comprised of that scene write the large "one." But let's say the scene starts at mid-page. Write ⅝ in the margin on the page where the scene begins. On the page where the scene ends, calculate the number of eighths from the top of the page to where the scene ends at your pencil-drawn line across the page. Approximate how many eighths of a page that is and place it in the upper right margin of that page.

Obviously, many scenes begin in mid-page. That means that the eighths designation should always appear at the beginning of the scene, or the top of the page when the scene consumes the entire page. The reason for this is simply that when you start to create the strips for your board it will make it easier to calculate the length of that scene.

Here's an example. A scene starts two eighths of the way down the page. The scene you are concerned with, therefore, took up six/eighths of the remainder of the page. It continues on for three complete pages and ends on the fifth page three eights of the way down. When you go to create the strip for this scene you will add the six/eighths from the first page to the three/eighths from the last page. This will add up to nine/eighths or one and one/eighth pages. Remember you had three pages that were all in this same scene. In order to determine how many pages this scene took on paper you add the three complete pages to your one and one/eighth pages. The length of this scene is four and one/eighths pages. You can write that number in the upper right margin of the top of the scene or wait until later when you are creating the individual strips to do the math for that particular scene.

In terms of creating the board, once you have numbered the script the numbers cannot be changed. Rewrites are handled by a system called *omits* and *additions*. For example, we have scene twelve, thirteen and fourteen. A rewrite page is distributed and scene thirteen has been cut. We would write the word "Omit" where scene thirteen had been. The page would read: scene twelve, omit, scene fourteen, and so on.

What if a scene were added later that was to precede scene fourteen? We would show it as scene A14. This system of omits and additions is designed to maintain the integrity of the board. If we simply reassigned old numbers to new scenes it wouldn't be long before the scene numbers and the strips did not match.

If all this seems complicated, read it again. The good news is that it is far easier to do what I just described than to describe what I have just described.

In other words: *Just do it.*

Number the scenes, underline them at the end, compute or judge the number of eighths, and write whatever you come up with in the high right margin. Before long it will seem like second nature to you.

Once we have identified the critical assumptions, numbered and lined the script, and dealt with the omits and additions, it's time to break it down.

ISOLATING ELEMENTS OF THE SCRIPT

This is the fun part: the script breakdown. This is where you identify and isolate every element within your screenplay. Remember those fine-tipped, multi-colored pens? Well, gather them near. Turn back to your title page. You are going to create a color index. That is, we are going to write down what each colored pen will record.

Here's the color index I use: make a red mark of approximately one inch in length on the left-hand margin of the page. Next to it write: *Cast, Extras and Stunts.* Do the same with green for *Props.* Blue for *Vehicles,* including *Trains, Planes and Automobiles.* Purple for *Special Effects.* Orange for *Musicians;* and finally, brown for *Livestock* (in *The English Lady* that will be confined to dogs and ducks).

Let's break down *The English Lady* together.

Page one, scene one: The film begins at a party in the Chancellery Ballroom in Berlin in 1933. Here, for the first time, we meet our heroine and the world's most reviled man. Instantly we sense that this will be a story imbued with considerable tension and intrigue.

```
FADE IN:


INT. CHANCELLERY BALLROOM, BERLIN, 1933 - NIGHT

A state ball. Between courses, between announcements, between
musical selections.  House lights off: candles the only
illumination.  Nicely modulated chatter, tinkly sounds of
crystal and china.

In the near-darkness, we can make out a huge swastika banner
behind the orchestra.  Two flags -- a Union Jack and the flag
of Lufthansa -- are lowered into place, one on either side of
the Nazi flag; then a SPOTLIGHT comes on and lights up the
three-flag configuration.  The guests APPLAUD.

The Orchestra CONDUCTOR looks toward CAMERA.  Someone
enshadowed by the CAMERA nods.  The Conductor turns to face
the orchestra, conducts.  The MUSIC is the first movement, a
jig, of Gustav Holst's ST. PAUL'S SUITE for strings.

The enshadowed figure who gave the go-ahead turns his profile
into FRAME: ADOLF HITLER looks to a guest for approval.

The guest is LADY NANCY BROOKEFORD, scarcely more than a girl
but elegant and poised, every inch a well-bred English
noblewoman. Recognizing the music, drawn from English folk
tunes, she smiles, nods at the Fuhrer, acknowledging.

Hitler beams. MOVE IN on the orchestra, then past it to the
huge German flag and Union Jack.

FADE to WHITE and

                                        DISSOLVE TO:
```

Figure 3. An unmarked scene from *The English Lady.*

INT. CHANCELLERY BALLROOM, BERLIN, 1933 — NIGHT

With black pen in hand, underline the scene heading. This isolates several pieces of information. 1— this is an interior scene. 2 — the set, where we will be shooting is the *Chancellery Ballroom in the city of Berlin, Germany.* 3 — this is an historical piece, as it takes place in 1933. 4 — the scene occurs at night.

The second line of the first paragraph says: *House lights off: candles the only illumination.*

This is one of those relatively rare instances where you will need two pens to correctly identify this element. With your green pen (for props) underline the word <u>candles</u>. Now circle the word with your purple pen. Why? Green because the candles are props specifically identified in the script. Purple because of the candle's fire. Fire is a special effect and will be the responsibility of the special effects crew.

In the second paragraph it says: <u>two flags — a Union Jack and the flag of Lufthansa are lowered into place beside the Nazi flag.</u> While these are tech-

```
FADE IN:


INT. CHANCELLERY BALLROOM, BERLIN, 1933 - NIGHT

A state ball. Between courses, between announcements, between
musical selections.  House lights off, candles the only
illumination.  Nicely modulated chatter, tinkly sounds of
crystal and china.

In the near-darkness, we can make out a huge swastika banner
behind the orchestra.  Two flags -- a Union Jack and the flag
of Lufthansa -- are lowered into place, one on either side of
the Nazi flag; then a SPOTLIGHT comes on and lights up the
three-flag configuration.  The guests APPLAUD.

The Orchestra CONDUCTOR looks toward CAMERA.  Someone
enshadowed by the CAMERA nods.  The Conductor turns to face
the orchestra, conducts.  The MUSIC is the first movement, a
jig, of Gustav Holst's ST. PAUL'S SUITE for strings.

The enshadowed figure who gave the go-ahead turns his profile
into FRAME: ADOLF HITLER looks to a guest for approval.

The guest is LADY NANCY BROOKEFORD, scarcely more than a girl
but elegant and poised, every inch a well-bred English
noblewoman. Recognizing the music, drawn from English folk
tunes, she smiles, nods at the Fuhrer, acknowledging.

Hitler beams. MOVE IN on the orchestra, then past it to the
huge German flag and Union Jack.

FADE to WHITE and

                                            DISSOLVE TO:
```

Figure 4. Starting a scene breakdown, with elements marked according to color legend.

nically the responsibility of the set dressers, we will underline them in green because they were specifically identified in the script and for now are props.

The last sentence of the second paragraph says: The <u>guests</u> applaud. Underline the word <u>guests</u> in red. These are *extras* (or background performers). How many will be determined at a later date. For now, we just want to acknowledge that they are present in the scene.

The third paragraph begins: *The Orchestra Conductor looks toward camera.* Underline both the words <u>orchestra</u> and <u>conductor</u> with your red pen. They are extras.

Now, at the end of the fourth paragraph it says: *FRAME: Adolf Hitler looks to a guest for approval.* Underline <u>Adolf Hitler</u> in red. Write <u>Hitler</u> along the margin of the scene. In addition, with your pencil write Adolf Hitler on the yellow pad of paper.

The next paragraph begins: *The guest is LADY NANCY BROOKEFORD.* Underline Lady Nancy <u>Brookeford</u> in red. Write her name in the margin and on the yellow pad in pencil.

```
FADE IN:


INT. CHANCELLERY BALLROOM, BERLIN, 1933 - NIGHT

A state ball. Between courses, between announcements, between
musical selections.  House lights off, candles the only
illumination.  Nicely modulated chatter, tinkly sounds of
crystal and china.

In the near-darkness, we can make out a huge swastika banner
behind the orchestra.  Two flags -- a Union Jack and the flag
of Lufthansa -- are lowered into place, one on either side of
the Nazi flag; then a SPOTLIGHT comes on and lights up the
three-flag configuration.  The guests APPLAUD.        HiTLER

The Orchestra CONDUCTOR looks toward CAMERA.  Someone
enshadowed by the CAMERA nods.  The Conductor turns to face
the orchestra  conducts.  The MUSIC is the first movement, a
jig, of Gustav Holst's ST. PAUL'S SUITE for strings.
                                             LADY NANCY
The enshadowed figure who gave the go-ahead turns his profile
into FRAME: ADOLF HITLER looks to a guest for approval.

The guest is LADY NANCY BROOKEFORD, scarcely more than a girl
but elegant and poised, every inch a well-bred English
noblewoman. Recognizing the music, drawn from English folk
tunes, she smiles, nods at the Fuhrer, acknowledging.

Hitler beams. MOVE IN on the orchestra, then past it to the
huge German flag and Union Jack.

FADE to WHITE and

                                               DISSOLVE TO:
```

Figure 5. Same scene with complete breakdown.

Congratulations. You have just broken down your first scene.

What do we know about that first scene? Quite a lot. We know its principal cast consists of Lady Nancy Brookeford and Adolf Hitler. We know there are a good number of extras, including an orchestra and a conductor. We know where it is to be shot and when. We know we will need several special effects people to light the candles, and there are to be three very large and descriptive banners present. We can surmise from the year, 1933, that the extras and actors will be dressed in appropriate period attire. We know that, in terms of the lighting, it takes place at night. That's an awful lot to know about a scene that is only ⅝ of a page in length.

On to the next scene. The heading reads: EXT. THREE MALLARDS IN FLIGHT,

Underline it. The text reads: *Descending from a cloud-white sky, touching down on the glassy surface of a pond, cruising near the dense foliage near the shore. The birds are visiting...*

DISSOLVE TO:

EXT. THREE MALLARDS IN FLIGHT

Descending from a cloud-white sky, touching down on the glassy surface of a pond, cruising toward the dense foliage near the shore. The birds are visiting ...

Figure 6. The first scene in a story with the first element underlined before location is pulled from body of text.

And then it goes to : *EXT. WICKSTONE — ENGLAND — (1932) — DAY.* The first thing we do is underline: Three Mallards in Flight. But in what color? Remember our color chart or index? Let's look at it again:

This is telling us we need three mallard ducks. Perhaps we could find stock footage. Maybe we could go out and wait for these birds to fly over. However, the most likely scenario is that we will employ trained ducks for this action.

We still haven't identified the locale of this shot: *Descending from a cloud-white sky, touching down on the glassy surface of ... A POND.* The location is a pond — preferably, but not necessarily, adjacent to the next location, which is Wickstone Estate. Which, by the way, is why it carries its own scene number, as opposed to just being the prelude to the next scene.

Underline the word pond in black. Now draw a line up alongside three mallards and write the word "Pond." In essence, you have created your own scene locale identification by pulling it up from the body of the scene description.

There is still one other piece of information germane to this scene. Did you spot it? As far as this script is concerned, Scene 2, *Three mallards in flight*, is the first scene of the first day in the continuity of our film. This does not mean the first day of filming. It means the first day story-wise.

```
EXT. THREE MALLARDS IN FLIGHT   Pond
Descending from a cloud-white sky, touching down on the glassy
surface of a pond, cruising toward the dense foliage near the
shore.  The birds are visiting ...

EXT. WICKSTONE - ENGLAND [1932] - DAY

...the estate of the Earl of Edham.  As the mallards seek the
camouflaged safety of the foliage, whispered VOICES alert us
to SPORTSMEN, waiting in ambush.

MOVING IN toward the voices, we first find an Irish setter,
poised to do his duty, then a portly man of 58, with a big
cigar and a moon-round face, intelligent and witty: WINSTON
CHURCHILL.

                                             (CONTINUED)
```

Figure 7. The location of this scene is pulled from the body of the text. Note the marking of the location is underlined and added to the log line.

How did I know it was a day shot when the log line doesn't list it as such? By reading ahead to the next scene that is a continuation of the action and is also the first day story-wise in our film. Thus, after the description *three mallards in flight*, add the word "DAY" in the log line and place the number "1" alongside it.

This scene is ⅛ of a page in length. Write "⅛" in the right margin alongside the log line of the scene.

The next scene, scene 3, reads: EXT. WICKSTONE — ENGLAND (1932) — DAY. The description reads: *The estate of the Earl of Edham. The mallards seek the safety of the foliage. Whispered voices alert us to Sportsmen waiting in ambush.* Moving in toward the voices we find an *Irish Setter*, then *Winston Churchill*. At the top of the next page there is some dialogue, followed by this description: *With him is Sir Henry Brookeford, Earl of Edham.* The Earl has some dialogue, and then the description says: *The Earl's son Herbert, 30s, much stuffier than his stuffy father.* The three men converse until the next page. In the description it states: *Herbert shoots.*

There is a lot of information in this scene. It takes place during the day. We are on the Wickstone Estate, even if not at the main house. Theoretically, this could be a location that is not attached to the estate. However, visually it will be preferable that this scene be shot somewhere on the actual estate. We know it is Daytime, and more specifically it is Day 1.

There is a piece of information not indicted on the page but important to the scene. The three men are hunting. Therefore, they must have guns. Because *guns* doesn't appear in writing, it must be gleaned from the action and indicated. We will take our green pen and write the words "three hunting rifles" in the margin.

Finally, we want to know how long the scene is. Starting at *EXT. WICKSTONE* near the bottom of page one, I estimate it to be ⅜ of a page. The next whole page that contains the scene is one page long. When the scene ends on page three, I estimate it to be ⅜ of the way down the page. When you add ⅝ and ⅜ to one page you come up with 1⅛ pages.

Write "1⅛" in the upper right margin of the start of the scene.

EXT. WICKSTONE - ENGLAND [1932] - DAY

...the estate of the Earl of Edham. As <u>the mallards</u> seek the camouflaged safety of the foliage, whispered VOICES alert us to SPORTSMEN, waiting in ambush.

MOVING IN toward the voices, we first find an <u>Irish setter,</u> poised to do his duty, then a portly man of 58, with a big cigar and a moon-round face, intelligent and witty: <u>WINSTON CHURCHILL</u>.

(CONTINUED)

Figure 8. Pulling the underlined elements of a scene from the text.

On to scene 4. It reads: *EXT. WICKSTONE—THE HOUSE—DAY.* (See Fig. 11.) Tea time — present are the Earl's daughter Lady Violet, her husband Nathan, Herbert's wife, Lady Random, Lady Churchill and Nancy, age 20.

What do we know so far? We know we are at the Wickstone Estate, at the House. It is still Day one. We are going to underline in red <u>Lady Violet, Nathan, Lady Random, Lady Churchill</u> and <u>Nancy</u>. Write their names on your yellow pad. (Nancy's name should already be on your yellow pad from the opening.)

What else do we already know from reading the scene description? It is *tea-time.* Which means part of the set dressing must consist of a tea service, tea cups, doilies, scones, biscuits and the like. Underline those two words in green. Even though at the start of the scene they are technically the responsibility of the set dressers, the minute the actors begin to use them they become *hands props.*

Further into the scene it says: *Nancy plops a glob of clotted cream on her scone.* Underline <u>clotted cream</u> and <u>scone</u> in green.

To this point the scene is ⅝ of a page in length.

2.

CONTINUED:

3 GUNS

3 Because he is ostensibly out shooting, his distinctive cat's-**3**
roar voice is reduced to a ~~whisper.~~

                    CHURCHILL
          She's said nothing about it?

With him is SIR HENRY BROOKEFORD, EARL OF EDHAM, 60s, crusty,
opinionated, ~~a Tory, clubman,~~ patriot and snob -- English.

                    THE EARL
                 (too loudly)
          What could she say? If the Prince of
          Wales does not wish Nancy to be the
          Princess of Wales...

The Earl's son, HERBERT, at 30 much stuffier than his stuffy
father, implores Sir Henry to keep his voice down.

                    HERBERT
          Please, Father...

                    CHURCHILL
          I had heard the opposite. I had
          heard that Nancy discouraged His
          Royal Highness.

                    THE EARL
          Winston: My daughter is headstrong
          and independent...

A FLUTTER of wings from the pond; Herbert tenses...

                    THE EARL
                 (continuing)
          ...but she is not stupid.

A duck rises; Herbert takes aim... FIRES.

                    HERBERT
          Aha!

He starts to move off, snaps his fingers for the dog.

                    THE EARL
          No, Herbert.

                    HERBERT
          I'm quite certain...

                    THE EARL
          He is more certain.

The Earl is referring to the dog, who, rather than following
Herbert, yawns and sits.

                                        (CONTINUED)

**Figure 9. Assuring continuity on set. When breaking down you have to add
what isn't necessarily written by making logical connections with the action.
Notice that guns are not written; you must add them.**

CONTINUED: (2)

3   CHURCHILL   3
      The King is disappointed.   He
      approved of the romance.   2/8

Herbert resumes his posture, his aim.

                  THE EARL
      So did I.

Another flutter of wings as another mallard takes flight.
Herbert shoots. The dog doesn't budge. The Earl frowns,
looks up at the sky, SEES...

The reprieved mallard flies over the low-rolling hills of the
big country estate. We go with it to...

Figure 10. This is the end of a scene. You will need to add the page length to the pages that come before.

Nancy heaps strawberry preserves onto the clotted cream. Underline <u>strawberry preserves</u> in green.

    <u>The Earl, Herbert, Churchill and the Dog approach</u>. They should all be underlined in red except the <u>dog</u>, who should be underlined in brown.

    You do not need to add the Earl, Herbert and Winston Churchill to the list on the yellow pad because you should have already done that when they appeared earlier. You might, however, want to consider writing all eight cast members somewhere on the page. It will make it easier to identify them when it comes time to create the strips for the Board.

    Finally, *Churchill sticks a cigar in his mouth.* Underline <u>Churchill's cigar</u> in green.

    Note: The Earl says in the dialogue that he will send Nancy to Germany to visit her distant cousins the Von Bachfurts. Therefore, when the very next scene says *EXT. SKY—A BI-PLANE IN FLIGHT—DAY* (see Fig. 12), we know that the scene takes place in Germany and probably on another day, which makes this Day Two. However, we cannot be absolutely certain that we will shoot this scene in Germany.

    <u>Nancy</u> and <u>Kurt Von Bachfurt</u> are in the scene and should be underlined in red. Kurt's name should go on your yellow pad. The <u>bi-plane</u> is (see Fig. 12) an action prop or vehicle and should be so noted by underlining it in blue.

    So far what we have done has been fairly straightforward. Now let's do a scene that has a few more elements.

    Five-eighths of the way down page 12 we come to a scene with the heading *INT. RESIDENCE OF THE REICHSTAG PRESIDENT—NIGHT.* (See Fig. 13.)

```
EXT. WICKSTONE - THE HOUSE - DAY
```

Tea time -- no conversation, uneasy. Present are the Earl's
daughter LADY VIOLET, late 20's slender, horsy; her husband,
NATHAN; Herbert's wife, LADY RANDOM, a pinched 30; LADY
CHURCHILL, and ...

NANCY, age 20, the cause of the uneasiness. She looks from
face to face; in each case the eyes are averted just before
Nancy's eyes make contact.

                    NANCY
          My dog has not died.

Everyone looks at her quizzically.

                    VIOLET
          Your <u>dog</u>, Nancy?

                    NANCY
          Yes, Violet. All of you have been
          looking at me as though my dog has
          just died. He has not. He is alive
          and well, hunting with Father,
          Herbert, and Mr Churchill. Hunting.
          He will return when they return.

Everyone smiles politely, sadly, admiringly -- as if to say:
Brave girl. Nancy plops a glob of clotted cream on her scone,
looks up to see Lady Random staring at her with tragic
sympathy. She tries again:

                    NANCY
                 (continuing)
          There was no romance. No love affair.
          My heart is not broken. I am not
          even disappointed.

                    LADY RANDOM
          You might have been Princess of Wales.

                                        (CONTINUED)

Handwritten margin notes:
4
6/8
1 6/8
NAN
CHURCHILL
LADY RANDOM
NATHAN
HERBERT
The EARL
LADY VIOLET
MRS. CHURCHILL

Figure 11. A broken down scene with the total page count. Note all the cast placed in one spot for ease of transferring to the strips of the Board.

By this time in the story, Lady Nan has ingratiated herself with the German military hierarchy. Her cousin Kurt is actually designing advanced aircraft, and she is a fairly talented pilot. She and Kurt have been invited to a party at the residence of the Reichstag President.

The description begins: *Large rooms, lit by candles, gracefully furnished in Louis XV. A small crowd in white tie, a few in field-gray uniforms with medals. The women are more likely to be mistresses than wives.*

There is a lot of information in that short paragraph. First of all, underline the heading. This is a practical location in Germany, and we will have to go there to film it. Second, I know by tracking the days that have transpired

EXT. SKY - A BI-PLANE IN FLIGHT - DAY 2   5

A wood and canvas bi-plane climbs, dives, loops. It's an open-cockpit two seater, one seat behind the other-- and something of a crate.

In the cockpit, Nancy, a bit apprehensive and very excited, occupies the front seat; behind her is the pilot, her distant cousin KURT VON BACHFURT. Nancy's hair is tucked into a leather flying helmet. Kurt is hatless. Otherwise they are dressed alike in flying clothes, goggles pushed up.

Kurt is 35, handsome, smiling, the image of a daredevil, German-style -- which means that he is 100% confident as he risks their lives.

Presently the aerobatics are replaced by simpler maneuvers until they are flying straight and level.

Because they can't speak over the ROAR of the engine, Kurt extends his riding crop and taps Nancy on her shoulder.

Nancy turns, SEES that he has taken his hands off the controls. A momentary horror crosses her face but she does as Kurt gestures: puts her hands on the control stick and throttle.

The bi-plane tips and jerks... then gradually straightens.

Her terror quickly dissolves into determination and as Kurt instructs her, she steers, she climbs. As she gains control we can SEE her confidence growing. Indeed, what she's experiencing is more than confidence, more than control; it's the joy of discovery. She's obviously a beginner, but she's beginning an adventure she's meant to take.

                                                    CUT TO:

Figure 12. Another scene broken down, introducing a new character and raising the possibility of filming either on-location in Germany or creating it as a visual effect. It is important to note that we know it's Day Two based on the wording of the prior scene.

in the script that this scene is the fifth night scene in the movie. Write the number "5" next to the word "Night."

Large rooms, lit by candles. Underline <u>candles</u> in green and <u>lit</u> in purple (for special effects).

The furniture is Louis XV. This is a set dressing note but informational all the same.

A small crowd of extras, a few in field-gray uniforms with medals. Underline <u>a small crowd</u> in red, <u>with medals</u> in green.

Nancy and Kurt hesitate at the door. Underline <u>Nancy</u> and <u>Kurt</u> in red. It is not necessary to write their names on the infamous yellow pad because they have appeared in the script before. However, I would write their names in the margin of the script.

Göring approaches. Underline <u>Göring</u> in red and add his name to the yellow pad. *At his throat he wears the Blue Max — pour le mérite.* Underline <u>pour le mérite</u> in green.

    Left on his own, Kurt crosses to the bar for a drink, finds himself next to a portly, scholarly looking man named MILCH. Underline <u>Milch</u> in red and add his name to the yellow pad. *A heavily rouged TART staggers over to Milch.* The woman is an extra. Underline <u>Tart</u> in red but do not add her to the yellow pad. The scene as written ends with the word <u>drinks</u>, which should be underlined in green.

```
INT. RESIDENCE OF THE REICHSTAG PRESIDENT - NIGHT            /2

Large rooms, lit by candles, gracefully furnished in Louis XV.    3/8
A small crowd in white tie, a few in field-gray uniforms with
medals.  The women are more likely to be mistresses than wives.

Nancy and Kurt hesitate at the door, taking in the show, as
Goring approaches, greets them.  Goring's tailor has kept on      7/8
top of the man's formal wardrobe: his clothes fit perfectly.
At his throat he wears the Blue Max -- Pour le Mérite.
Perfunctorily shaking hands with Kurt, he takes Nancy by the
arm and leads her into the crowd.

Left on his own, Kurt crosses to the bar for a drink, finds
himself next to a portly, scholarly looking man named MILCH.

                         MILCH
              Herr Bachfurt.                      NAN
                                                  KURT
                         KURT                   GoRiNG
              Herr Doctor Milch.                   MiLcH

                                              (CONTINUED)
```

Above and top of following page: **Figure 13. Examples of a properly broken down scene.**

Next:

Cut To: *INT. PARTY — LATER.* (See Fig. 14.) We are at the same party, and at first glance it is a continuation of the same scene. However, two things are significantly different. The first is the condition of the people and the room. The second is the introduction of a major character — namely, Adolf Hitler. For both these reasons this scene bears a separate scene number and will require its own strip on the board.

Why? Aren't we going to film this scene at the same time as the prior one? The answer is probably yes. However, it may require more than one day. The character of Adolf Hitler doesn't appear in the first piece and would not be called in or paid. But what if, for reasons not apparent to us now, the scene needed to be rescheduled at a later date? By breaking the sequence into two distinct pieces we allow for this possibility. Remember *anticipation?* This merely anticipates the possibility of filming the sequence at two different times.

CONTINUED:

12

Kurt is attentive but never loses sight of Nancy.   12

                    MILCH
                  (German)
          I have seen your designs. Goring
          thinks highly of them. So do I.

Goring introduces Nancy to several OFFICERS.

                    MILCH
              (continuing; German)
          Versatile. Just what we need to
          rebuild German aviation. We should
          make an appointment to discuss them.

Kurt marvels at how Nancy maintains her poise: even surrounded
by debauchery she is an aristocrat.

                    KURT
                  (German)
          Certainly, Herr Doctor.

A heavily rouged, partly drunken TART staggers over to Milch,
takes his arm, flings it over her shoulders as if it were a
fox stole, kisses him on the neck.

The tart staggers off with Milch in tow. Kurt watches Nancy;
she glances his way. He toasts her, drinks.

                                                  CUT TO:

The scene begins: *The air is heavy with cigar smoke.* Green for *cigar.* Purple for *heavy with smoke.*

At the top of the next page it says: <u>A Motion Picture Screen is lowered into place</u>. Underline it in green.

The next paragraph states: *TWO SERVING WOMEN ENTER. They are almost naked.* Underline them in red and add their description to the yellow pad. Why them? They don't speak. Why would we add them to our cast list? The answer is their state of undress. This is not normal attire for general extras. Many performers are reluctant to appear nude in a film. These two women will have to be cast and, in all probability, paid more than what a general extra would receive. We add them to the yellow pad to single them out for specific casting purposes.

When in the next paragraph it says: *A SERVANT—less revealingly clothed—places a love seat into place for them,* we underline her in red but do not add her to the yellow pad. She is a general extra.

Six-eighths of the way down the page the description says: *The lights dim, the projector whirs, the movie starts. It is a silent, black and white, old-style hard-core, pornographic film.** Underline that description and asterisk it. There are two ways to deal with this pornographic film. It can be purchased or it can be produced. Whichever way it is accomplished, it will have to be acquired before shooting this scene.

The good news is that this scene is not about showing pornography but about Nancy's innocence and reaction to seeing it. Therefore, most of this portion of the scene will be played on Nancy's face, showing her reacting to the film. From a production point of view you will only have to create or acquire a small piece of black and white footage to establish what the movie is.

When Hitler enters the scene he is *flanked by two bodyguards*. They are extras. Of course both <u>Hitler</u> and the <u>bodyguards</u> are underlined in red.

Another note about this sequence: When calculating the page count, be sure to treat the two pieces as individual scenes. While both pieces together come to 4⅞ pages, the first part is 1 page and the second is 3⅞.

```
INT. PARTY - LATER   NS                                  13

The air is heavy with cigar smoke.  Hair has mussed, ties have
slipped, buttons have popped, feet are unsteady.

Nancy is surrounded by men.  When a hand drapes over her
shoulder, she unceremoniously removes it, excuses herself,
rejoins Kurt.
                         NANCY
                You told me that decadence was dead
                in Germany.

                         KURT
                This is not decadence.  This is
                vulgarity.

                         NANCY
                You are a snob, Kurt. The only
                difference between the decadent and
                the vulgar is class.

                         KURT
                      (not denying it)
                You're handling this well.

                                            (CONTINUED)
```

Figure 14. Note here the word Later is very important. It shows the same people and the same place but later in time. This means a separate strip is needed for a scene that may or many not be filmed at the same time as the previous scene. It also introduces a new (and in this story) significant character — Adolf Hitler.

You should now be able to break/down the rest of the screenplay page-by-page, scene-by-scene.

A note here about dialogue: Notice that the German characters speak to Nancy in German. That is significant, as there will be translation involved. It is possible a Dialogue Coach will need to be hired. A good First Assistant Director will make note of that and ask the Producer about it. This is yet another example of anticipation and communication.

Now it is time to create *the Board.*

CONTINUED: (2)

Göring extricates his hand from the open neckline of his
bleary-eyed partner's gown, gets to his feet, gives orders to
servants and guests.

                        NANCY
                     (continuing)
               What's happening?

A SERIES OF SHOTS...

Cigars and cigarettes are crushed out.

Drinks are quickly finished, the empty glasses quickly
collected.

Windows are thrown open.

The two near-naked servant girls are hustled from the room.

Göring indicates a few of the farther-gone women guests, the
drunkest and most undressed -- they're hustled out, too.

A couple of military officers watch with contempt.

The windows are closed.

The room is now smokeless, sexless, and immaculate for the
arrival of...

ADOLF HITLER

Dressed in a blue suit and flanked by a PAIR OF BODYGUARDS, he
enters with the restless air of a man paying a duty call to an
affair where he feels out of place.

People rush to greet him, deferential. He is perfunctorily
cordial, anxious to get away as soon as he can -- until he
SEES Nancy, clearly the class act of the room.

Göring takes Nancy's arm, leads her to Hitler.

                        GÖRING
                     (German)
               Mein Führer, allow me the honor of
               presenting Lady Nancy Brookeford,
               daughter of the Earl of Edham.

That Nancy is titled English aristocracy impresses Hitler, an
Anglophile, but it also intimidates him a little: never a
social butterfly, he becomes even stiffer and more formal.

                        HITLER
                     (German)
               An honor and pleasure, Lady Nancy.
               Is this your first visit to Germany?

                                        (CONTINUED)

**Figure 15. A breakdown showing the necessity of creating a second strip
within the same scene due to the deterioration of the room and anticipating
the possibility of filming this scene at a later time.**

Creating the
Production Board

You have gone through your script, underlining, writing, calculating and making note of things.

Let me first start out by saying that in my day a Production Board was done by hand. It was a tangible thing that you could hold and carry around. Today, most productions are "boarded" using a computer. It is easy to use a computer to board your film, but to really understand the process you have to know how to do it manually. I will walk you through the process by hand. It's a process that you can easily transfer to one of the several available software packets on the market.

The Cast List

First you must organize your cast list. Your yellow pad, upon which you have written names, now shows its true significance.

This is how you will prioritize your cast. Some characters work in every scene and are so prevalent that common sense demands their placement near the top. A little trickier is using a character's significance to your story. If, in our sample, Lady Nan is number one because she appears in every scene and also is the most important character, what should we do with Adolf Hitler? He is clearly a larger-than-life figure, but he only appears a few times. Believe it or not, I relegated *Der Führer* to number 15 — just to keep him humble. So who was number 2 and number 3? Number two we have already met — Lady Nancy's dashing first cousin, Kurt Von Bachfort. Number three is a man we have not yet introduced. He is Reinhard Heydrich, or "the Monster of Prague," Heinrich Himmler's second-in-command of the Gestapo, the man with whom Lady Nan will have a torrid affair and through whom she will gain access to

Hitler's inner circle later in the film. His presence in the film — although he appears halfway through — is so significant that it demands placement near the top. Another character, little seen but highly relevant, is a Jewish photographer named "Leinberg," a man Nancy tries to rescue. He earns the number four spot on our list.

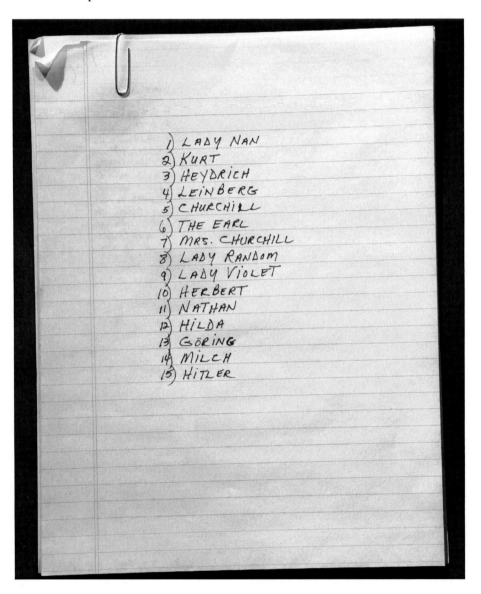

1) LADY NAN
2) KURT
3) HEYDRICH
4) LEINBERG
5) CHURCHILL
6) THE EARL
7) MRS. CHURCHILL
8) LADY RANDOM
9) LADY VIOLET
10) HERBERT
11) NATHAN
12) HILDA
13) GÖRING
14) MILCH
15) HITLER

Figure 16. The Cast List organized into a pecking order.

"Hey, Joe, what do I do with 'the Butler'? He is in half of all the scenes."

"Yes," but is he the most important character or just living set dressing? My guess is that in the final analysis he will be far down the list.

The good news is: there is no right or wrong way to list your characters. The selection process is purely subjective. Here's even better news: The reason we wrote the names in pencil in the first place is so you can change your mind, try different orders of listing and develop an internal sense of what is the correct order of numbering for your project. Subjectivity will rear its wonderful head over and over again on this journey.

By now you have gone through the script two very intense times. You are starting to develop an instinct for what is best for your film. Go with your feelings here. It's not that big a deal.

The Header Board

The Header Board is a piece of white cardboard anywhere from fourteen to twenty-one inches in length and roughly three to four inches in width. Along its svelte body will be found all the information from the script you just disassembled. It exists as the master list against which all the strips, once created, will be juxtaposed. Like the index of colors you created when you first began to break down your screenplay, the *Header Board* will serve as your guide when creating the strips of the Board.

Breakdown Page	
Day or Nite	*D/N*
Location or Studio	*Loc/STD*
Sequence	*SND/MOS*
No. of Pages	
Prod. No.	*PAGE COUNT*
	Sc. #
Title	*THE ENGLISH LADY*
Director	
Producer	*JOE WALLENSTEIN*
Asst. Dir.	

Figure 17. The start of a Header Board.

Breakdown Page

Day or Nite	D/N
Location or Studio	LOC/STD
Sequence	SND/MOS
No. of Pages	
Prod. No.	PAGE COUNT
	SC. #

Title _THE ENGLISH LADY_

Director

Producer _JOE WALLENSTEIN_

Asst. Dir.

Script Dated

Character	Artist	No.
	LADY NAN	1
	KURT	2
	HEYDRICH	3
	LEINBERG	4
	CHURCHILL	5
	THE EARL	6
	MRS. CHURCHILL	7
	LADY RANDOM	8
	LADY VIOLET	9
	HERBERT	10
	NATHAN	11
	HILDA	12
	GORING	13
	MILCH	14
	HITLER	15
	HANS	16
	BINGHAMTON	17
	SCHMIDT	18
	SS MAN	19
	AIDE	20
		21
		22
		23
		24
	EXTRAS	25
	MUSICIANS	26
	ANIMALS	27
	SP. EFFEX	28
	VEHICLES	29
	GUNS	30

Figure 18. A complete Header Board.

At the very top will be the words "Breakdown Page." Below it, on the next line down, will be the words "Day or Night." Beneath them will appear "Location or Studio." One line down will be written the word "Sequences." I replace that with the designation "Sound or no Sound," written as "snd/mos." The last line of the top grouping will read "No. of pages" or "Page count."

Below that will be the designation "Sc. #," or scene number or numbers. There will then be a break, an open space of about three inches, whose significance we will get to shortly. Below that will come the words "Title," followed, one beneath the other, by "Director," "Producer" and "Assistant Director."

There will be an empty line, and below that the words "Script dated." At long last there will be a line on which is written first "Character," then "Actor," and finally, "No." (for "Number").

Now we are getting somewhere. The rest of the board will consist of narrow lines and numbers from one to forty or more. This entire description of what a Header Board looks like is another example of a picture being worth a thousand words. You will now transfer, or write the Characters, in the order you assembled them on your yellow pad. And "Voila," you have a Header Board.

The Strips

I wish to pause here a moment and call this _the coal mine of production._ Here is where you learn a great deal about yourself. Do you have what it takes to be a physical filmmaker? Do you have the patience to transfer all the information of your breakdown to about a hundred narrow strips of cardboard?

Of course you do. Get started!

Strips come in many colors. They are bought in bundles of 25 or 50. I use the following formula for my shows:

Yellow for day exterior, because yellow reminds me of sunlight.

Light blue for night exterior, because light blue reminds me of night.

I use white for day interior, whether on a stage or at a practical location, because white reminds me of fluorescent lighting.

How do I differentiate between night and day? I use red and blue ink. Blue for day, red for night.

What's the difference when you're on a stage? The answer is lighting. If you are doing two or three scenes on the same day, and one is day and the other night, knowing which is which will help you schedule them efficiently. For example, it is time consuming to light for night, then tear it down to light for day, only to go back and re-light for night. Start with both your night scenes and peel away the extra light as you go for day lighting.

The one remaining strip is for "practical"—not on a stage, location, night interior. I use green. No clever explanation here, other than it's not white, yellow or blue.

Can you use other colors? Sure! Why not? It's up to you. I try to narrow the number because one of the best things about the board is that when you have finished you can look at it from across the room and just by the colors of the strips tell a great deal about what you will be doing. The colors themselves become a kind of shorthand.

If you line up any strip, regardless of color, against the Header Board, the lines on the strip should perfectly match the lines of the Header Board. This is important because being "out-of-sync" by even one line can cause confusion and delay in the Board Creation process.

Back to *The English Lady.*

Fade In: INT. CHANCELLERY BALLROOM, BERLIN, 1933 — NIGHT.

Here's where all your underlining, margin writing and page count estimation comes into play. With the strip lined up perfectly with the Header Board, write the number "1" in the very top box. This is the first strip, and it coincides with the first scene in the movie. From here on in you will number in ascending order every strip, even though it is unlikely that the board will end up in sequential order. The reason for this is that should a change occur in personnel, actor availability or even a page-one rewrite, you will be able to lay out the board in scene continuity. In effect, you will have gone back to square one and built your schedule anew.

In the next box down you will place an "N" for night. In the next box, place the letters "LOC" for location. It is my belief that we are more likely to find and secure a practical location than have to incur the costs of constructing this set.

Next box? *Sound* or *MOS* (a Hollywoodism for No Sound). The film world has it's own language, one you will have to know. A word here about the expression "MOS." It stands for "mit out sound," and its exact origins are still debated. The story goes that German-born director Ernst Lubitsch (although some say it was Fritz Lang) was asked by his script supervisor how he wanted to shoot an upcoming scene. The director said he wanted it "mit out sound" that is, "without sound." Thus, it was written down that way on the production reports. It's a great story and may be true. Others say it comes from an old abbreviation of "motor only shot." In the early days of Hollywood, when a shot was planned without sound, the Sound Mixer would tell the production Sound Recorder to roll the motor only. He would start the camera's motor without starting the matching sound recording equipment. They would write down MOS to indicate this. Who knows today? Perhaps it's a combination of the two.

In the next-to-last box of the upper group is "page count." Now all the discussion about calculating eighths and where you list them will come into play. Hopefully you wrote the final number — one-and-one-eighth, three-and-three-eighths, or whatever — in the upper right margin near the start of the scene.

In the case of *The English Lady,* the page count for the first scene is ⅝, written as "⅝." Here, unlike in other places, I would strongly suggest you write the number in pencil as opposed to ink. The reason is that if the scene is rewritten you will only have to adjust this one box instead of throwing out the strip entirely and having to make another one. It may not seem like a big deal until the script undergoes a substantial rewrite that changes most, if not all, of the page counts.

Now, in the space beneath the last box, the space that is part of the three-inch open space, write the scene number in pencil. Clearly, both yours and mine will be the number "1."

Turning the strip sideways so I can write in the open space, I put: "INT. CHANCELLORY 1933"

The strip is now realigned with the Header Board, and if exactly in sync, in the second little box write the number "1." For me that would be Lady Nan. Why the second box and not the first? The answer is that when correctly aligned, the first little box will abut the line that says "character," "actor" and "no." (or number).

In my first scene Adolf Hitler also appears. But remember I relegated him to the number 15 slot. Moving down the board until I reach his name, I write the number "15" in the little box alongside.

Now, because of the many other elements present in this scene, I need to take a moment and explain the rest of the Header Board creation.

Go to the bottom of the header board and move your pen upward approximately one-quarter of the length of the header board. Pick a numbered line. Write the word "Extras," then "Musicians," "Animals," "Sp. Effex," "Vehicles," "Guns," and so on. Hopefully you still have some open space on your Header Board. I will explain why this is necessary very shortly.

Alongside the box marked "Extras," I draw a diagonal line in pencil going from lower left to upper right. The boxes are small so you had better have a sharp pencil and neat handwriting. I pencil in the area to the right of the line and I approximate and write the number of extras I think the scene will have in the left side of the box. This is difficult to do on a 15-inch board, but easier on an 18- or 21-inch board.

I move down to the box marked "Special Effects." I pencil it in. All this tells me is that I will need a special effects person at some point in this scene. As it happens, it will be the unfurling of the two large swastikas that have prompted this necessity.

The only other unrecorded element in this scene are the musicians, who I would lump in with the extras since they do not speak but are an integral part of the tapestry of this scene.

I suggested a moment ago that you leave a space beneath the "element" designations. Here's why. Again, turn the strip sideways and write a very brief synopsis of what the scene contains. In our case I would write "Hitler's party for Nan." This is yet another way of quickly calling to mind the scene and its contents that you are trying to capture and record.

All right. Hooray for us; we have just created our first strip. We are moviemakers. We still have a hundred or so more to make.

Just so you know, when I broke down *The English Lady* for the first time, it took one hundred and thirty-seven strips. And yes, it took me several days to do it. I will say that once your board is completed, you will have a

		23
		24
	EXTRAS	25
	MUSICIANS	26
	ANIMALS	27
	SP. EFFEX	28
	VEHICLES	29
	GUNS	30

Figure 19. A closer look at a list of elements listed on a Header Board.

deeper sense of your film, and a feeling of organization and control like none other. This is what makes the process worth it.

Remember: Fast is not our goal, our goal is accuracy.

For those interested in understanding this crucial part of filmmaking, Chairman Joe has included additional strip creation examples in Appendix A.

Scheduling

So you have trudged through the grunt work of strip creation. Now is the time for all your hard work to begin to take shape and form. But how do you begin? What are the priorities? There are two major views of filmmaking.

1. Start with a small crew doing small scenes close to home. This way the cast and crew will get to know each other and get their collective sea legs. Then move farther away from home base with a progressively larger crew, or...

2. Jump in with both feet. Start with the biggest, most difficult scene; get it out of the way and move to progressively easier scenes, dropping excess crewmembers along the way.

I prefer the second option. My philosophy of filmmaking goes: "Start far, end close. Start big, work down."

In other words, you should come out of the gate running. Don't be afraid to do your most difficult and largest scenes early on. Most crews will step up to the challenge. Would it be better for everyone to work together for a while and get to know one another? It would be okay, but professional crews pride themselves on getting the job done at the highest possible level. Personalities will work themselves out or collide in such a way that changes will have to be made anyway. Plus, there's nothing like a well-earned challenge to bring a crew together. I also believe that once a work pace is established, it is harder to ramp it up than tamp it down.

There is another reason — a performance reason — why I prefer starting big and working down. Intimate, two-people scenes between actors should not be rushed. Trying to film intimate love scenes with the pressure of much larger, more expensive scenes looming over their heads is uncomfortable for actors and may force them to subconsciously rush their performances.

Okay, Chairman, you've convinced us. Now what?

Now go back to your list of "critical assumptions" and remember the word *tentative*. It's that word that means "likely to have many changes before becoming final and complete." You are about to create your "tentative schedule."

Returning to *The English Lady*, our very first critical assumption was that we would film in Germany and England. Separate out from the board all strips that are not scenes in Germany. Having done that, there is one other thing you should do: Remove all the interior Apartment scenes of Nancy and Kurt, Nancy and Leinberg and Nancy and Heydrich. These sets will be built in England, probably at Shepperton Studios.

What about all the flying scenes? Where will they be filmed and will they be considered "2nd unit?" For the purposes of this pass, we will treat all the flying sequences as 1st unit in Germany.

(NOTE: There is also the distinct possibility, in the modern world, that the flying sequences with be the result of visual effects work. That would mean getting a Green Screen Stage and would have both scheduling and budgetary ramifications.)

Now line up the biggest, most people-heavy scenes in Germany. Begin to lay them out side-by-side. That seems easy enough, except you're not going to film them all in one day, and in all probability not even in one week.

I probably should have mentioned this earlier, but it wasn't germane at the time. Along with the bundle of colored strips, you will also purchase a bundle of narrower black and white strips known as "day separator strips." It is these black strips that will be placed at the end of each prospective shooting day. Sometimes the black strip will be placed behind just one strip if the scene is large enough to take an entire day, or behind six or eight strips if the scenes are short in duration and easy to accomplish.

My advice to you would be to start with exterior scenes. There is a good term to learn now: *the cover set.*

A cover set is a set — be it built or practical — to which the company will move in order to continue filming in the event of inclement weather. For example, in *The English Lady*, if the scene of the Hitler Youth marching through the streets of Berlin was scheduled but rain forced the company inside, it would be possible to film some (or all) of the scenes in the K-Dam Bar.

On *The Godfather*, the company was scheduled to go to the Bronx to record the scene where Sonny beats up his brother-in-law. Rain precluded that.

Figure 20. A day separator strip.

Instead, the company moved onto a sound stage in mid-town Manhattan where the interior of the Corleone house had been built. Actors who had not been previously scheduled to work that day were called in, and a scene was rehearsed. It was the scene where Michael says he will kill the Captain and Solazzo. It is the scene where Jimmy Caan says, "You. You, who didn't want to be involved in the family business, you're gonna get blood all over your nice Ivy-league suit?" They rehearsed the scene over and over, and at around four in the afternoon they began filming. It was one of the great scenes in the picture, but it sure as hell wasn't the one they set out to do in the morning.

I should note here that. I like to speak about *The Godfather* as if I was one of the prime movers of the project. The fact is, I was called in as a young man to be a second Second Assistant Director, primarily for the wedding sequence, but stayed on for a few weeks. I was so far down the food chain that I was akin to the red lantern on the caboose.

But I was there.

Back to *The English Lady.*

Even though the two-people interior scenes could be shot on a sound stage or even a practical location in Germany, we will move them back to England. The reason for this is that it is cheaper to fly and house the actors playing Kurt, Heydrich and Leinburg in England than it is to keep the English crew and actors on location in Germany.

Let's take a look at the scene in the Reichstag that is broken into two parts. The second, longer portion is where Hitler makes an appearance. How much time or how many days would you allot to complete those two pieces? If you looked solely at the page count and you surmised that a project of this magnitude would probably average one-and-a-half to two-and-a-half pages a day, and the combined page count of the two pieces was four-and-some-odd pages, it would be tempting to just say that these two scenes would take two days to film. But remember, page count alone does not tell the whole story.

My advice is to play the scenes in your head. Look at the room and the condition of the actors at the start of the first piece and at the commencement of the second. There is a marked difference in the appearance of both the wardrobe and the condition of the room itself. *What you are doing is estimating time.*

When I first scheduled these two pieces, I had not seen the location and could not answer the following questions: How large was the room, and therefore how many extras could it reasonably hold? How high were the ceilings? Would everything be lit from the floor or would we have to send in a rigging crew to erect spreaders across the ceiling in order to hang our lights overhead?

I scheduled the Reichstag Party scenes for three days. What was it that ultimately got me to make that decision? I decided that if I was going to be wrong, I would rather the company was a day ahead than a day behind.

In the chapter about producing, I stated, "Production is like a smooth lake into which a pebble is dropped. The ripples go out and become wider." And the ripple effect of going over a day early on in your production could have enormous ramifications down the line. It is important to learn that a day over is not just a day over. In film, when the dominos of production begin to fall, they fall in a geometric progression: two, four, eight, and sixteen — just like ripples in a pond get wider and go out. This is why I say start big!

I would isolate the two or three biggest scenes or sequences. There is a scene in *The English Lady* where Lady Nan walks through a typical Berlin neighborhood. It is dusk, and people are sitting outside their apartments. People are strolling and children are playing. Into the scene comes a marching band, followed by a procession of "Hitler Youth." When the elderly couple in the middle of the scene sees the Hitler Youth they become afraid and move inside. The scene is meant to indicate the impending horrors of fascism.

Of the major cast, only Lady Nan needed to work. The rest of the elements, large as they were, would not interfere with accomplishing the scene in one day. It was the perfect scene with which to start the film — an abundance of production values, a compilation of wardrobed extras, and a makeable day — while the crew settled in with one another.

Next I isolated the sequence titled "Kristallnacht" (historically, "the Night of the Broken Glass"). It was a horrific series of shots, short on page count but extremely heavy on elements. There were extras, cars, fires, stunts, special effects, and breaking glass, all of which would have to be reset for each take. The sequence should be storyboarded — that is, each shot should be drawn on a sheet of paper, approved by the Director and distributed to the company. That way everyone will know the approximate shot the Director is looking for throughout the entire sequence.

I allowed for five nights of filming. Might it have taken less? Perhaps, but I would rather be safe than sorry.

After many hours of looking and "guesstimating" what it will take to accomplish each scene, you have now put together your "tentative shooting schedule." This is what we've just done looks like.

Now comes something that is little discussed but vitally important to both your schedule and your budget. It is known as the "day-out-of-days."

When hiring actors, particularly ones you will be taking to distant locations, you must know more than just how many days they will work and when those days are. You have to know when they will travel, when they will be fitted for wardrobe at the location, or when will they require a few days of

Figure 21. A first assembly of the created strips on our Production Board.

shopping with a costume designer. You must know. Will they work the first day or the second or the third? Will they be required to sit around a hotel until day four? When their work assignment is finished will they be flying home the same day or the next morning?

Let's, for argument's sake, say that your actor travels one day, then works the next. They do not work for the next two days but work for three after that. They have two days off then work one more half day before flying home. Here is what your day-out-of-days will look like for that particular actor:

Day 1	Day 2	D3/D4	D5/6/7/8/9/10
T (Travel)	SW(Start Work)	H/H/(Hold)	W/W/W/H/H/WFT (Work Finish Travel)

That is a total of ten days, not including Sunday. You can either make a deal for ten days or, more likely, pay the actor for two weeks.

You will do this sort of calculation for each and every actor on your Board. It is time consuming and subject to change; but it is one of the key components of the budgeting process, and it is driven by the flexibility of the Board.

One other note about scheduling prior to the day-out-of-days: there are two or three ways to look at a schedule. It can be driven by cast, locations, or unique circumstances (snow — or the lack thereof— would be a good example). Don't bother scheduling a movie that relies on snow and hope to film it in the Mojave Desert in July.

New filmmakers often ask, "Is a film ever scheduled in strict continuity?" If the Director and the actors had their way, they would always be scheduled that way. It is, however, the reality of production that a film is rarely shot in continuity, and almost always the actors are forced to jump around within their characters.

The reason for this is purely logistical (and therefore financial). Imagine that you have three scenes in the same restaurant but they are spread throughout the script — one happens early on, the second 50 pages in, and the last at the end of the film. Would you really go back to the same place three different times when you could shoot them all at once? That is what is known as "a false move."

A false move is having to do twice or three times what can and should be done once.

Movies are expense and false moves are bad money. A perfect example: As an Assistant Director I worked on an Elaine May/Walter Matthau film titled *A New Leaf*. It was Elaine's directorial debut, and she wore three hats. She had written the script, was co-starring as an actor, and she was the Director — a heavy load for anyone. We were filming in a mansion on Long Island.

It was a three-page dialogue scene between Elaine and Walter, and it took place in the opulent dining room. There were mirrors on one wall that created a lighting problem. It took three hours to light the room so that the lights would not be seen in the mirrors.

We were finally ready to film. Walter said his first speech and Elaine called "Cut." "Okay," she said confidently, "around on me." Everyone was astonished. Were we really going to tear down the lights and re-light for the opposite direction? Yes we were. Three hours later we shot her first group of lines. It went like that for three days, tearing down and re-lighting in the opposite direction.

When her First Assistant Director tried to tell her she was making it more complicated than it needed to be, she fired him. I became her First A.D. but had learned that if someone was going to complain about waste and amateurism in filmmaking, it wasn't going to be me.

Several months later the head of Paramount flew to Jamaica and literally unplugged the battery cable from the camera and said, "Everyone go home."

Elaine worked in the editing room for a year until she got yanked off the project. She sued Paramount and they sued her. The picture came out to good reviews, and they signed her to a three-picture deal. You gotta love the film business!

Another note on this film: The hours were so horrific that even though my salary was fairly low, by the time it was over I was walking around with thousands of dollars of cash in my pockets. On the last day of filming we shot for twenty-two hours, until the sun came up.

I wandered back toward my neighborhood in a disoriented stupor brought about by physical and mental fatigue. I passed a Cadillac showroom. In the showroom was a white Deville convertible. I stumbled in. The salesman looked like he didn't know whether to assist me or call the cops. The sticker on the window of the convertible read $7,500 (it was 1972).

I said to the salesman, "If I paid cash would you take seven thousand?"

He looked at me in my disheveled condition and said, "Kid, if you got 7Gs, you can have it."

"Really," I said and began counting out the money. His eyes got as big as saucers, and I got the car.

I had the car for one year before some members of the Mafia stole it. It was tracked down and I was offered the car ... sort of. The exact words were, "Wees can get it back for ya, but yer gonna make somebody look bad and ya know ... weees don't know." But that's another story for another time.

One other point before we leave scheduling. When scheduling their shoots, film students tend to place a great emphasis on page count. A student will come to me with a Board on which there are six strips or scenes scheduled for one day. When questioned, they invariably say, "Well, the page count is only one and a half pages." I try to tell them just how misleading that can be. The real way to look at it is: six rehearsals, six times lighting the scene, set-ups and camera moves, dollies, and the like. It all translates into time.

A good example of how words on the page will translate into work time can be found on page 10 of *The English Lady* in Appendix A. You will note in the scene at "Tempelhof Airport" one sentence that will drive the entire day's filming. It is: "Concluding his inspection, Göring notices Kurt watching Nancy's takeoff." In terms of page count, "Nancy's takeoff" is barely ⅛ of a page. However, its accomplishment could take an entire day. In fact, when I scheduled that scene originally, that is exactly what I allowed. In terms of strip creation, I could even have made a separate strip and given it an "A" designation.

Locations

There are two ways to approach the subject of *locations*. There is *the* location, as in a park, the beach, a restaurant, an apartment, a house — that place where a particular scene in your movie will be shot. And then there is being *on* location. The latter is completely different from the former, and it is crucial to know the difference. For the moment lets stick with *the* location.

How to Find Them

Finding *the* location is generally the easiest part. You can literally drive around and look for it. You can search the yellow pages of the phone book. In most cities and states there are film commissions with large location databases. You can speak with other producers or directors about a particularly attractive or amenable location. You can go online and search for it. If your budget allows, you can even contract with a location service. They not only have a significant database of interested locations, they can also work out the financial arrangement for you.

I am not a big fan of location services because they tend to be expensive. It is also a little murky as to whose interests they are really committed to guard.

Let's say you have been driving around and found a fabulous house in California's Encino Hills. You can't wait to show it to the Director, Producer and Production Designer. First, you have to ask the homeowner whether he or she will allow filmmaking in the living room. If the answer is "NO!" do not — let me repeat, do *not*— show it to your Director. Along with Murphy's Law (anything that can go wrong will go wrong) there is this karmic axiom: "The Director will fall in love with a location in direct proportion to your inability to secure it." Never show a Director a location you aren't already certain you can get.

But you've seen this fabulous house in Encino and the owner will allow you to film there. Take pictures first. If you and the Director are not on the same page, don't waste his time by taking him there. Well, if I don't take the Director first, who should I take? My answer is that you take your Transportation Captain. Here's why. The house you love is up a narrow winding road at the top of a hill. It is a large, beautiful estate with a high-ceilinged living room. One wall is all glass. There is a magnificent tree outside that breaks up the sunlight streaming in and creates a dappled pattern on the far wall. Breathtaking!

That is exactly the description of a home I once shot at. The Location Manager, trying to score points with the Director, took him to the house over the weekend. Of course, the Director fell in love with it. The Location Manager had already positioned a deal, so he thought everything was set.

The various department heads went to look at it as well. I was seated in the van with the Transportation Captain. We got out of the van, took one step, and the "Transpo" turned to me and said, "You must be joking."

Due to the narrow winding road, there was no way to get our trucks up to the house. Professional shows travel with anywhere from six to twelve trucks; sometimes even more. There is the camera truck, the grip and electric truck, the prop truck, the production truck, the honey wagons ... the list goes on.

Since the Director insisted on the location, we had to leave the large trucks at the bottom of the driveway. In addition to the disruption this caused other people in the neighborhood, we had the added expense of having to "off-load" all the equipment onto smaller trucks via additional manpower, which was not in the budget. And it was also extremely time consuming.

By the time we were ready to film in the house, the sun had moved to the other side. Rather than the beautiful dappled living room, we were left with a large uninteresting room with a dark object looming outside the window — all this because the Location Manager had jumped a step. In other words, it is not enough to know you can get the location, you must be sure the location is *logistically achievable.*

How to Scout Them

Learning to find perfect filmic locations takes practice and common sense. When scouting for a location, stand still and listen as well as look. Is it near a freeway, a river, a schoolyard, a construction site, the practice field for a marching band? If you are indoors, is there a hollow sound or an echo? These are all conditions that might compromise the viability of the location that should be taken into account (because they compromise the purity of your dialogue or production sound). By-and-large, Directors and actors do not like to ADR scenes. That means pulling your actors onto a looping stage, running the scene just shot without sound, listening through the headset for three beeps and then trying to replace the dialogue with the same reading, fervor or intensity of the original — a royal, and sometimes expensive, pain.

Film companies have a natural proclivity to shoot beneath the glide paths of major airports. I don't know why this is ... it just is.

Thinking about location scouts makes me remember a moment in Texas on *Dallas: The Early Years*. David and I needed to scout an open field where "Digger" would stumble upon the oil that should have rightfully been his but was stolen away by Jock Ewing. We set out across a bog in a wide open field. It was a drizzly, humid, generally uncomfortable day. Our location lady, a lovely young thing with an amusingly clichéd Texas twang, hung back as we began to traverse the quagmire. David had on his shit-kicker boots and I had mine. We both wore cowboy hats and heavy woolen jackets. Now, I should mention that David grew up in the wilds of Baltimore, and me, well, I was a Brooklyn kid.

We were halfway across the bog when the Lovely Young Location Lady with the clichéd Texas twang called out, "Watch out for snikes."

I looked at David and he looked at me and said, "What the hell is a snike?"

As it turns out, "snikes" is Texas for "snakes."

We both looked down at the same time and had the exact same reaction. Ever see a movie or hear the phrase "feet don't fail me now?" Just two East Coast Jews running for their lives through a Texas bog — a picture no artist could paint.

But I digress.

The actual "set" on your location is but the "tip of the iceberg." The entire outer perimeter, if you will, is also crucial as well. You have to consider those people and equipment that do not actually enter the set but are necessary to the project. The drivers, the additional assistant directors and production assistants, second and third make-up artists, hair and wardrobe people, background performers, even additional location managers. Where will they congregate? Where will the entire company eat? What happens if it rains?

It is not enough to acquire the filming location; you must also be cognizant of the surrounding area. In the example of the house up the narrow road in Encino, everyone had to be transported to a lunch several blocks away — a colossal waste of time. On *Seventh Heaven* we made a deal with neighbors to set up our lunch tables in their adjacent driveways. Of course, those lunch tables and chairs had to be rented. Sometimes the caterer will provide them (for a fee); other times you will have to find them, rent them and arrange for their delivery and pick up.

It is not uncommon to contract with a school gymnasium or local community center to set up lunch or dinner tables when there are a significant number of background players or crew.

When filming at the church on *Seventh Heaven,* we ate in the adjacent parking lot in tents rented by the location manager. The tent provided shelter when it rained and relief from stifling heat in the summer. When working in a cold climate, space heaters or warmers may also have to be rented, delivered and returned.

When a film company comes to a neighborhood, regardless of the size of the production, it is a gigantic disruption to everyday life, and the absolute definition of inconvenient. Film companies take up parking spaces, act as if they are on a sound stage created solely for them, and generally antagonize the locals.

In Los Angeles, a growing number of neighborhood associations have made the process of location procurement extremely bureaucratic. Permission from surrounding neighbors must be sought, parking adjustments must be posted in advance, and noise abatement laws must be followed. The film industry works on the same hours as the construction industry: "not before seven nor after ten." Admittedly, this is a little tricky when trying to get your trucks settled in anticipation of a seven A.M. crew call. But do not take for granted that you can just roll into a neighborhood and go to work whenever you choose.

On *Malibu Shores* we filmed on a street adjacent to the Colony, an extremely difficult location to obtain and retain. It was "tail lights at ten." Every evening at precisely ten P.M. I stood and watched our last truck, a forty-foot production van, back slowly down the street and disappear around the corner. Malibu, home to the stars, is an extremely difficult and expensive place to shoot. Most of the people who live there have made their fortunes in the entertainment business but are the most anti-filmmaking bunch in the state. In addition, any time a television show follows a major film into a location you had better get out your checkbook.

Okay, so you have thought of everything. You have the location, all the correct permits, permission from the neighbors to set up lunch tables in their driveway, and a plan to keep the noise level low. You've got it knocked, right? Well ... maybe.

Never underestimate the ability of the locals and the crew to clash. This is particularly true when dealing with "day checkers" — individuals hired just for the day and not part of the regular crew. They do not have the same vested interest in location peace that your regulars do. Respect is key. A man's home is his castle, and this includes the neighborhood around it.

I once lost a location because a day driver got into a verbal altercation with a homeowner in front of whose house he had parked. The verbal exchanges escalated until the police were summoned. The police revoked our permit on the spot.

How to Maintain Them

In short, the Location Manager's job is to find and secure the location, then be able to maintain it. S/he must be able to manage the surrounding area, keep peace with the neighbors, and accomplish one last but vitally important item. When the day is over, the exterior of the location must be spotless. No trash, no cigarette butts or coffee cups lying on the ground. If there was any exterior filming, all the tape used as "marks" for the actors must be picked up and disposed of. Being able to return to a location is as important as finding it in the first place.

Hear this well: *You can break something, and so long as you are willing to repair it or pay for the repairs, you will be allowed to continue filming. Disrespect the location and it is no longer a money issue.*

My good friend Denis McCallion, a brilliant Location Manager in his time, would make that point to me over and over again. Respect the location and the people who grant it.

Two examples should make my point. We were filming at a house in Burbank. The lady of the house was lovely, upbeat, and happy to have us in her home. She was accommodating in every way ... until she walked into her kitchen and found the First Assistant Cameraman sitting with his feet up on her breakfast nook table.

The very person who had only moments before been Doris Day–lovely came to me like Linda Blair in the *Exorcist* head spinning, spitting pea soup, and rasped, "You have violated my soul. You will have to leave."

To which I very producerishly replied, "Yes, but..."

And she said, "That's okay. You can sue me."

And just like that ... woosh! We were gone.

An even more egregious example of a disrespected location happened on my set for *Malibu Shores*. We were paying twenty-five thousand dollars a day for an incredible hilltop home overlooking the Pacific Ocean. The furnishings in this home were amazing. We had to take extraordinary steps to insure that no surface would be scratched or furniture nicked. We put down poster board all over the floor to avoid scuffmarks from our shoes. We were filming in the master bedroom when one of our actors, a kid in his early twenties, needed to use the rest room. However, to do so would have meant he would have had to go downstairs, get in the van, drive to the bottom of the hill (where the honey wagon was), and be driven back up. That seemed a bridge too far for our young prince, so he just proceeded to enter the master bathroom and urinate in the sink.

When the lady of the house discovered what he had done she very sweetly explained to me that we were done filming in her home, then and forever, and I could take my twenty-five thousand dollars and stick it where the sun never shined. She ended our somewhat time-shortened discussion with the words, "You people are animals and you can't get back in here for a million dollars an hour."

I had the honor of telling Aaron Spelling we had been tossed from the location, and he said, "Why did you let him do that?" If it had been anyone other than Mister Spelling, the answer would have gone something like: "We were trying to get him to piss on her rug but he insisted on using the bathroom, sir!" But this was *the* Aaron Spelling, so I simply said, "I was downstairs when it happened, and frankly, it never occurred to me that he would do that." He shrugged and replied, "Yeah, Kids, huh." To Spelling, who was all about glitz and glamour, actors could do no wrong (short of unscripted pregnancy and maybe murder, although even that might have been negotiable).

So two things to remember about maintaining a location: keep your feet off the kitchen table and don't piss in the sink.

Again: *Break it and you can fit it, disrespect it and it's gone.*

Being *on location* is an entirely different animal. There is an expression in the biz that goes: "There are no last names on location." This is a reference to the sometimes indiscriminate way people far from home — and from the constraints of marriage — will change sexual partners. Clearly, the majority of film people do not behave that way. However, I literally stood in the doorway of a motel room in Santa Fe, New Mexico, one night and watched crewmembers sneak from one room to another like something out of an "Inspector Clousseau" movie. The best example of location romance is depicted in the Francois Truffaut film *Day for Night*. Of course, there are very legitimate romances that form on a film set.

Sexual misadventure is not the only danger in location work. When a show goes to Las Vegas it is not uncommon for the spouse to request that the weekly paycheck be sent directly home, as opposed to given out near the casinos. The industry is rife with examples of film crews being paid large amounts of money only to lose it at the tables, or worse — come home with new debt.

However, by far the most dangerous way to go *on location* is to go uninformed. Let me give an example.

I was working in my office on a Friday afternoon around five-thirty of a three-day Christmas weekend. I was just leaving when the phone rang. The voice on the other end said, "Have you ever worked in Hawaii?"

I replied, "I have been there a half-dozen times but I have not worked there." There was a prolonged silence.

This is "an aside." The industry always prefers to use people with previous experience when going *on location*. If you think about this mindset, you will quickly conclude that you are only qualified to work in the city in which you were born.

"Would you like to?" came the voice on the other end.

"Sure," I said, knowing full well that if this call had been made at eleven-thirty on a Tuesday, their next words would have been, "Well, we need someone who knows Hawaii."

We discussed salary, flight information, and the reason the Producer I was going to replace had been fired. In fact, we chatted for a good half hour, but they left out one critical piece of information. My sudden benefactor had neglected to mention that he was dropping me into the middle of a Teamster dispute. For those of you who think you have led an adventurous life, until you have been dropped into the middle of a Hawaiian Teamster dispute, you cannot say you have truly lived.

Let me just say a word about Teamsters in general and Hawaiian Teamsters in particular. First of all, they are a talented bunch. They are hard working, professional and the butt of many unfounded jokes in Hollywood (like this one: How can you tell which child is a Teamster's son? He's the kid who rides his bike all the way to the park only to watch the other kids play.) Nonetheless, they are not the sort to be trifled with.

First of all, they are mostly Samoan, the size of redwood trees and if hungry, they can eat the tires off your catering truck. In addition, their views on violence and yours are probably different. They are just big, physical, athletic guys who like to hit and be hit. And they can be incredibly intimidating. They also make loyal friends and can be a lot of fun.

I landed in Hawaii with no clue as to what was going on. The problem was this: Many of the guys who had come over for the job from the mainland had once worked for Art Rutledge. Art was the business agent for the local Hawaiian Teamster's chapter. He looked like a beach ball with Coke-bottle glasses, was a part of labor history, and very proud of his prior relationship with Dave Beck and Jimmy Hoffa. He also was one of the most powerful men on the Islands. An associate of his once said to me, "If you're gonna have the arm, you gotta have the charm"—meaning that muscle alone wouldn't get the job done; it was always better to talk first.

Technically, Local 399 in Hollywood has jurisdiction over Hawaii (jurisdiction over the thirteen Western states). However, Art didn't see it that way.

To Art, when you were in Honolulu you were in *his* territory. The guys from the mainland, his former "associates," had shipped over trucks that they owned. Art wanted his drivers on them. The guys from the mainland wanted to drive them themselves. It was, as they say in the trade, "a problem."

On set, Art came by and said to me, "Get in, I'm gonna take you for a ride."

Now I'm just a kid from Brooklyn. When someone says you're being "taken for a ride," it means something uncomfortably different. However, since it seemed unlikely Art would do anything drastic to a Producer from Hollywood, I got in.

We drove to the airport where we weaved around the various airline buildings. Next we drove into Honolulu and parked across from the Department of Transportation offices. We watched the city buses pull in and pull out. We drove past Honolulu Hospital and finally up the crescent of Waikiki. At long last we returned to where we had started, and Art said to me, "I just want you to know that if I said so, all of it would stop."

It was his way of saying that with a wave of the hand he could shut us down. That would have been the "charm" part, I supposed.

Art had a daughter (and probably still does) named Anna. Anna was hard-core Teamsters. I had a kid from the University of Hawaii who interned in our offices. He came in each evening at six and worked until nine. At around eight he would walk three blocks to a Chinese restaurant and pick me up a container of won ton soup. One day Anna came in and told me we would have to put a car and driver on the kid when he retrieved my soup. I bitched to Art.

Art chuckled and said, "How do ya like that? The only kid I got with balls don't have any." He waived the car and driver. It was the only negotiation with him that I ever won.

One Sunday night, as I lay down to sleep at about eleven o'clock, my phone rang. It was one of my mainland drivers, a very nice, quiet and small man named Harry who drove the production van.

"You've got to help me," he rasped.

"Help you with what?"

"They're going to kill me," he said.

"Who is?" I replied, perplexed.

"You know who. They threatened to kill me if I don't go home. I'm on an eight o'clock flight back to Los Angeles, but I've got to live to get to the airport."

"I... I...," I cleverly replied, trying to fathom if this was some kind of practical joke.

"Meet me at the Illiki, by the pool. Please. I'm begging you."

Not sure what was really going on, and not willing to ignore the possibility that Harry wasn't just a raving paranoid, I got up, re-dressed and drove down to the Illiki.

I found Harry standing by the pool, looking remarkably like a lawn jockey. He was standing so still I almost mistook him for a statue. I should say that the reason Harry wanted me to meet him by the pool at the Illiki was that it was in the open and surrounded by four tall residential towers. If anyone really did try to harm him it would be witnessed by literally hundreds of people.

"You've got to drive me around until I can get to the airport," he half demanded, half pleaded. We argued for several minutes about that, and I finally agreed I would. I naively thought, "What-the-heck, we'll drive and talk and drink coffee and talk and, generally, just wile away the night." But as Humphrey Bogart said to Claude Rains in *Casablanca* when asked how he could have thought it was near the ocean, "I was misinformed."

When we got to my car, Harry asked for my keys, opened the trunk, climbed inside, tossed me the keys back and slammed the trunk. That's right. I was going to be riding around Honolulu with a grown man in the trunk of my car. I had visions of being pulled over by the police and having to explain how it happened that there was a guy in my trunk.

I decided to drive over to Pearl City to a place called The Monkey Bar. The Monkey Bar is just that — a bar with monkeys. They reside in a large glass atrium behind the main bar.

Now, for the record, let me say there are only three reasons to be in *The Monkey Bar* in Pearl City at twelve-thirty on a Monday morning: You are either a sailor on shore leave, drunk out of your mind, or you are another monkey.

I sat at the bar nursing a drink, trying to decide what to do with the rest of my night, when a guy sat down beside me. "Joe," he said, "what brings you to this neck of the woods?" It was Jimmy, our craft services man.

For a split second I considered saying, "Harry's in my trunk but I decided to stop for a drink." I wisely only said the part about the drink.

One thing led to another, and by two A.M. both Jimmy and I were feeling no pain.

"Hey Joe," he started, "I'm hammered. I don't think I should drive. Can you run me home?" Running Jimmy home meant driving up to the North Shore. But since I still had six hours to go, I said, "Suurreee, why not."

We drove up the Pali Highway, through the sugar cane fields towards the North Shore. It was pitch black, a starless night and no lights on the highway. Halfway across the cane fields, Harry must have gotten a cramp in his leg. He began to kick at the trunk lid. The sound completely freaked Jimmy out.

"What was that?" he gasped.

And, I said, "Oh, that's just Harry. He's in the trunk."

I swear, in the dark, I could see the hair on Jimmy's head go up like a Chia Pet on steroids. He looked at me as if I had suddenly become Joe Pesce in *Goodfellas* and would shortly pull a gun and shoot him dead. He didn't say another word.

When I got to his place, he jumped out, slammed the door and fled. No "Good night," no "Thanks for the lift," nothing. Just ... gone.

It was three o'clock, and I had only four more hours to kill. I spent those hours driving around the entire island twice, stopping only to get gas at a place that looked like a set left behind from filming *South Pacific.*

At seven A.M. I pulled up to the Sky Cap counter at Honolulu Airport. I got out, opened my trunk and let Harry out.

"Thanks," he said and disappeared into the terminal. I looked up. Two-dozen people waiting to deposit their luggage were staring at me, no doubt wondering how it was that my passenger had gotten out of the trunk rather than the passenger or rear door. It was one of those moments that begged for an explanation. However, I knew nothing I could say was going to make it better, so I just left.

I returned to my apartment, showered and got ready for bed. Just before my sleepy head touched my fluffy pillow, I said to myself: "Whhuuut ... and give up show business?"

Things turned considerably more serious after that. Art was growing frustrated with the lack of resolution to the staffing question.

I should say that for the most part, the two groups of the International Brotherhood of Teamsters got on famously. They were, after all, cut from the same cloth — just a bunch of big, happy-go-lucky guys who liked hackey-sack, Liar's Poker and banging into each other. There were twenty-five or thirty of them. They would cluster together, holding up their thumb and pinky finger and saying "Brah" this and "brah" that until Art showed up.

When Art drove up it was like Moses parting the Red Sea. The guys from the mainland would drift away from the locals, and out would come all the black intimidator sunglasses. When Art left the glasses would disappear, and the two sides would re-form as one.

It all came to a head one day in the parking lot at Turtle Bay. Art walked up to the head "Haoli" (Hawaiin for *asshole from the mainland*) and asserted, "I want you off my island."

The Haoli replied, "Sorry, Art. It ain't your island anymore."

To which Art just nodded and said, "Okay ... I accept your challenge."

At this point I went to the phone and called my employer. "You'd better straighten this thing out before the actors get spooked and want to come home," was the advice I received.

To his credit, "the Voice on the Phone" and several other executives flew over. In the end, it got settled; how or at what cost, I do not know to this day. And frankly, I don't care.

To be totally fair to Hawaii and the Hawaiian Teamsters, in spite of all the drama and angst, not one person nor one piece of equipment ever got touched. I had a wonderful time in Hawaii, and except for the fact that I have written this book and am now probably *persona non grata* for doing so, I would go back in a heartbeat.

I liked and admired Art Rutledge. He was as tough a guy as I ever met. He was totally fearless. He was passionate and relentless in his loyalty to his men, his union and his place in history. He was fair but firm, and I count my time with him as some of the most interesting in my whole career. Sadly, Art died in 1997 at the age of ninety.

The people of Hawaii were wonderful, the place was gorgeous, and it is still a terrific place to film. It is also the only place I have ever been that is prettier in person than it is in its travel brochures. So, "'Aloha' ... and 'mahalo' for not smoking."

I want to share one last story with you before we leave "Locations."

Because of the nature of the show, *Dallas: The Early Years* was scheduled without stage-built cover sets. Our first location was at Southfork, on the opposite side of Dallas from all our other locations, and miles from the nearest one.

It was our first day of filming. We had tons of extras, a large crew, two catering trucks to accommodate both crew and extras, and virtually our entire principal cast. It was big. I stood in the driveway of the location feeling confidant that we were off to a good start, smoother than I had any right to expect.

And then it snowed.

I couldn't believe it. We were stuck. The very first day, and the dominoes that had been so carefully arranged on the show we had worked so hard to get green-lit were about to tumble. I walked down the road from the house, and for the first and only time in my career, tears began to well up in my eyes. I felt totally betrayed.

Now, for the record, I am not a particularly religious guy. I don't believe God favors Notre Dame over Ohio State or even good over evil; but standing in that driveway I looked up and wailed, "How could you have done this to me?"

I knew it was only a matter of minutes before Mister Curmudgeon, Larry Elikann, would come up to me and say, "You—you screwed this up." I could handle him. I was more concerned with what I was going to tell the bosses back in town.

David came up to me and put his arm around my shoulders. "What could you do," he asked comfortingly?

I felt awful.

"C'mon, I'll buy you a cup of coffee."

We started for the chow wagon. I looked up again. The sky was lightening. I could make out a patch of blue in the distance. The snow was falling slower. We might just make it.

A car pulled up and Larry got out. He was ten minutes late. He took one look at me and barked, "Ya gave my driver the wrong directions." I looked at his driver. The man just shook his head "no," surreptitiously David and I both laughed. I wiped my eyes, hoping they would believe it was amusement and not a flood of relief.

I looked back up at the heavens and murmured, "Thank you."

No cover sets.

Cranky Directors.

Sliding down the razor blade of life.

Producing.

Budgeting

It is important to understand that there is no single way to format a budget. That is why there are at least twenty-eight different budget formats included with industry-standard budgeting software. There was a time when an United Artists production budget was expected to be ninety-six pages long. Talk about being precise. When budgeting a movie, you will always hear Producers talk about items that are above-the-line and below-the-line. This is a little movie lingo that you should know.

The line and those costs that appear above or below it are a throwback to the days when the major film studios ruled the world. In the studio days, Writers, Producers, Directors and Casting Executives were under contract and on salary. The studios paid them whether they were on a project or not. However, the Production Manager and all those below him on the totem pole were only paid when they were hired for a specific project. It was the studio version of *fixed costs* versus *variable costs*. Hence, the infamous "line" was what separated the two.

Generally, the above-the-line budget today consists of the story rights, Writer fees, Producers' salaries, the Director's budget, the cast and Casting Director costs, stunts and, if going on location, all these people's airfares, lodging, meals and car rentals. This also includes any other negotiated "perks." There are usually fringe benefits attached to most of the aforementioned line items: pensions, welfare (health benefits) and the like.

Below-the-line begins with the Production Manager and encompasses all the other departments — camera, grip, electric, props, set dressing, set construction, wardrobe, transportation, set operations, locations, and so on.

Let me quote me, Chairman Joe: "The budget is a living, breathing document that does not meet its final resting place until just before the green light." It's a good quote but an obscure reference. Let me explain. Just because you throw some numbers on a piece of paper does not mean you have accurately budgeted your project. No matter how skilled you are, your first pass at the budget is just that — your first attempt. There are three reasons for this. Despite your best guesses, you cannot know precise budgets for actors, locations and departmental needs. Let's take one at a time.

Actors' salaries are negotiable. They are based on their demand, the last time they worked and how valuable they are to the picture. Heck, often you don't even know who is going to be in the film at this stage.

You may or may not have your locations locked down, so you can't accurately input all the variables that might apply to any one of them. Just like with that nice house up the narrow road I told you about, how will your chosen location impact your equipment and manpower needs? It's all a guess at this point.

And finally, you do not yet have your department heads on board. It is the rare (and maybe nonexistent) Line Producer who can speak with absolute authority about every category in the budget. It never failed that I would make out a budget and underestimate, thinking, for instance, we needed twelve trucks, one catering truck and five additional vans to transport actors. When my Transportation Captain came on board, his detailed breakdown of equipment needs would show that twenty trucks were necessary, along with two catering trucks for heavy background performer days and a dozen extra vans. His numbers were always more accurate than mine because they are based on scouted knowledge and his expertise in this special area.

So the long and the short of it is this: Your numbers will change each time you get more specific information about the project. It's part of the business. Don't let this fact upset you.

Remember: Accuracy is your goal, not expedience.

But there you are with a semi-green-lit project. The powers-that-be are just waiting to see if the project can be done for a price they are willing to pay.

Lean on the three elements of budgeting: the schedule, the day-out-of-days and the hard facts. Let me explain more about the *hard facts.*

Basically there are costs that won't change no matter who is in charge. If you know that you need to rent a jib arm for three weeks, get on the phone and call an equipment house. Need to transport airplanes from Czechoslovakia to Budapest to be repainted to look like Storches? Call a vintage plane transporting company and get their fees. Don't know where to find such a company? Get on the Internet. Still no answer? Track down another film company that made a movie with vintage aircraft and ask them who they dealt with. Don't be lazy. I knew a Location Manager who spent a year and a half traveling all over the world to find the yacht they used in *Murder by Death.* While that's an extreme example, you can still start with the costs you already know. How much will you pay for the script? What will be your Producer fee? What is the Director's salary? Plug those numbers into the budget. What will you pay a Casting Director? How about her assistant? I'd stay away from stunt costs at this point because they are always schedule-contingent.

Once you have these costs, there are still other areas you can prepare. Will you and your director be on-location? If so, for how long? Will you just go to the location and stay, or will you and the director makes several trips before filming commences? These are all costs you can budget.

Again, let's use *Dallas: The Early Years* as our template.

For argument's sake, you and the director will make three trips before staying for the shoot. You will be casting in L.A. but needing to check locations in Texas. How much are the round trip airline tickets? Call the airlines, duhhh? No, call an airline and see if they will cut a deal with you. Tell them that you and the Director will be flying three times, but your cast and crew — and that could number in the sixties or seventies — will also be traveling to Texas as well.

You will be surprised at what you can come up with.

Whatever the final number is, place it in its own "above-the-line-travel" account. Break it out by the number of tickets and who will be using them. The reason for this is that some may be traveling coach and some may, by contract, be traveling first or business class. Also, don't discount the possibility that before the negotiation with actors is done, you may also be flying spouses to and from the location.

The next item is a little trickier. How many "man days" in a hotel? Each night's stay for each person is a "man day."

You and the Director alone could account for a significant number of "man days" before the camera even turns. Remember, when it comes to staying on location you must also count the days you stay in a hotel that are non-shooting days, like Saturday or Sunday.

How about "per diem," the money given to each cast and crewmember to cover food costs while on location? Those numbers can range from a low, across-the-board rate for most of your non-star actors to some amazingly high, agent-negotiated rates for your big stars. Again, the number of days for per diem will match the actual number of days while on location, not just while filming.

By the way, while speaking about your stars, it will be helpful to know just how outrageous the "perks" can be. I know of one movie several years ago where the lead actor's cars had to be flown to the location, half way around the world. Hopefully, for your sake, those days of wretched excess are gone. In addition, some union contracts may have clauses that guarantee "incidentals," meaning "laundry allowance."

At this point your above-the-line will look fairly meager because you have yet to add cast costs. What to do? You guess, assume, project. You anticipate and you communicate. It's a living, breathing document, right? Even if you are wildly wrong, at the end of the day you can simply go back and provide the real numbers. This is where working with a knowledgeable Casting Director, even if he or she is not yet on salary, can be a big help.

Whenever I see the words *allowance* or *miscellaneous* in a budget, I really see the word *lazy.* That is the connection I make. As Director of Physical Production at the University of Southern California's School of Cinematic Arts, I will not green-light a master's thesis film that has those words in the budget. There's no excuse. Do your research. Get the best numbers you can. You budget is alive, it will change, but often for the better.

Film is a business where "perception is reality" (another quote from Chairman Joe). If you appear lazy or unknowledgeable you will seriously undermine your own credibility. Horses smell fear; Hollywood smells incompetence.

We've talked about perks, but one word more about fringes. The Writer's Guild, Director's Guild and the Screen Actor's Guild all demand fringe benefits by contract. Find out what they are and what percentage you should input into your budget. And by the way, if you are budgeting a totally union film, *all* the department contracts contain "fringe benefits." Learn what they are because they vary from department to department.

That's a lot to wrap your head around, and we haven't even tackled below-the-line. Before we do that, you must make a basic decision. Are you paying *scale*— the minimum allowed by — or are you paying above scale? Believe it or not, sometimes paying only the contractual rate works against you. Like in any other business, the cream rises to the top. The better or more talented the individual, the more money he or she can demand in the open marketplace.

You will see a lot of *globals* when working below-the-line. A global is a number, once determined and put into the budget, that will be the calculus for that department, individual or group of individuals. This is the one thing about modern computerized budgeting systems that I really like.

For instance, you have decided to pay your electricians $19.76 an hour. Instead of constantly having to do the math for every hour of straight time, time-and-a-half and double-time, your computer will use the *global* number to figure out the details. You will have globals for every crewmember in every department. It is the one timesaving break you get in this entire process.

Let's drop down to the location account budget. Since you have not yet hired a Production Designer or a Location Manager, it's all right to speculate on your location costs. Pick a number. $5,000 a day? $10,000 a day? Who knows? Just plug in something. But be careful. Don't be so extravagant that you drive the bottom line of the budget through the roof. "Sophrosyne," as one of my high school teachers used to say: "Everything in moderation."

Globals and guessing will prevail through your post-production budget as well. What about music? Say no more. Will the picture be scored or will it depend on published music? And at what price? Post-production music is affectionately known as "the black hole of production." Along this path so many good filmmakers have lost their way that most studios have a separate music department.

Now we come to the *others* portion of the budget. The first *other* is the word *contingency*. In the biz, the contingency account is also referred to as "the dumbshit account" because it exists to repair and recover from all the "dumbshit" things that happen on any film. A nicer way to say it is: "The account of unanticipated events." But when you need to dip into it because one of your Teamsters backs into a prized and highly trained stunt camel, sending her by air express to the veterinarian two States away, you too will start calling it the "dumbshit" account. Stuff happens. Take the classic example of when the Assistant Cameraman loads a thousand-foot magazine of thirty-five millimeter film into the camera and, instead of opening the opposite side to position the film through the pull-down mechanisms, reopens the same side and exposes the negative — five hundred dollars gone, poof, just like that. Nobody could have anticipated it, not even Murphy.

I once worked on a pilot for television called *Bravo Two*. It was about the Los Angeles Harbor Patrol. We filmed it in Marina Del Rey. At one point the script called for a boater with severe diabetes to pass out at the helm of his boat as it roared through the marina. The boat ran up the loading ramp and flew into the parking lot where it crashed to the pavement. It was a dangerous and expensive stunt.

We planned to cover it with six cameras. We had to be careful that the boat had enough fuel to make it up the ramp but not so much that the fumes could ignite if the heavy landing caused sparks to fly. To say it was a tense time is to greatly understate the situation.

We rolled cameras; the stunt man hit the throttle. The boat roared through the Marina, went up the ramp, flew into the parking lot and crashed on the pavement. The stunt man got bounced around pretty good, but he was okay.

We were beginning to set up for the next shot when the Assistant Cameraman of the A-camera, the one with the widest and therefore most essential angle, walked toward us. He was pale as a ghost. Allow me to just say that an Assistant Cameraman walking towards you with an absence of blood beneath his skin is never a good sign.

"I don't know how to tell you this," he began, as my bowels started to loosen. "I forgot to thread the A-camera."

You would think that the crew would get together and beat this individual profusely about the head and shoulders. However, it was such a stunning admission that all I could do was turn to the stunt man and say, "How much to do it again?" Stuff happens.

This allows me to segue to insurance.

Insurance is a big issue and therefore has its own chapter. However, for this discussion, take the figure of 2 percent of the *all in* (or total) budget and add it to the cost of your film. You may also need a completion bond. Allow 6 percent for budgeting purposes, although you will probably be able to negotiate that down.

What else goes into the "other" account? Publicity, legal services, promotional DVDs and accounting services.

If you are going to a foreign country you may be required to post a surety bond with their local unions. DGA Canada comes to mind. This is money you will have to raise, but since under normal circumstances you will get it back, you may or may not show it as a line item in your budget. This is also true of refundable taxes like the V.A.T. If you are going to a foreign country you must account for costs of bank charges and be cognizant of the exchange rate.

Okay, the first pass of your budget is way more than the money people are prepared to put up. So what? Go back to the beginning. Call your proposed Casting Director. Ask for some random quotes for actors on your "wish list." Make some calls. See if you can get a sense of what locations similar to yours have cost other filmmakers. Both of these figures will be better than the ones you had. Replace your old numbers with these new ones.

You have overlooked one enormous piece of the puzzle. You have not spoken to your Director to ask if the 40-day schedule you are proposing is something he or she can accomplish. You take her to lunch. You mention in passing that you have scheduled the shoot for 40 days. At this point she will say to you, "Oh my heavens, I can't possibly shoot this in less than 50 days. In fact, if you schedule it for 40 days, I don't want to direct it."

Welcome to your new 50-day schedule and all the attendant problems that creates, not the least of which is actor availability.

On the other hand, perhaps she will say, "Wonderful! I can certainly do it in that time." Congratulations. Lean back and enjoy the rest of your lunch. You have just passed one giant hurdle and entered the realm of what it is actually going to cost. Now you can really project your actor, location, truck and equipment rental costs.

I want to say something before going further. Another quote from Chairman Joe: "Your budget will go up before it comes down." Remember, you heard it here first.

As more people are hired and asked to provide what they think their various departments will need, out of a sense of self-preservation they will overestimate their costs. Don't get upset or anxious. I told you before that this would happen. They are subject to the same ebb and flow of information as you are. It never fails that, as information becomes more solid, their costs will decrease. And if they don't, it will be a good thing that someone caught something you overlooked or underestimated.

Let's revisit "the house up a narrow road" from earlier. Any Transportation Captain not having seen the locations is going to budget for the worst possible scenario. He's "covering his ass." Once the Transpo can actually see the location, much of what he budgeted for may not be necessary. His budget can only go down, not up. Multiply that tendency by the number of department heads, and you will understand my point.

And while Chairman Joe is spouting quotes, here's another one: "If your budget is accurate and your film is accomplished on schedule, it is difficult (though not impossible) to be over-budget."

I know this sounds a little like the theological argument between free will and predestination, but think about it. The key is *accurately budgeted*. If it is, you will be within the margin of acceptable over/unders. That margin is usually 3 percent either way, above or below the budget. Never vastly overestimate your costs so you can come in under budget. It will make you look dishonest or unknowledgeable.

Here's the good news. The Casting Director, to whom you have sent the script, is eager to cast your film. He or she will provide you with some preliminary cast numbers. You input them into your budget. They will change as your day-out-of-days takes hold, but they are better numbers than you had before — primarily because you had none.

Slowly, as your above-the-line figures are accurately taking shape, your below-the-line numbers will as well. When figuring logistics (like location and others), you have come to a crossroads. Do you schedule favoring locations or do you budget for the most efficient day-out-of-days spread for your cast. Because this was such an undertaking, when scheduling and budgeting *The English Lady* I made the assumption we would start in Germany and end in England. Fortunately for the budget, that would have entailed making only three *run-of-the-show* deals. Let us suppose you are not that fortunate. When you budget favoring locations, it plays havoc with your cast budget. You have too many expensive actors sitting in hotel rooms not working. You go back in, schedule the most efficient day-out-of-days, and step back. You now have to make three trips back to a distant location to accommodate the needed scenes. You will then have to weigh the cost of logistics versus tighter actor costs. It is a tough decision, but money talks. In the end you will do what is right for your budget. The only real exception here could be the lead actor who, for reasons of prior commitment, forces you to conform to his or her schedule.

At long last you come to a conclusion — a road map, if you will. You will start far and work back, carrying two or three actors. Hopefully they are not too expensive, and their deals won't force you to put them in five-star hotels.

One other thing has happened. Because you have a game plan you can now schedule and budget your stunt players. Voila, you have a fairly accurate (but sure to change) above-the-line budget. This is because the actual negotiations between you and the various agents and managers can alter your numbers. The good news is that you can say "no" if the demands are too far from what you can afford.

When budgeting below-the-line costs, remember that each account will consist of *labor,* meaning salaries and *materials*— that which is purchased, rented or manufactured. All of it will be a function of time — prep time, shooting time and wrap time. Each of these — rentals, purchases, and manufacturing — should have its own line in the applicable category of your budget.

Your first below-the-line account, that of the Production Manager, will also include a Unit Manager (if one is to be hired), the First and Second Assistant Directors, and any additional *man days* for other Assistant Directors or Production Assistants as needed. It will include a Production Secretary and a Production Coordinator. The subject of who will prep where and for how long will affect not only salary but travel, lodging and per diem as well.

Since the First Assistant Director, and conceivably the key Second Assistant Director, will be the choice of the Director, they will probably be hired locally and flown to the location, with all the attendant travel, lodging and per diem of everyone else. Theoretically, the Production Secretary and Coordinator can be picked up on location, but sometimes not.

A word here about Directors selecting or not selecting their own First Assistant Directors. By DGA contract, Directors have the right to choose their own A.D.s. Sometimes they will defer to the Producer. That is what happened with me and Larry Elikann on *The Early Years.* I got him a good one named Freddy. But their styles clashed.

On shooting days we had six o'clock-leaving calls from the hotel. Larry would come down to the lobby at five-thirty and read the day's scenes ... the only time he would have read them. That was a good thing to realize because most of the time planning shots with Larry went something like this: "Joe, what the hell should I do here?"

I would make a suggestion based on actually having read the scene.

Larry: "Naw, naw, that's a terrible idea. You're killin' me. You're killin' me."

Of course, two days later we would do the shots I suggested, word for word. But by that time he would be on to the next way to torture me.

By now I was wise to all Larry's tricks, and I tried to advise Freddy.

"Freddy, get down there by five-thirty. Sit with him. Bond with him."

Freddy: "Nope. Call is six. I'll be down at six."

Yikes. A big mistake. Larry decided he didn't like him and wasn't going to deal with him.

We came to the biggest night of the show. We had built oil rigs; now we were going to blow them up and burn them. We had five "six-ups" — rigs pulled by six mules bound together by a heavy wooden through-rod or beam, guys on horseback, people dressed as Klansmen and black sharecroppers. We had bulldozers to pull the legs out from under the oil rigs if the explosion didn't topple them. We had guns, flaming torches, fire, squib hits and more.

Larry walked up to Freddy and said, "I know what the next shot is, but I'm not telling you."

Freddy came running over to me and said, "That son-of-a-bitch won't tell me what the next shots are."

That is about the worst scenario from a safety standpoint that there is. However, by this time I knew from experience that if I just went to Larry and asked what the shots were, I would be treated to the same maddening answers as Freddy. I decided on a different approach.

I went to Larry and said, "Hey, Chief, the guy with the horses thinks you don't need him tonight. He's taking his horses and going home."

Larry freaked.

"Naw, naw, he can't go home. He's killin' me. I need him. He works in the next five shots." And he began to rattle them off.

"Kay," I said. "I'll tell 'im to stay."

I walked off. Passing Freddy, I articulated the five shots as Larry had stated them. A half hour later Larry glowered at me and said, "You'll pay for that, too." Producing.

Back to the budget.

What other costs might attend the Production Manager's account? The cost of several Production Boards and strips, if done by hand, or computer fees if done electronically. The production accounting department may also appear in the Production Manager category, but I prefer to treat that separately.

The production accounting account consists of the Production Accountant, Accounts Payable Clerk, Estimator, Payroll Coordinator, and Office Runner (often known as your gofer or Production Assistant). What is a "gofer?" Someone who "goes for this or goes for that." The materials and supplies will consist of computers and general office supplies, like stationary, envelopes, stamps, etc. Their purpose can't be overstated. This team will refine the budget, keep track of the costs during production, and create, track and authenticate your estimated costs to complete your film. They will also define and administer your "draw down" account.

More on this subject later.

All personnel in this department reports to the Production Accountant and the Production Manager. Obviously, as the Producer you are entitled to (and must avail yourself of) their information on a constant basis.

Accounts Payable will track, record and pay the incoming bills. The Estimator constantly estimates whether the outlay of money is consistent with the schedule and the budget. There is a piece of paper called a *hot sheet* that lists certain *bell-wether* accounts. If these accounts are in line with your budget, you are probably in reasonably good shape. The accounts are crew overtime, extras, set dressing and meals. If any of these accounts suddenly or unexpectedly spike, you will want to investigate why. Are you using more extras than you budgeted? Are you working too much overtime?" Are your sets costing more to dress than you originally anticipated?

The Payroll Coordinator prepares the time cards for payment. You will probably employ a payroll service for your cast and crew pay. You will want your records as accurate, neat and organized as humanly possible.

I have learned: "From chaos come costs."

And, before you ask, the answer is "yes" ... Chairman Joe.

Your production design account is where you budget the needs required for the look, style, and physical location of your film. This account will consist of Production Designer, Art Director, Assistant Art Director, Set Designer, Assistant Set Designer, Researcher or Researchers (if your film is a period piece), Sketch Artists; Art Department Runners, and, significantly, the Construction Coordinator. It is perfectly okay to treat construction as its own account, and we will do so here.

Let's back up. The Production Designer will be one of the first people hired — right after your Casting Director, Production Manager and Production Accountant. He or she will need an office and very probably an art department. This is a room large enough to hold research books and drawn sketches of sets, locations, vehicles and wardrobe.

The Production Designer may hire (unless you have one of your own) the Location Manager. They do not belong to the same guild or union, but the LM will report in the early stages to the Production Designer.

The construction account covers manpower, materials and incidentals related to both the building of sets and the alteration of practical locations. What does this mean? Case in point: The Corleone Compound in the *Godfather* was not really a compound at all. It just appeared that way onscreen.

The location was a cul-de-sac street one block above the Staten Island Community College. The Production Designer had a wall constructed from one side of the street to the other, walling off the remaining homes in the cul-de-sac. An imposing iron gate was added as the entrance, and the street was completely covered with gravel. The net result was that it all seemed like part of one compound. That's the magic of moviemaking.

Your construction account consists of the Construction Coordinator, Construction Accountant (depending on the size of your production), Carpenters, prop-makers, Scenic Artists (painters), Greens Persons (handles flowers, plants, trees and shrubs), Construction Medic (builders bang themselves up at an alarming rate), and others specific to your film. They will need tools, both large and small, lumber, a place to build, lunch while working or a meal allowance to get their own food, and incidentals (nails, paint brushes and the like).

The construction department will work building sets during prep and maintaining them through production. The number of bodies may shrink while filming, but the department itself will remain viable throughout the shoot and must be budgeted accordingly.

Your set dressing account will consist of the Set Decorator, Lead Man, Charge (the rough equivalent to the Best Boy), and additional Dressers. They will need their own truck, although that money will probably be accounted for out of the transportation account. It is possible that you will want two trucks and two complete dressing crews. Set dressing kept on rental beyond the point it is needed can get pricey. If you have two crews, one can be setting up while the other one is taking down and returning items to the rental house. This is not essential in every situation, but it is worth considering, particularly in the early stages of your budget before reality — and a budget too large for the company — takes hold.

Next will be the cinematography account, consisting of the Director of Cinematography, the Camera Operator, the First Assistant Cameraman, the Second Assistant Cameraman, and, if shooting 35 millimeter film, a Loader (someone whose function it is to load camera magazines and *can* the exposed film). In this account may also appear a Still or Production Stills Photographer. This individual will record the entire process of making the picture, usually photographing the rehearsals and other "around-the-set" goings on. These pictures can either be used as a record of the process or for publicity. The latter is why in some budgets the "Still Photographer" comes out of the publicity account. The camera, all the lenses and any other gear necessary to support the camera's needs (all the way down to rolls of tape to secure the film cans for transport to the lab) goes in the cinematography account.

You must take into account that your Cinematographer and other department heads may need prep time. Clearly, the Production Designer, Art Director and Location Manager or Managers will require prep time because they are the very essence of generating the look and logistics of your film. However, so too will the Electric Gaffer, the Key Grip and even the set dressing department. It is for you to assess what reasonable amount of preparation time they will require, but you do need to ask and budget for it.

Not all of these individuals, with the possible exception of the Location Manager and construction department, will prep on location. Your Gaffer and Key Grip may prep locally by rounding up equipment and putting it in supply racks in rented trucks. These people aren't paid for travel, lodging or per diem until they actually go to the location, but they do receive pay for prepping. If you are shooting locally, their travel and other costs will not exist. That is obviously true of everyone else on your show as well.

While you are still in the camera account, you must ask yourself, "Will the picture require a second unit camera crew? Will it have additional cameras for some heavy first unit days? Will there be helicopter work?" If the answer to any or all of these is "yes," it must be included in this account. It should be broken out and identified specifically. No "allows" or "miscellaneous" here.

It is possible, depending on the size of your project, that you will need a Second Unit Director. I would put his salary and travel needs in this account as well. It can be argued that a Director is an above-the-line cost. However, without knowing how long or how big the second unit will be, it is possible that the job will go to another cinematographer. The specifics of your individual project will drive how you input information. And, by the way, it may be wrong, and you will have to go back in to your budget at a later date and fix it.

Let's move on.

The electric department account consists of the Gaffer, the Electric Best Boy, electricians and additional electric man-days.

The Gaffer is the boss of the electrical department. The Best Boy is responsible for men and material. The electricians run cable and set the lights. Additional man-days speaks for themselves. Well, almost.

Take the following scenario: You have a split call — one that starts at noon and runs until midnight. You have day work and night work. However, your normal ten-man electrical crew will need help when the sun goes down. Do you simply hire four more guys and have them sit around until dusk? No, that's bad money. You call them at 4 P.M. Why is that significant? Because you will only have to pay them for eight hours of straight time. The rest of your electrical crew, the ones that started at noon, will receive time-and-a-half for their ninth and tenth hour of work, and double time for the eleventh and twelfth hours. Get it?

The point is: These late-call man-days should be listed separately in the electrical account. If you simply add twelve-hour man-days you won't use, you run the risk of looking sloppy or unknowledgeable to the "Powers That Be." This input is different from the days when you legitimately need to up the manpower projection for additional electricians on a twelve-hour day.

What else goes into the electrical budget? Rented lights. How many and for how long? Then there is the sub-account titled *expendables.* This covers items like gels: sheer plastic sheets of various colors — orange for sunlight, black for night-light — placed over window glass or in front of lights. Once these are used, they are thrown away and, therefore, replaced. Globes or light blubs burn out and need to be replaced. You will want the electricians to physically give you the "burn outs" that they are asking to replace. Both of the above should be anticipated and listed as line items in the electric sub-account. There are other expendables as well: rope, tape, chalk, and so on. Think of anything they might need that is used once or twice and then replaced.

The grip department account consists of the Key Grip (boss of the grips), the Grip Best Boy (responsible for men and material of the grip department), the Dolly Grip and grip crew. It can be as few as two or three, or as many as ten or twelve. Only you can determine the right size of your crew, but a word of caution here. I have seen it a hundred times. It's a bad philosophy to think: *Any money for cast, no money for crew.* Don't make this fatal mistake. Don't underestimate either the importance or the correct size of your crew. You can't make a movie without them.

There may also be days when your grip requirements mirror those of the electric department, meaning additional manpower either for a full twelve hours or on a delayed call.

There should be a line item in the grip budget for *additional equipment.* Things like a jib arm, scissor lifts, car mounts, cranes, etc. And speaking of cranes, I should mention the "c word."

Eddie Denault, the Head of Production at Lorimar, had a great dislike for cranes. He called them the "c word." We were not allowed to mention the "c word" anywhere near him. I suspect that the genesis of Eddie's dislike was both the cost and the fact that it came with a Teamster driver and at least one grip. That made the crane an expensive toy in the hands of directors who didn't really know how to use it or when to employ it.

The Titan Crane was a remarkable piece of equipment. It could work in the desert, on the beach, on steep inclines, in rain, sleet and snow. Its wheels could rotate to a forty-five degree angle, making it the perfect large crab dolly. This was great because most dollies move forward and back, side-to-side or along rail track, some of which may be curved. "Crabbing" or turning the dolly's wheels, allows the dolly to move in a diagonal direction.

On my second job at Lorimar, my director insisted that he needed a Titan Crane for a night shot that involved rain. In order to see rain on the screen when shooting in 35 MM, the rain must be backlit. The director wanted to be up high, looking down on the water-soaked street. Given that scenario, the Titan seemed appropriate, so I fought for it. Because Eddie liked and trusted me, he grudgingly gave in.

Friday night, after a long day of filming, the Titan and two extra grips arrived for the night shot. Our special effects team ran Rain Birds around the intersection. Rain Birds look like lawn sprinklers, only they are strung much higher and form a perimeter around the area to be filmed. When they are fired up, heavy rain falls over the set, perfectly mimicking a real downpour.

As we set for the shot, I got called to a home a few doors down the street. The woman was upset about the lights shining towards her house. After assuring her we would make the adjustment, I headed back to the set. When I got there I was dumbstruck to observe that rather than using the crane for the camera, they had placed one of the arch lights on it.

An arch light is a very large and heavy light, sometimes called a Brute. I started for the director to protest when a car pulled up and Eddie Denault got out. First he looked up at the light on the crane, then straight at me. He looked as if I had just killed his dog while saying the "c word." I felt terrible. I was going to explain, but he just ducked back into his car and drove off. I was in big trouble.

Needless to say, I spent a long worrisome weekend until I could get to him and try to explain. Monday morning, first thing, I dashed up to his office.

Hat-in-hand, I began, "Eddie... I ..."

He looked at me and said, "Next time a director wants a crane, tell 'em to get a ladder and a pogo stick."

He never said another word about it.

Sure enough, on the very next picture the director wanted a crane — but not just for a shot. He wanted it for the entire shoot. Mindful of Eddie's admonition, I argued against it. The director was certain he needed it. He was so sure, in fact, that if he had had to choose between me and the equipment, he would have given me up in a heartbeat.

I went to Eddie.

The film was titled *Desperate Women*. Unfortunately, the picture wasn't nearly as good as the title. It was going to be shot in the Mexican dessert in summer where only Hell is hotter, and that's a big maybe.

Earl Bellamy Senior was the director. Eddie liked and trusted him, and allowed us to take the dreaded piece of equipment. If you ever have to shoot in the box canyons and snake-infested landscapes of northern Mexico, Earl is the guy you want to go with. The camera was never off the back of the crane. We were scheduled to shoot twenty-one days. Because of Earl's acumen and exhaustive preparation we finished in twenty. We also saved on a considerable amount of additional grip manpower.

So sometimes the "c word" isn't so terrible after all.

By the way, this was also the show on which I got talked into the one really big and embarrassing mistake of my career as an Assistant Director.

We were housed in Mexicali but drove out each morning sixty miles south to a Hell-on-Earth place called Laguna Salada. How anybody ever found this place I do not know. In the mornings it was a lake fed by underground springs; by dusk it would evaporate to little more than a puddle. We, however, didn't film near the water. Oh no, we turned north and drove up into the box canyons. Hell is at least twenty degrees cooler than that place.

We had contracted with local farmers to employ twenty-one of their horses. They were transported to and from the location in large horse transport vehicles, seven to a truck. We had to pay for the trucks, the drivers, the gas, the horses, the wranglers, the hay and, in a deal unique to Mexico, the farmers whose horses we hadn't selected so they wouldn't "lose face." The point is, the number of horses we used varied from day to day, and how many we used was in large part determined by cost.

Lorimar, in its wisdom, had understaffed the production department. I was out their basically alone. I did have two Mexican Assistant Directors, but neither one of them spoke English and I couldn't speak Spanish. A marriage, as they say, made in heaven. I called back to L.A. for help. And they sent me help, all right.

Enter blond, curly-haired Jamie. He was relentlessly upbeat, ingratiatingly good-natured, and unendingly energetic. He was also a spiraling dust devil of bad ideas, poor judgment, and hasty decision making — a whirling dervish of catastrophe.

He had heard it was hot in the desert (imagine that), so he bought a pair of sun glasses. Not dark ones to cut the desert glare — oh no, not Jamie. He bought yellow ones because he thought they looked cooler. And they did, only they acted like magnifying glasses, and after only two hours Jamie's eyes puffed up and swelled shut. He ended up back at the hotel, resting on a comfortable bed in an air-conditioned room, while I trudged on alone in the Devil's furnace.

His return to work coincided with a series of scenes with all twenty-one horses. Normally we put the next day's call sheet out around four in the afternoon. On this particular day, Earl told me he would only be looking into the canyons and not the reverse. That meant we would only need two thirds, or fourteen, of the rented horses. We would save considerable money on that third truck. However, as an Assistant Director I knew that the Director had the prerogative to change his mind. I listed all three trucks and all twenty-one horses on the call sheet. Re-enter blond, disastrous Jamie.

"Joe, he only needs fourteen. He'll never see the other way. Why spend the money on the third truck if he's never going to do a reverse?" Maybe it was the heat, maybe it was the fact we were close to going over-budget, but I allowed Jamie's logic to override my instincts ... and I got what I deserved.

Right on cue, mid-way through the next day Earl turned to me and said, "Joe, I've changed my mind. I have one shot in the opposite direction. I'm going to need three more horses."

I could feel my heart sink. I had to tell him I had not called the third truck. Nevermind it was because of his assurance we wouldn't need it. I had undermined one of the basic Director/A.D. tenants of production: *Never short-circuit the Director's prerogative.* He knew it and I knew it.

To Earl's credit he never scolded me or criticized my decision. We both knew we could get the shot by re-allocating the horses we did have. Matching horses is not as obvious as matching actors or wardrobe. No. It was in the way he looked at me. I had let him down. To this day, if I think of that moment I get a queasy feeling in the pit of my stomach.

Jamie, of course, was conspicuously absent from that discussion; he was probably back in the make-up trailer chatting up one of the actresses. Telling stories about Jamie is a little like an alcoholic taking just one drink — it forms an irresistible compulsion. And so...

We drove back from Mexicali to the United States in a convoy of fifteen seat vans. Jamie and I were in the last one, with three of the young women stars of the film. At the border one of the women got caught with a small amount of marijuana. Jamie was out of the van like he'd been fired from a cannon.

"Jamie, Jamie," I called to him, "let the Baja Film Rep deal with it. You stay out of it."

"Don't worry," the blond Flash reassured me. "I know how to deal with these guys." And off he went.

The upshot of this little vignette is that we didn't see Jamie or the actress for the next six months. Prison, I suspect, but I don't know for certain. One more Jamie story (the last — I promise).

A year later I was producing a series on the Warner Brothers Ranch, a block north of the main studio, called *Married: The First Year.* The interior of the lead house was on a stage. Every night at six, like clockwork, Jamie would tool up in his yellow Karmen Ghia. He had developed a crush on one of the young actresses. He would roll up, park right in the front of the elephant doors and disappear inside. The elephant doors are those large stage doors through which all manpower and equipment come and go. We asked him over and over again not to park there, but it fell on deaf ears. One evening the Teamster captain said to him nicely, "Jamie, your car is in the way when we try to wrap. Please don't park it there. It makes my job that much more difficult."

And Jamie said, "Sounds like you've got a problem."

Oh boy!

One week later Jamie rolled up and parked. He went inside. When he came out this time, his car was gone. At first he laughed, thinking it was only a practical joke and the guys had just pushed it around the side of the stage. However, a rapid trip around the building quickly dispelled that notion. He returned to where his car normally resided and noticed a large chalk arrow on the ground and the words "Follow the arrows and find Jamie's car." He began to do just that. He followed a trail of arrows, each propelling him onward to the next — through the parking lot, past other stages and finally back toward his point of origination. But instead of ending at the elephant doors, the last arrow directed him to a large industrial dumpster. Amused, as if he were on some hyper-charged Easter egg hunt, Jamie climbed up and looked in. Sure enough, there lay his car. It had been fork-lifted in, and only a fork lift would get it out. That's when it dawned on Wonder Boy that he was going to need help retrieving it.

The show wrapped for the day, the elephant doors opened and people began to file out. Jamie called to everyone within earshot to help him rescue his car. To a man they ignored him. One by one the crew left until finally only he and the Teamster captain remained.

"Look," said Jamie. "That was funny, but I've got to get my car back. I need to go home. I will need it for work tomorrow."

The Teamster captain simply replied, "Sounds like you got a problem." And left for the day.

Lest you think I have been too harsh on poor old Jamie, he eventually calmed down and gradually grew up and actually went on to a pretty big career. He was, in spite of himself, likable. He didn't have a mean bone in his body, and it was hard to stay angry at him for very long.

Back to the budget.

The grip department will have expendables as well. Here I will mention the kit fee. Kits are personal supplies that will, in time, have to be replaced and therefore paid for by the show. Sandbags are a good example of something a grip might own and bring but have to re-buy because of wear and tear during the course of your film. The kit fee is usually paid at the same time as salary but is generally not subject to tax. The kit fee is usually between fifty and a hundred dollars per week.

Other departments may have kit fees as well, such as make up, hair, wardrobe and assistant camera. In truth, the kit fee is another one of those little *industry subterfuges*. You want to pay an individual a little more than you are paying others, but you don't want to set off another round of negotiations.

The sound department will consist of the boom operator, the mixer, and a cable man. The longest-running argument in the business is whether a television company is required to have a two-man or a three-man sound crew. Three is better. I used to say, "Don't trip over hundred dollar bills picking up nickels."

Items to be budgeted for this department will be equipment, sound tape, travel, lodging and per diem. While you're at it, you might want to add an assistant or gofer to this account as well. The reason being that this department is wedded to the set. If they need something that's not at their immediate beck and call, they can't leave to get it. The entire production would sit around and wait for their return. That is death to your budget.

I've been waiting to get to the locations account. This consists of the Location Manager, the Assistant Location Manager, the Permit Administrator (a fancy way to say *the gofer who files and retrieves filming permits*), and perhaps Location Scouts. One or all of them may get a "car allowance" because of the amount of running around town they will have to do.

You may end up paying "drive to" money to some cast and crew. This mileage money should be anticipated as a line item in this account. Every location that is not being built on a sound stage should be listed in this account. In addition, parking, filming permits, police and other security, fire officers (if applicable), and lunch set-up rental (including eating location, tents, chairs, tables and space heaters), should be anticipated in this account.

Also there is petty cash. Much of what the Location Managers have to deal with are unexpected intrusions. What does that mean? You're filming on a residential street. The guy down the block is mowing his lawn. The sound intrudes on the intimate scene you are filming. The Director yells, "Turn that damn thing off."

Easier said then done.

The guy on the lawnmower may want to continue. It is the Location Manager who will have to approach the happy gardener and say, "If you would be so kind as to do that in an hour, we would like to give you twenty dollars for your trouble." Ninety-nine percent of the time, when given the choice between continuing and getting twenty bucks for postponing what he didn't really want to do in the first place, the homeowner will stop mowing. Multiply that by two or three times every day, and you can see why petty cash is essential to a smooth-running show. Jackhammers on commercial streets, loud blaring radios on window ledges, taxicabs in the middle of your shot, and on and on and on. All, by the way, are legitimate expenditures in the process of getting the day's work done.

One major word of caution: Some of the best fiction in the history of the world has been written in the petty cash account. Here's what I mean: On the very first job I did in motion pictures, the one for the guy who only wanted to know if I had a pulse, I misplaced the very first hundred dollars of petty cash that I was given. I was mortified. It was beyond stupid. But I knew enough not to try and bluff Mr. Vreeland.

I went to him, with head down in shame, and told him I had lost my petty cash. I was sure he would be angry with me. Instead, without missing a beat, he said, "Oh you didn't lose it. You gave twenty dollars to the cab guy who blocked our shot. And you probably had to give at least ten dollars to the kid with the loud radio. And what about the store we blocked? The owner must have been given at least thirty bucks for that inconvenience." And quicker than you could say, "Schmuck, how could you lose the money?" Roger had explained away every cent and became a hero in a young man's eyes.

I contrast that with a job I did several months later for a commercial outfit called Audio Productions. It was a commercial for a bank. It shot for three weeks (which is long for a commercial), and I had over three thousand dollars in petty cash run through my hands. But I had learned my lesson. I was scrupulous in accounting for every last cent. I had receipts and explanations up the wazoo. When the job finished, I went to the Vice-President of Production to account for the money. He looked over my receipts, then at me. "You mean to tell me you had three grand go through your fingers and you've accounted for every penny," he asked incredulously?

"Yes," said I, puffing out my chest. "And you didn't help yourself to at least a couple of hundred?"

"No, sir," I replied indignantly.

The executive stared at me for a moment and then said simply, "Schmuck."

There it was. I was a schmuck for losing the money and a schmuck for accounting for every dime. Schmuck in, schmuck out. Hollywood is a strange place indeed.

During the eighties, when I was with Lorimar Productions, we used to have a saying about petty cash: "No tire marks." In other words, you could turn in almost any receipt and explain it away, but the accountants would take a dim view of receipts you had obviously just picked up off the floor. If you've ever been to the race track and seen guys gathering losing tickets up off the floor so they can write off the supposed loss on their income tax, you will have some idea of the filmmaking equivalent.

I worked with a Location Manager named Mike Beche. I loved Mike.

He was a great guy and a great asset to our shows, but Mike had more curves than a Formula One raceway. He figured out that it took the accountants at Spelling Productions approximately six weeks to reconcile the expenses for any one episode of a series. Mike would put in receipts early, late or not at all. Six weeks after the scout lunch no one could remember what show it was supposed to be charged to. Clever, yes. Honest? Mmm...

The accountants soon got wise. They said to themselves, "Ah hah another wise guy who thinks he's gonna tinker with the system." They decided that Mike could no longer charge things on his own charge card. They figured there was too great a likelihood that his bills would get commingled with theirs. They insisted that he get a separate card just for the show. Whereupon Mike got a charge card that offered one frequent flyer mile for every dollar spent. By the end of the show there was no place on Earth he couldn't fly for free. Talk about "Don't throw me into the Briar Patch."

I had the exact opposite situation on *Dallas: The Early Years.* Lorimar insisted that I use my own charge card in Texas, and they would reimburse me. They were the masters of hanging onto money and the interest it generated. We stayed at the Marriott Hotel on the LBJ Highway. We were treated like royalty. Since my charge card was paying for the rooms, I got all the Marriot stay-free points. The show went well, the cast and crew were happy, and I didn't pay for a room in a Marriott Hotel for a long time. You gotta love this business.

The Wardrobe account is for the Costume Designer. On a large epic period piece this is the person who designs and draws the look of the clothes. On a smaller show she may be the one who goes shopping with the stars. It's not uncommon to have both a male wardrobe person and a female wardrobe person, seamstresses (costumes tear or need to be altered, sometimes overnight), and a runner — someone who takes the clothes to the dry cleaners and picks them up and returns them to the wardrobe department. On a large period piece you may have several male and female wardrobe personnel.

In this account will appear the dry cleaning allowance. The word *allowance* in this context is legitimate because you have no way of knowing how many trips to the cleaners any one garment will require. All you can do is guess.

You will need a line item for shipping here. Unless you are filming locally, you will either have to send your wardrobe people on ahead to shop with the actors, or you will have to ship the wardrobe acquired locally. Clothing tends to be heavy, and shipping it is expensive. Do your research carefully before you just throw a number into the budget. Believe it or not, I have worked on shows where the wardrobe budget equaled or beat the transportation budget.

One other note about wardrobe: It is entirely possible you will need multiples of your costumes. Weather, stunts, or simple wear and tear can result in the necessity of anywhere from two to twenty or more of a particular piece of wardrobe.

The transportation account consists of the needs of the Transportation Coordinator; Captain; Co-Captain; Dispatcher; and Drivers, which in itself consists of the production van (including sound equipment), camera truck, electric trucks, grip trucks, prop trucks, honey wagons, star motor homes, set dressing trucks, special effects forty-footers, set vans; make-up trailers, wardrobe trailers, generators, motor homes, and production cars.

All the aforementioned vehicles will have at least one driver. Production rentals are cars assigned to individual crewmembers by contract. It is also possible that you will need a standby mechanic. Trucks break down, but the circus keeps rolling. Here comes another violation of my own rule about slinging terms like "miscellaneous." Unforeseen expenses may plague the transportation department as well. It's okay to budget for a few.

I'll never forget how on *Dallas: The Early Years* we filmed in an open field. It was where Digger, drunken and forlorn, stumbles on the black gold that should have made his family rich beyond measure. We finished the day's work around seven, packed up the trucks and prepared to depart. From out of nowhere we were overwhelmed with a torrential rainfall. The heaviest trucks sank to their axles in the mud. The trucks weren't going anywhere.

To his everlasting credit, the Transportation Captain stayed out all night locating and contracting for giant tow trucks capable of extricating our vehicles. The next morning we were out and shooting as if nothing had happened. It did, however, come at considerable financial cost—almost five thousand dollars.

The long and the short of it is: Murphy's Law roams the transportation account. An allowance for the unforeseen (say shit happens) is acceptable in this account.

Gas and overnight parking should be anticipated here as well. In New York they would always say the trucks were "going back to the barn." The "barn" was a fenced in area on Tenth Avenue whose rental was passed on to the shooting company.

Tires, off-site repairs and overnight security should be in this account as separate items too.

Your project may have one or more special effects forty-footers. Will you have vintage cars? Perhaps you will have ten. Will you pay ten people plus gas to drive to your location? Think car carrier. A car carrier can usually hold up to ten cars and requires only one driver. This equates to quicker, safer, cheaper. Will they have to use toll roads and therefore pay tolls to get to a location? It goes in the budget.

Will you be paying for people's cell phones as they drive? If so, make a reasonable estimate and put it in your budget.

Before leaving this department, I would like to share another true episode in my life. Hopefully you won't deem it inappropriate. Just rest assured I could not make this stuff up. It happened down in Dallas. I had invited Alvin Milliken, head of the Dallas Teamsters, and an associate of his to have drinks in the lobby of our hotel. Alvin had been appreciative of the fact that I had contacted him early in the process. I felt this was my moment to make a reasonable deal with him on the number of trucks and drivers we would require for *Dallas: The Early Years.*

Alvin was, and is, a very good guy but a little too serious at times. He was big, intense and slightly intimidating. He was also a little square, all business and not a man to be taken lightly. It was Halloween night. I never realized that in North Dallas Halloween is akin to a national holiday. People down there took it extremely seriously. The place was flooded with people in costume — bumble bees, princesses and gorillas abounded. I was immersed in a serious negotiation with Alvin when behind him, across the lobby, came an enormous giant phallus. It had two pillows attached to a string to simulate testicles and they were dragging along the floor.

All I can say is: You try negotiating with a Teamster official under those conditions. I completely lost my concentration. I was also afraid Alvin would turn around, see it and be insulted that I had arranged to meet him in such an undignified place. I was also certain that if I didn't have a witness, I would never be sure I hadn't just dreamt the whole thing.

I excused myself, went to the house phone and called upstairs to my Production Manager, a lovely man named Robert Schneider. I asked him if he wouldn't mind joining us. Bob walked into the lobby, saw the giant phallus, and burst out laughing. That caused Alvin to look as well. It was at that precise moment that the giant phallus, which, as it turned out, was constructed of two pieces, grew larger and spewed talcum powder from the tip all over the lobby. I was mortified. I was sure Alvin would be furious.

Instead, he turned to his assistant and said, "Not him again." Say what you will about the event, the guy did win for best costume. Just for the record, we only used nineteen drivers, down from twenty-six for the series. In the end, Alvin was straight up with us, bad phallus puns aside.

The prop department budget consists of Property Master, Key Set Prop, Second Prop, Shopper (in Europe she has a different title but the job is the same), and additional prop persons (as the size and scope demands).

What is the difference between Set Dressers and property people? Set Dressers dress the set then turn it over to the prop people. Once an actor touches the item, its resettlement at the start of the shot falls to the prop department. Here I am speaking in a union context. In a non-union film the distinctions may be a bit more blurred due to budget constraints.

Under *materials* will be the line items of purchase, rental, and manufacture. There should also be a line item for loss and damage, as small hand props very often become damaged. Loss and damage can occur in any department, depending on the nature of the show. There is no down side to having this designation in all your other accounts.

Let's talk about the set operations account. In this account will be found the catering truck and the chef but not necessarily his helper. The helper may be on the company payroll and on a time card like everyone else. This is a mantra for my USC film students: "The Army runs on its stomach." This is most definitely a quote from Chairman Joe. It means this: A crew's first question is always, "Who's catering?" Their second is, "What time is lunch?" The former is negotiable and subject to personal preference, the latter is mandated by union contract. You will always have to break for lunch six hours after the crew call. It doesn't matter what six hours. If you call the main body of the crew for 10 A.M., then you must break for lunch at 4 P.M. Similarly, if you go longer than 12½ hours you will have to provide a second meal. Even non-union shows adhere to this general guideline, and it is not a capricious concept. Food equals energy. If you've ever been on a set where people's blood sugar is crashing, you will quickly grasp the significance of food. Not to mention it is the right and humane way to treat people.

On union shows, if you pass the six-hour mark you get charged a penalty. How much varies from department to department, but if the crew is large enough the amount can be significant.

Still and all, there are times when it is better to take the penalty than to break and come back after lunch. The most obvious one concerns the close-up that completes a scene. It will take you perhaps five or ten minutes to accomplish before lunch, but you will have to pay the penalty. However, if you break for lunch still owing that close-up, you will have to do it first thing upon returning. And that will take time. Why? The answer: the process of re-assembling the elements.

How does this affect make-up, hair and wardrobe? Don't they come in earlier? What about the actors? Women may be called two hours before the main body of the crew. Why doesn't their six-hour rule interfere with filming? The answer comes in the form of the "rolling" or "walking" breakfast. The Production Assistant rounds up a small breakfast that can be eaten while working. This "walking breakfast" then brings the early calls into sync with the rest of the crew.

Lorimar was housed at MGM studios, now Sony Pictures, in Culver City. We were shooting up in Burbank at the Burbank studios. I was under strict orders not to take a lunch penalty. In union contracts if the company does not break for a meal after six hours of work, the company must pay a financial penalty to each and every crewmember and actor. The prices vary by position, but the cumulative effect can be substantial. It was ten to one, which meant I had only ten minutes to decide whether or not to take the penalty to finish the first scene of the day. It was a close-up of the lead actor. I called the production office to let Eddie know I was going to go into penalty to finish.

Eddie said my name with a decided Midwestern twang that made it sound like "Jow."

"No, Jow, I wouldn't do that."

"But Eddie, it will go faster if we do it now instead of owing it for after lunch." "You may be right, Jow, but I don't want you to take anymore penalty."

"Eddie, I gotta say I love ya, but you're wrong."

To which Eddie replied, "You may be right, Jow. But there's one thing I gotta say and that is I'm the boss and I say break."

To which I replied, "Ya know, Eddie, when you explain it that way, you add a certain irrefutable logic to the decision-making process."

We broke for lunch.

I produced a pilot for Fox Television. It was called *The Covenant*. It was an unsuccessful attempt to marry a soap drama to a horror film. Our director was a feisty, short-tempered, little guy named Walter. He was talented and generally responsible.

There was a story in the business that he and another Producer had ended up in a fist fight that caused both combatants to tumble into a canoe, which then broke loose from its mooring and carried both men out into a lake. I don't know if that's a true story, but I still laugh thinking about it.

What I do know is, that every day Walter came to work wearing the same outfit — grey slacks, white shirt, and blue blazer. He always brought fresh clothes in a garment bag that he left in my office until the evening. He would go into another room where he would change into his fresh garb — grey slacks, white shirt, and blue blazer.

The pilot for *The Covenant* was shot mostly at night. We had a very slow Cinematographer. He was a good guy, but watching him light a set was like watching wallpaper dry. Walter tended to be a little cavalier about taking overtime penalties. Consequently, two weeks into production we had spent thirty thousand dollars (non-budgeted) on meal penalties.

The then head of Fox production was having none of it. He called me. "I don't care what you do, but you may not take another dime in meal penalty."

Five to one in the morning I went to Walter and said, "Walter, we are going to have to break in five minutes."

"What," screamed Walter? "No way. We are finishing the scene."

"I'm sorry, Walter, we are under strict orders not to do that."

"I don't give a damn what the suits say. I'm shooting."

Five minutes later, at one o'clock, I said to Walter, "I'm sorry, Walter, I'm breaking."

"No way," he hollered. "Roll camera."

There is nothing worse on set than for someone to publicly challenge the director. I had no choice. I stepped onto the set and declared, "Ladies and Gentlemen, we are at lunch. As the representative of Fox Television, anyone who works beyond this point will not be paid for their time."

There was a Whoosh! Walter was standing there by himself. He turned to me with such anger in his eyes that for a second I thought he was going to punch me.

"Get him on the phone," he demanded.

"Walter," I replied, "it's one o'clock in the morning. You sure you want to do that?"

"Damn right," he yelled. "Just get 'im on the phone."

Reluctantly, and with considerable trepidation, I went to a nearby pay phone. I started to dial. Walter came over just as it started to ring. He took the phone from my hand and hung it up.

"I'll call him myself," he pronounced and stormed off.

At six-thirty in the morning when we wrapped, he patted me on the back and said, "Good night's work," and toddled off. And yes, he was wearing grey slacks, a white shirt and a blue blazer.

Two days later I ran into the Production Chief and asked if Walter had called him.

He had no idea what I was talking about.

While we are on the subject of phone calls, here's a doozy. Alex November (not his real name) was a good director, a terrific guy and a nervous wreck. I worked with him several times and never once saw him without a neck brace. He had a great sense of humor and was a practical joker. Irwin Allen was a big-time old-fashioned producer. He Produced *Poseidon Adventure*, *Towering Inferno* and just about every other disaster movie ever made. He took himself really seriously. He also had just about the worst hair of anyone in Hollywood. He would comb it over his bald spot from left to right. One day, on a Warner Bros. stage, he was standing in front of a large fan. Alex snuck around behind him and plugged it in. The blades began to whir, Irwin's hair shot out straight forward and began to flap around in the breeze. He looked like something out of a bad Felix the Cat cartoon. He was, to put it mildly, not amused. A few weeks later, Alex literally crawled across the floor to sneak up to Irwin's refrigerator on the second floor of his offices. It seems

Irwin, for reasons known only to himself, kept a ten-pound salami in the fridge. Alex took a humongous bite out of the center and turned it back around so it looked like it was still intact. I happened to be in the office the day he discovered the damage. My wife was working for I.A. (Irwin Allen) at that time. His outburst made Captain Queeg's tirade about his strawberries pale by comparison.

So what does this have to do with the telephone?

This is just background.

One day I was working with Alex on the Warner Brother's Ranch. It is a smaller version of the studio and its back lot about one block north of the Burbank Studios. We were filming by the swimming pool in the middle of the lot. It was five o'clock and we were a couple of hours behind schedule. Every day at five, every one of Lorimar's shows would call in to the production department to let them know how we were doing. It was routinely referred to as the "five o'clock report." I went to call it in. Alex was deathly afraid of our Head of Production, a real tough son-of-a-bitch named Neal Mafeo. It was an ironic name because, in those days, Lorimar was quietly thought of as a being a "mob" company, an assertion they went to court to dispel. Neal was the guy who sent me to Mexico with the promise that if I brought the show in under budget I would get a bonus. When I went to collect he told me, "Bonus, my ass. You're lucky to be off the streets."

This day Neal was out of the office when I called. Out of the corner of my eye I could see Alex watching me, apprehension written all over his face. It was too good a moment to pass up. No sooner did the phone disconnect at their end then I went into my own tirade.

"Do not ever question a Director like Alex November. If he wants to stay here until midnight, that's where we'll be. He's getting sick and tired of you getting on his back because we're a little behind."

I could see the color draining from Alex's face like soda through a straw.

"You're lucky he's willing to work for this company. How dare you question when he wants to wrap. He'll wrap when he's good and goddamned ready."

After another few seconds of insane babble I slammed the phone down hard.

By the time I reached Alex, his legs looked so wobbly I didn't think they would hold him.

"That was a joke," he half-stated, half-begged. "You're only kidding with that, right?"

"You know, Alex, here's the thing. If they think you're crazy, they leave you alone."

And I kept going.

He literally ran after me. He finally grabbed me and spun me around. He began to shake me. Hysteria rang from his voice.

"Tell me you're kidding. Tell me you're kidding."

I burst out laughing. I laughed so hard I fell to the ground and continued laughing. Alex just stood there, giggling, drooling, wobbling then giggling some more.

We finished on time.

Where was I? How do you estimate the number of meals to be served? Estimating is easy. Negotiating a "per head" price and multiplying it by the number of bodies is the killer. $17 or $20 a head? There will be separate add-ons, like soda if not supplied by the prop department. And the estimate is rarely what the final price will be, because hungry people standing and working on their feet for twelve or more hours a day go back for seconds and even thirds. Then there are unexpected guests. Actors invite their agents to the set, the money guys might drop in, neighbors of your location join you. How do you identify the costs before you get a nasty surprise? You count plates. Production companies will literally station someone in the catering truck from the production department to count the number of plates given out.

Just thinking about catering makes me think of a day when we almost ran out of food. We were filming at the Warner Grand Theater in San Pedro. It is a beautiful old art deco theater, but it is cavernous. It took a lot of extras, today we say background performers, to fill up the auditorium.

We were scheduled to start in the theater, release the background players and retreat to the lobby for another scene. Had we stayed with that plan, we would have finished in plenty of time. But someone decided it would be quicker to start in the lobby and then move in. It was a big mistake. It kept the extras around much, much longer than they should have stayed. Worse, the day got slower and slower, and it was clear we were headed for a second meal. The caterer only had enough food on the truck for one meal, and not nearly enough for all the additional background players. We were too far away from his purveyors to run for the additional provisions. We were stuck — until the Production Manager hit on an idea, part inspiration, part desperation. We had had steak for lunch, and had just enough for the bare bones crew for dinner. He ordered the chef to cut the remaining steaks in half, thereby doubling our food capacity.

"Won't they squawk," I asked him?

"Na," was his confident reply. "Who's gonna complain over the size of the steak at ten at night?"

He turned out to be right. By the time the second meal rolled around, they were just grateful to have something to eat. All they really wanted was to go home, but we lucked out on that one.

In this account should go your Set Medic, a standby nurse, if you will, who represents an alternative to sending someone to the hospital.

On *Married: The First Year* Linda Hamilton cut her foot. It hurt, it bled, it could have gotten infected. Had we not had a Set Medic we would have had to put her in another car and take her to the hospital. When you lose an actor to the hospital you are losing them for at least three or four hours. On an episodic show, taking four hours out of the middle of the day is death.

Our Medic cleaned her wound, bandaged her foot and gave her two Tylenols. Ever the trooper, Linda went back to work, a little embarrassed but none the worse for wear. We finished the day on time.

There are days, particularly when doing stunts, when you may be required to have an ambulance on standby. The driver will not be a teamster, and you will not need it every day. Therefore I put the ambulance and its driver in this account rather than in transportation. Should you choose to do it differently, that is perfectly all right, just so you anticipate its necessity.

Now comes the line item everyone waits for: craft services. Crafty (for short) are the men or women who supply a constant stream of set snacks. They generate the perpetual supply of coffee and pastries. From herbal tea to red licorice, from Swedish meatballs to cocktail franks, they are your army's unending supply of rations. They burn through a lot of money, so you had better hire someone who is both honest and capable of keeping track of a great number of receipts.

What just a minute, you say. Let me get this straight. You mean to tell me you have a catering truck in the morning that feeds them breakfast, a catering truck that supplies them lunch, a catering truck if a second meal or dinner is required, *and* you have craft services doling out other foods all day long? Yes, yes we do. "But, but, but..." you stammer, to no avail.

Have you ever spent twelve hours hauling cable, moving furniture, pushing a dolly, setting lights, or holding a boom mike over your head? Have you ever worked in freezing cold, stifling heat, wind-blown rain? In real estate it's "Location. Location. Location." In film it's "Food. Food. Food."

I'll say it to you again:

"The Army runs on its stomach."

There is one last item in this account: Laborer. On many, but not all, sets there will be someone who cleans up the area, keeps the facilities stocked with toilet paper and paper towels, disposes of cigarette butts, and throws out used coffee cups. This person tends to have a greater shelf life on a sound stage than on location. However, this individual can really save your bacon by sweeping up cigarettes and Styrofoam cups and picking up the tape from the actor's marks at a location. I know I've already said it, but when it comes to locations, "Break it and you can fix it, disrespect it and it's gone."

A final word before leaving the below-the-line portion of the budget; for everything I have just written there is an alternative way to input your information. Did I just abrogate everything I've told you? No, just don't get hung up thinking there is only one right or wrong way to do your budget.

The bottom line is this: "Does this budget accurately reflect my film, and can I substantiate everything I have placed into it?"

Clearly your sense of your film will lead you to the right way to do it. Hallelujah, we are finally out of the "below-the-line."

Post-production is where your film is really made. It is, however, tricky because it is difficult to predict how long *post* will take.

Director Hal Ashby, of *The Last Detail, Shampoo,* and *Being There,* had been an editor before he became a director. He was famous for shooting a million feet of film, taking a year to sort it out and then finding his movie in post.

Elaine May on *A New Leaf* spent so much time editing that Charles Bludorn had to shut her down. Juxtapose that with my old friend Larry Elikann's experience on *The Menendez Brothers* a four-hour mini-series. I ran into Larry in Beverly Hills. He was happy to see me and invited me into his trailer. He proudly asserted, "I finished shooting the first part four days ago." He hit a button on his computer and showed a rough cut of the film he had just barely finished shooting.

So how long will it take you? Who knows? But one thing you do know: Your Editor and his Assistant, and perhaps even an apprentice, will start when filming starts and end when the picture is mixed ... a long period to have people on the payroll.

Opticals sound design; sound effects editing; music; music editing, ADR (automated dialogue replacement); foley; walla (background babble) color correction mixing (dialogue, sound effects and music), answer prints, S x S cards, screen credits, and main titles all go into post-production budgets.

What about related costs? Depending on whether you shoot film or digital, they would be raw stock, lab (develop and print), telecine (converting film to tape) visual special effects, rentals on editing suites, equipment, and, of course, food.

And in our constantly evolving technological world, there are new jobs and people with new disciplines that you have to consider. For example, today you have to budget for the new kid in town — the digital imaging technician (or DIT). His job is to work with the Cinematographer and help achieve the best digital results. This includes monitoring exposure, setting the look up tables (or LUTs), establishing camera settings, and so forth. In the end, the image integrity is the main focus of this new job.

My point here is not to overwhelm you but highlight just how involved the post area of your budget will be. You can certainly throw numbers together for the sake of a final figure, but in my opinion a better way to proceed is to hire a Post-Production Supervisor or an Associate Producer. This person will oversee the creation, execution and accounting of everything in post. That doesn't mean you won't oversee it or be intricately involved, just free of its capacity to be overwhelming.

Music is a tricky area. That is why on many films you will see the credit "Music Supervisor." He will oversee the Composer, the Arranger, the Music Producer, the licenses, any publishing, the sync rights, the master licensing rights, the needle drop, the Contracts, and the two scariest words in the world of film: *favored nations.*

I can't give you the historical origins or dictionary meaning of this film term, but I can tell you its practical effect on your budget. Basically, favored nations means: what one gets, they all get. No individual can be favored over any other. So if you make a deal with one recording artist or one record company, and a more favorable deal with another, you may have to up your first deal to match the second. Multiply that by the twenty or thirty pieces of music your film may require, and you get some idea of the scope and complexity of the issue.

By the way, it can happen in other areas of your budget too. *Knots Landing* had an ensemble cast. Our regulars numbered eight or ten. Many of them, particularly the ones represented by the same agency, had favored nations clauses in their contracts.

At the start of every year, Lorimar's business office would send us the pattern budget (the budget for which we were supposed to produce every episode). It would not have the cast salaries. We would call the head of the business office, a lovely, buttoned-up executive named Julie.

"Julie," we would say, "what are we paying the actors?"

To which Julie would reply, "I can't tell you."

"Why?" we would inquire politely.

"Because you might slip and tell one of them what another one is making," would come her response.

Never mind that it was insulting that she thought our loyalty to the company was so thin that we would run to the actors for the sake of stirring the pot, it also overlooked the most obvious scenario in the world.

On the first morning of the first episode of each and every season, the entire cast would be called for make-up at 6 A.M. They would sit side by side in the make-up trailer, and by 6:01 A.M. one of them would turn to the other and ask, "So how did you do in the off season?"

To which the other would say proudly, "Oh, my agent got me seventeen five per" (meaning $17,500 dollars per episode).

The first actress, who was only paid $15,000, would say, "How fabulous. Good for you... Uh... I think I need to make a phone call."

She would go to her trailer, call her agent, wake him up, and scream at him for not doing enough to protect her star status. By 10 A.M. every one of their agents was calling Julie on the phone.

The "favored nations" concept even exists in union contracts. Not precisely as stated above, but most have clauses that say if another union negotiates a more favorable contract, they retain the right to reopen negotiations.

Rod Serling was a brilliant creator who wrote and ran a series called *The Twilight Zone*. One of the quirky characteristics of that show was its titles. One in particular captured my imagination: "The Horse Has a Big Head ... Let Him Worry."

I say that to you now in the context of your post-production budget. Hire a Music Supervisor and a Post-Production Supervisor. They have big heads ... let them worry about all of this.

Congratulations! You put together your budget. Never mind that it is probably two million dollars more than your investors wanted to spend. Even if you had gotten green-lit with your $14,000,000 budget, the Money Source will not just cut you a check for the whole amount and say, "See you when the film is done." The trick is to get them to the next step. That is simply this: to get them to extend you enough money to get started. We call this the "draw down projection."

Simply put, it is a document that projects your financial needs on a week-by-week basis. Remember, your money people can pull the plug on your project at any time because you are not officially green-lit. Have your Production Accountant estimate your cash flow needs for the first few weeks. This might include:

Week 1: Producer weekly salary
Partial Director compensation
Open production office
Rent production office equipment
Phone lines installed
Computers, printers and copiers rented
Total: $25,000.00 (numbers made up for this example)

Week 2: Producer's Assistant hired
Casting Director hired
Production Accountant hired
Open bank account
Producer's weekly salary
Total: $35,000.000

Week 3:   Hire Production Designer
          Hire Casting Assistant
          Open casting office
          Casting Director salary
          Production Accountant salary
          Accounting department equipment rentals
          Total $65,000.00

One of the things these early hires are going to do is help you plug in better numbers. With the help of a Casting Director you may get a better sense of what your talent is really going to cost. My bet is those numbers will be less than you originally thought, since you can now marry them to your shooting schedule. An actor at $10,000 a week that you thought you would need for seven weeks, may end up costing a flat fee of $50,000. An actress you are desperate to have has a last quote of fifty thousand a week but you only need her for three weeks. You might end up paying her much less than she received on her last job because you need her for a shorter period. And on and on it goes — negotiating, reconfiguring, juxtaposing your day-out-of-days against your locations and coming up with more palatable figures.

The same is true with the addition of the Production Designer, although it may take slightly longer to materialize. I like to say you are in the process of getting your money people "slightly pregnant."

Getting people, whether they be studio or network execs, or simply your twenty closest doctor friends, to actually spend money is a very good thing. The more money they spend, the more likely they are to press forward. Of course, if you are unable to lower your budget or they begin to suspect that your $14,000,000 budget could easily balloon to twenty, they might pull the plug to cut their losses. But that will not happen to you. You are too smart and well prepared.

The first thing you do now is announce a shooting start date. Creating a *commencement of principal photography* date focuses your energy on making it happen.

You meet with your Director and Production Designer to discuss the look, style, tone and general landscape of the picture. You agree on what will be built and what will be a practical location. This accomplishes several things. It sets in motion the search for locations. It also identifies the next round of hires — Art Director, Set Designer, Construction Coordinator — and opens up dialogue about Cinematographers and Editors.

At this point, because you are starting to anticipate your below-the-line hires, you should seek the services of a good Production Manager. At this moment of trying to close your financiers and set up the look of your film, you do not want to get sucked into the vortex of below-the-line minutia. That's not to say you won't be paying very careful attention to it — just don't take your eye off the bigger ball at this juncture. This is about "mounting" your project.

By the way, if by some miracle when you showed the money people your $14,000,000 budget, they said, "Great. Let's do it. You're green-lit!" you would still follow the draw down projection and staffing scenario I just laid out. There will be interest charges on the money you spend. Don't start the clock running on interest before you need to.

Hey, I don't know about you, but I'm getting excited. I think this project is going to get made.

Casting

Imagine that every time you spoke, everything you wore and every move you made was judged by someone else. If you can imagine a lifetime of rejection, of criticism and personal failure, you will have a small inkling of what an actor goes through every day of his or her professional life.

Ask ten actors up for the same role whether they achieved their goal and they will say, "I didn't get the part." That simple phrase speaks volumes about an actor's psyche. A healthier way to think is, "Someone else got the part."

Most actors assume that the casting session is all about them. The truth is, it's partially about them. It is also how they play with other actors in the scene or script. A four-foot actress playing a scene against a six-foot-six actor will look strange. Think Charlene Tilton and James Brolin. Then there is the word *subjectivity*. Producers, Directors and Casting Directors are subject to its vicissitudes like no other.

Many years ago, I was in a casting session where the principal character was a high-fashion model. We looked at every pretty woman in Hollywood. We must have seen a dozen who could easily have fit the bill, but the process dragged on. Finally, a young woman named Nancy Blye came in. I knew her because she had dated a friend of mine. Nancy had been on the cover of every major fashion magazine in Europe. She was a slam-dunk. She didn't get the part. Instead, a blond (who I thought was a little out of shape) got the role. When I asked how they could not hire the number one model in Europe, the Director explained, "We're going to play against type."

If you are a "star" your agent sends you the script. You read it, discuss it, show it to your manager or whoever's opinion you hold dear, and then ask for a meeting with the Producer or Director.

If you are a "day player," a performer who may only work one or two days, you get sent "sides." Sides are just the scenes in which you will appear. It is true there is no compelling reason for you to read the entire script when you are only in four scenes with a total of twelve lines. However, you can't know the context in which your character appears or the tone of the film as a whole. Are they asking you to give a serious, dark reading or a lighter, more frivolous one?

Some Casting Directors will give actors limited instruction, some will not. The actor is left to guess at the intent or mood of the piece and give a completely out of context reading. This is known as a *cold reading*.

Another thing an actor doesn't know when leaving the casting session is that he may be wrong for that part but right for another one in the same film. It is a nerve-wracking process. That is the primary reason why you must respect what actors go through and why you must treat them with dignity and patience. Most of all, you must not waste their time. Never bring in an actor to read who isn't potentially right just for the power trip of it. It is unprofessional. Don't be talking or disengaged when they enter the room. Treat them like you would a friend you've invited to your home. If you have it, offer them water. Try to make the session as relaxed as you can, and, most of all, pay attention to them.

It is also not a bad idea to phone the performers who didn't get the part. Not only is it a humane thing to do, you may want to work with them at a later date on another project. A little kindness now can pay great dividends later, such as when that day player becomes a major star and only returns the phone calls of people who were nice to him when they were just starting out.

When I was a struggling Second Assistant Director in New York I worked on a picture called *Jenny,* starring Marlo Thomas. We shot part of it in Central Park. Every day this little guy in a trench coat would show up and just hang around. When questioned, he said he just loved to be around film. We talked to him, fed him and generally treated him with kindness. Five years later that awkward little guy in the trench coat turned out to be Dustin Hoffman.

An Actor's life in film is about time. Not just *time is money* but also *time is precious.* Think as an actor for a moment. They scan the casting web sites looking for potential jobs. They find one. They submit their picture and resume. They get called. Be here at ten tomorrow. They live in the San Fernando Valley. Maybe they get the sides the night before, maybe not. They get up early, dress, drive to the casting session, look for and possibly pay for parking, wait (hopefully not more than fifteen or twenty minutes), and sit with the other "potentials." When all is done they travel home or to their next audition, riddled with self-doubt and hope.

The worst thing you can do to that actor is cancel or change the casting session without notifying them. It shows an utter disregard for their time and emotion. Nothing says amateurism louder than non-communicating with your potential cast.

Never negotiate with an actor in a casting session. They have agents and managers, and *they* are the appropriate conduit for financial and work related matters.

It is not uncommon after a casting session to request footage of the performer from their agent. It is also legitimate to speak with other Producers who have worked with that actor to get a sense of their temperament and level of professionalism.

I once worked with an actress who was sweet as sugar but could not get the words out of her mouth unless she stood on the set and brushed her hair for forty strokes. That might sound like a minor annoyance until it comes up at two minutes before midnight on the Friday night you are shooting.

I once worked with an actor — who shall forever remain nameless — who would sit on the set until the Director called "Ready." At that point the actor would get up and walk to his trailer. It would then take us twenty minutes to get him back out on the set. It was the most infuriating kind of un-professionalism I have ever experienced. Production companies talk to each other, and you can bet that when asked, I warned the next Director what to expect.

At every job I ever held some Casting Directors would call me, desperate for availability dates for my actors that they were hoping to cast. Often I had not finished the Production Board and therefore had not constructed the day-out-of-days.

Don't be rushed into a premature day-out-of-days. Accuracy-over-convenience. Prematurely issuing a day-out-of-days could result in an Actor being hired for dates that are no longer applicable two weeks later. All start dates are listed as "on" or "about," which will give you at least one day leeway, maybe up to three. Remember, everything in film is negotiable.

When making a deal for an actor, be sure to include at least two, but maybe more, non-consecutive looping days. In post-production it may be necessary to perform what is called ADR (automated dialogue replacement). That means bringing the performer onto an ADR stage and replacing part of their dialogue. Directors generally don't like to do this, and actors like it even less because it is difficult to get back to the original level of performance. However, sometimes flubbed lines, sibilant sounds or noisy locations make it unavoidable.

A common example of this: people walking along the beach with the waves crashing against the shoreline. When the scene is cut together there is a good chance that the waves will crash at the wrong spots in the dialogue. Thus, the sound will have to be stripped out and replaced with new dialogue and pounding waves that break in the proper spots.

Don't forget to include travel days as workdays in your negotiations. Shopping days for wardrobe are workdays as well. So, actor "A" is hired and told to fly to Dallas on a Friday. A travel day is a workday, so the actor is paid to fly to Texas. Saturday the Costume Designer goes out with the actor and they shop for wardrobe. Saturday is a workday and the actor is paid. Sunday the actor stays in his hotel room and watches football. It's not a paid workday, but you will still have to pay for the hotel room and per diem.

There is a Screen Actors Guild minimum you must pay an actor, but there is no ceiling. Per diem, like everything else in the film business, is negotiable and should have some relation to the city or town in which you will be working. Obviously, Dallas or New York is a more expensive city to dine in than, say, most of Iowa.

The actor starts filming on Monday. Although this is his first day on the set, he has already been working two days and been on the location for three. Unless you know about the "wardrobe" day, you don't want to be telling the casting department the actor just travels and works.

A note about actors and lodging: On some shows the Producers will house the actors in a hotel more upscale than that provided for the crew. I am not a fan of this. It tends to create two classes of people. Just like how the terms "above-the-line" and "below-the-line," imply that some people have more worth than others, better and lesser living arrangements imply a judgment on status. You do not want to give the crew the impression you hold them in less regard than the actors and Director. Most crewmembers have tremendous professional pride. They will work their collective tails off for you — so long as you appreciate their talent and commitment. Give the crew the impression that you think of them as "second-class-citizens," and the job will be only about the money. This principal especially applies to feeding the actors and the crew. One table of gourmet food for the actors and another of slop for the crew is a spectacularly bad idea. Let me illuminate: It is Friday night around eight o'clock. You are about to go into *gold* (double-time pay for the entire crew) and *meal penalty.* It can amount to a tidy sum, depending on the size of the crew, but you have everyone housed in the same hotel. They have all eaten at the same table. The cast and crew have bonded. Some of them go to movies together, others play softball on Sunday. That crew will work harder to get your shot and not split hairs over ten or fifteen minutes extra.

The unappreciated crew will get you for every dime.

I call this "giving to get" or "giving a little to get a lot." It will appear again in the chapter about managing locations.

Actors can be difficult, and some people think they are a necessary evil of a film. Most believe the actors *are* your film. Either way, they're people, so treat them well.

Dealing with Actors

Earlier I tried to articulate how pressurized and stressful the actor's life can be. When I first started in the business I was relatively unsympathetic to their concerns. However, time and experience have given me a whole new and far more professional perspective.

First thing, no actors, no film. For that alone they should be treated with a modicum of respect. After the rigors of trying to get the job, now that they have it, the real angst begins. They are plagued with: Am I good enough? Am I handsome enough? Will I have to take my blouse off? What if I suck? Should I lose weight for the part? Should I gain weight for the part? Do I need a personal trainer? What if I can't remember my lines?

Neurotic is an understatement. They feel exposed and vulnerable. They are relying on the judgment of others to tell them they looked good or that their performance was just right. It is hard to quantify how much trust is transferred from the actor to the Director, Cinematographer and Editor. Unlike you and the rest of the crew, it is *their* face six feet high up on the screen.

I know from painful personal experience that trying to look natural or believable when the camera and forty people are standing very still, staring at you, is not easy. In fact, it can be downright terrifying.

Early on in my career I was working on a beer commercial as a Production Assistant. We were filming at a racetrack in southern New Jersey. At four in the afternoon, the Director got an inspiration. He wanted someone to walk up the aisle of the grandstand hawking beer. We were too far away from the city to cast someone, and all eyes fell on me. Would I play the part? It was simple enough. Don the appropriate wardrobe, carry a tray of unopened beer cans, and say, "Beer here. Get yer beer here." When it turned out they would pay me extra money, I quickly agreed.

They dressed me for the part, slung the tray around my neck and stood me on my mark. The Director said, "Roll 'em," the place fell silent, and I suddenly felt as if I had turned to stone. Just getting my lips to move was an event. In the course of the next twenty takes I spilled the beer four times, muffed my lines six times, squirted six people seated near me three times (they needed to be re-wardrobed each time), and came away with a new and healthy respect for the art and craft of acting.

Actors don't get the part just because. They get it due to talent, experience, and ability to convince an audience that they are the person they are portraying. They spend years and countless sums of money learning their craft and honing their skills. They pay gobs for "head shots," seek agents and managers, and go on endless auditions. They play in small regional theaters and college productions. They pound the pavement of Hollywood trying to catch the eye of a talent scout or Casting Director. The failure rate is staggering, yet they soldier on, convinced that, if only given a chance, they have what it takes to be a star — or at least a working actor. Opportunity does knock, but "lucky" you have to get. They say there are three things that you need for a career in Hollywood: luck, talent, and desire, any two of which will suffice.

There are basically two kinds of actors — those who are profoundly professional, with whom you will enjoy working, and those who will make your gums bleed and cause you to have dreams of personal violence. In my experience, stage-trained actors come to the table the most prepared and get to their performances the quickest. This is understandable. They come from a discipline that brooks none of the egocentric excesses of the film business.

There are method actors who will need to know what propels every moment of the scene. There is an industry story about an actor who asked Alfred Hitchcock what her motivation was for the scene they were about to do, and he replied, "Your paycheck." That may be a cute joke, but there are many actors who sincerely need back-story and motivation to unlock the full scope of their abilities.

Shelly Winters, in her later years, relied on music to bring her to the place she needed to be in an emotional scene. Then there are performers who can "just do it." Then there are situations that you could never anticipate, human nature being what it is.

I was called to New York to be one of the alternating First Assistant Directors on the TV series *Madigan,* starring Richard Widmark. It was the prequel to the movie of the same name. In the film version, Madigan gets killed in the end. The series was billed as his experiences before his death. We shot in Harlem, Greenwich Village and Spanish Harlem.

The first moment I got to the set someone pulled me aside and said, "Be prepared. This guy is a handful." Sure enough, when people approached him he would respond loudly, even rudely. No wonder people were afraid of him.

I noticed one exception. When the Script Supervisor spoke to him, he reacted like a perfectly normal human being. The only difference in their approach was that the Script Supervisor spoke to him on his right side.

I asked the Script Supervisor about that "He can barely hear out of his left ear," she replied. "It frustrates him and makes him irritable when they talk into his left ear." Armed with that information, I always spoke towards his right. We got along fine. So fine, in fact, that he started inviting me to his lovely home in Roxbury, Connecticut. We became dear friends. In the end, I really enjoyed knowing and working with him. I was sorry to learn of his death a few years ago. I hope his soul is at peace in his beloved Roxbury.

In my career I have had the privilege of working with some of the finest, most professional actresses ever to come down the pike: the legendary Helen Hayes, Mildred Natwick, the incredible Julie Harris, the wonderful Anne Baxter, and, of course, the amazing Jessica Tandy. But I have had my share of clunkers, too.

One that clunked hard (whose name I shall not mention) is still considered an "A-list performer." I was young, not yet a member of the Directors Guild. I was day-checking on a film in New York. It was the dead of winter, colder than cold. We were filming exteriors of Lincoln Center at night. Three Production Assistants, myself included, were waiting outside this particular diva's motor home to escort her to the set. The call had been for 7 P.M. By midnight she had yet to set foot outside the trailer. The temperature was falling and the wind was kicking up.

Although I was wearing Long Johns, and several scarves and sweatshirts bundled beneath an Eddie Bauer coat, the wind cut through me like a knife. Finally, at two o'clock in the morning, "Herself" stepped out. She was wrapped in a heavy fur coat. She took two steps, looked up and said, "You must be kidding. I'll freeze my tits." She turned around and went back inside. We did not see her for the rest of the night. We stood outside, incredulous, cursing with our frozen tongues.

No one dared challenge her because she was the star of the movie. Without her there would have been no film. The reason I tell you this story is that sometimes you have to be careful what you wish for. She was the reason the film got made, but that gave her all the power. Power in the hands of actors can be a dangerous and expensive thing. The money will want a star of some magnitude, but a star of some magnitude will rule your world. Look before you leap. Are you really so desperate to get your film made that you are willing to get led around by your nose for month after month by some spoiled diva?

Well, you probably are. Is there an in-between? Yes — directors who are not afraid to exert their authority when necessary can save the day. There was a film in the early seventies shooting in Boston in which the female lead was perpetually late to the set. If the call would be for seven, she would wander in at nine. With make-up and hair to be done, it was impossible to get a shot off before eleven. It played havoc with the schedule, negatively impacted crew morale and pissed off her co-star. Finally the director had had enough. He called the entire company together, including the tardy actress, and told her in front of everyone that from that moment on every dollar that her tardiness cost would come out of her salary.

She was embarrassed, angry and threatened to quit. She probably would have, except her agent reminded her that to do so would put her in breach of contract. She was never late to set again.

I once had the honor of working with the iconic John Huston, director of *The Maltese Falcon, Treasure of the Sierre Madre* and *Prizzi's Honor.* Our film was *Kremlin Letter.* Most of it had been shot in Rome. The company came to New York for three weeks of filming — mostly for the enormous excitement and publicity Mister Huston's presence generated.

We were filming at the Iberia Museum in upper Manhattan. All the cast was on the set, ready for the scene. Only the young starlet co-lead was in her dressing room taking her own sweet time getting ready. She was called to the set three times but failed to appear. Mr. Huston called me over and said, "Son, you tell Miss Starlet that if she isn't on the set in one minute I am going to recast her part."

I set off to deliver the message. I was halfway to her trailer when it dawned on me that they had already shot sixty percent of the movie. To recast her would be to practically shoot the film all over again. But *mine was not to reason why, mine was but to do or die.* I delivered the message.

I never saw someone move so quickly in my life. It was as if I had jabbed her with a hot poker. She literally ran to the set. I have always wondered, given the financial consequences, whether he would have made good on his threat. Wisely, the actress did not put him to the test. So why do I tell you all this?

The bottom line is that actors are the life's blood of your film. They must be treated with dignity, respect and kindness. They must be reassured that they are the perfect performer for the role. You must nurture them, communicate with them and make them feel they are an integral part of the team. You must also make sure they understand that they are also part of a large machine. They need to be respected and they need to show respect back. With that said, a simple gesture can mean a lot. When it comes to lunch, have a P.A. get it for them and bring it to their trailer. If they wish, and many will, to eat with the crew, place them at the head of the line. This is not so much an indication of status as it is a practical accommodation. They will have to get back into make-up after lunch and should be ready to do so the minute that lunch break is finished.

Make sure they get a call sheet for the next day's work before they leave at the end of the day. If you are on location and they are housed in a hotel, make sure someone slips the call sheets and the pages for the next day under the door. Always make sure the set is quiet when they are working. Most will respond like the professionals they are.

"Just remember that actors, with all their temperaments and egos, all their neuroses and talent, are the lead dogs in the Iditarod that is your film." Yup ... Chairman Joe, again.

Now let's talk about extras. Extras, have rightfully earned the name background performers. Here are two very different stories about extras and why I sometimes prefer the designation "background performers."

We were filming inside a concert hall. The background performers were all well-dressed society matrons. In the afternoon we filmed outside in the adjacent alley. I noticed a women, shabbily dressed and slightly stoop-shouldered, picking through the trash. I went to her and said, "Maam, we're going to be filming here and I need to place my extras." She smiled at me and replied, "I am one of your extras." It was one of the matron ladies. She had completely transformed herself— wardrobe, hair style, body language and all. "Wow," I said. She smiled again, sweetly. "After all," she said, "I'm an actress."

Now a completely different story.

I was twenty-two and a Second Assistant Director. We were filming in a seedy neighborhood. We had thirty-six women portraying prostitutes. At one point they were sent back to the bus to change wardrobe. The First Assistant Director sent me to find out how long before the ladies would be ready for the next scene.

I stepped onto the bus, unprepared for the sight that greeted me. The Extras Casting Director, a fellow named Marty, who until that moment I had no idea was gay, was seated among thirty-six attractive women in various stages of undress. I mean from topless to completely naked. He seemed completely oblivious. I, on the other hand, had a somewhat different reaction.

To me it was some sort of epiphany. For surely I had died, and God, who is benevolent, recognized that I was a good person on earth. He had whisked me to heaven, and while I had never contemplated that heaven might take the form of a city bus, who was I to judge?

"Hello Ladies," I offered suavely to cover my embarrassment.

I was greeted with, "Hi Cutie."

"Hi Baby."

"Hey Baby, c'mere, Mama wants to show you something."

That was it. I had died and gone to heaven. I had always heard that expression but could only now truly appreciate it. However, I was ripped from my reverie by the booming voice of the First Assistant Director standing outside the bus, who hollered, "Joe, get your ass back out here."

Ever hear of the movie *Heaven Can Wait?*

You get my drift.

Acquiring a Crew

When you were in film school you recruited your classmates for the various crew positions. Now you are in the real world with real money at stake. Friendship and familiarity may no longer be sufficient. Still, if you don't reach out to the people you know, how will you acquire a crew? This question is a little reminiscent of the axiom *You must have worked in a place once before in order to work in it again.* You are in the same boat as anyone else asked to produce a project in a city in which you have never shot. You must do your homework.

The first time I filmed in Toronto, I knew no one. I only got the job because Michael Filerman had two shows preparing simultaneously. Warren Littlefield, then head of NBC, agreed to green-light both projects provided I produced one in Canada. It was a big boost of support from a network executive and helped Mike because I was his first choice anyway. I didn't know a single soul in Toronto.

I put the word out and sought resumes, reels and recommendations for locals in every department. I placed phone calls to other Producers who had filmed before us. I looked at sample reels of Production Designers and Cinematographers. When I had narrowed the field to a few, I brought them in and interviewed them. An interview is more educational than you might think. You quickly get a sense of a person's style, personality, ideas and willingness to be a part of a team. Why is being part of a "team" so important?

When you were in film school your classmates were part of your group but they weren't a team. In film school the Cinematographers were the kings of your production. You were totally dependent on them for your film, and they ruled the roost. Outside film school your objective is to gather the most talented, professional and congenial roster available. This axiom is true: *The best musicians don't necessarily make the best orchestra.*

You want the most talented, professional, hard working *team* you can find. I've said it before, the hardest thing a Producer does is create an environment where all the elements can do their best work together. Nothing detracts from a film production like backbiting and bickering. It unsettles actors and other crewmembers, and places the energy in the wrong place. So find the most talented *and* likable people.

Here's the bottom line: Unlike actors, who after three weeks will prove too costly to replace, you can reorganize your crew if it becomes a necessity. Nobody likes to fire people in mid-stream, I'll grant that. But if it's in the best interest of the film, you can. The good news is that very often you will assemble a fabulous crew — a bunch of professionals who love each other, hang out on the weekend, and even play ball after work.

When I started in New York in the seventies, every Production Manager I worked for was either terrified of or extremely leery of the teamsters. Grips and electricians were routinely referred to as "the Gorillas." I couldn't really grasp the divide. I supposed it was because production guys were money-managers and schmoozers. I guessed it was a kind of grudging admiration for the bigger, more physical guys who got things done. But it sure sounded like arrogant denigration to me, and I didn't like it.

Over the years I have worked with teamsters in Dallas, Boston, New York and Honolulu. Each one of those groups has a reputation for being tough. Yet I have had a good — and I mean really good — experience with all of them. I believe it is in the mindset. My mother taught me to "Never judge the book by its cover."

I have had some of the toughest, meanest-looking men read or write me the most beautiful poetry, show me their amazing art work and help construct things I am way too clumsy to ever have built by myself. I had a driver track down and buy a very hard-to-find album of Latin music merely because I mentioned in passing one day that as a youngster I would go the Village Gate in Greenwich Village, New York, on Monday evenings to listen to Latin jazz.

I have had them come to my rescue in street confrontations in bad neighborhoods and access some of the most difficult locations in the dead of night. How could you have anything but the utmost respect for them?

To me, teamsters, grips, electricians — in fact, every crew member — are talented professionals filled with personal pride. Your movie doesn't get made in spite of them ... your movie gets made because of them.

Oddly enough, if pressed to identify the one group I have had some less-than-positive experiences with, it would be Camera Assistants. Don't ask me why. To be fair, I have worked with a lot of wonderful assistant camera people, some who are friends to this day. However, I have had a disproportionate number of run-ins with ACs. Perhaps it has just been the luck of the draw.

There is one thing as a Producer I will absolutely not tolerate. No one, and I mean no one, can stand in the middle of the set and bad-mouth the production company. That is poison to morale, and it will not stand on any of my shows.

Clearly, from time to time, people have legitimate complaints about one company policy or another. However, airing one's grievances in front of crew and performers is not the appropriate action. Any crew member who feels so wronged that they must share their discontent publicly has two options: They can go to management, softly and professionally, and state their case; or they can separate from the show.

In my career I have let go stand-ins, Assistant Cameramen and electricians for what I have defined as "conduct disruptive to the flow of production." I never did it lightly.

In my view, leadership is crucial. Groups with a common purpose (i.e. a film or TV show) need to be led. You bring sixty or eighty strangers together, and one of two things will happen. The grumbling naysayers will set the tone of the set; or the upbeat, consensus-building team-creator will lead.

You must always be the latter.

For years my reputation was: "Joe is tough, but he's fair." Or: "Joe runs a tight ship."

Wow, Joe, when did you become such a bad-ass? Oh I'm tough, all right. I'll tell you how tough.

We had a prop man on Knots Landing who was a bloody disaster. I will call him Chester. If it could be dropped, lost or ordered for the wrong episode, Chester was your man. He was always over budget and rarely correctly prepared. My bosses had had enough. Chester had to go. "Joe, see to it."

It was two days before Christmas. I saw Chester headed my way outside one of the stages. "Chester," I started authoritatively.

"Hi Joe" he greeted sweetly.

"Chester ... I ... I ... I ..."

"What is it, Joe? Is something the matter?"

"Chester ... I ... I...," I croaked. "I have to let you go."

It looked for a moment as if he didn't comprehend what I had just said. Then his face sort of turned down like a Bassett hound who'd just stepped on one of his own ears.

"I understand, Joe. I'm kinda a screw up. It's all right, I understand."

We fell silent, during which time I, staying with the canine metaphor, began to feel like utter dog shit.

Finally, with eyes that were little more than limpid pools of pathetic liquid, Chester said:

"Thing is, Joe. It's two days until Christmas and I don't have the money for a Christmas present for my son. And I won't know what to tell him."

And what did Joe the-tough-guy do?

How did that runner-of-tight-ships navigate the situation?
Not only didn't I fire him ... I gave him a fifty dollar raise.
I know. You laugh.
That's what happens when humanity rears its ugly head.
To continue:
Start and maintain a database of crew. Put their names in your whatever-the-latest-gadget is. The point is to keep them available to you as a future resource. Why do big time filmmakers use the same crews over and over again? They like working with them. They have established a working rapport. They know each other's likes and dislikes. They have developed a kind of working shorthand. They can anticipate each other's needs. Here comes a big quote from Chairman Joe, "A happy crew equals a well-mounted film."

With an apology to all film school cinematographers and their egos, "The set belongs to the director and the actors." And one last dig at Camera people: "No one ever came out of the theater humming the dolly shots." You can chalk that one up to Chairman Joe, as well. However, lest you think I am being unduly harsh on the camera department, let me just say that the best possible partnership is the one between the Director and the Cinematographer. It should be one of the most symbiotic relationship on the film, second only to that of the Director and the Assistant Director.

When I was first starting out, I had the good fortune to work on films where that was the case. The Director and Cameraman worked closely designing shots, establishing a color palette and picking lenses. I felt that the Cinematographer really was instrumental in bringing the Director's vision to the screen and even improving on it. I loved the relationship and hoped one day I would get to experience such a wonderful partnership myself.

Twenty years later I got my chance. I was assigned to direct an episode of a one-hour television show. I arrived on the set excited to begin the collaborative process. Before I even got the chance to say "hello," the cameraman said to me, "Where do you want the camera, Mo?" I was stunned. I naively thought we would discuss it, toss around an idea or two, and come to a consensus. I was wrong. He had not one iota of collaboration in him.

His next line was: "And what lens do you want?"

I learned very quickly that developing a good working relationship with someone is easily as important as their native talent. Chairman Joe has since added this one. "Talent is not necessarily a predictor of temperament."

There are Cinematographers who sincerely want to be helpful and move quickly. However, they may be legitimately unable to light at any pace other than their own. I produced a television movie with one such Cinematographer. He was a wonderful guy, but he could only work at the pace he worked — slow. If he tried to go faster it threw him off his game and his work suffered.

We had to decide if the look we were getting was worth the struggle to achieve it. Remember, the longer it takes to light, the less time your actors have to do their thing, and "the set belongs to the Director and the actors."

Fortunately, we had a mostly British cast. The Brits are real pros who adapt and adjust if they believe they are doing it for the right reasons. In the end we rightly stayed with the guy. We ended up with a terrific-looking, well-acted show of which we were all proud.

What else is there to know when choosing a Cinematographer? While it is true that the set belongs to the Director and the actors, generally speaking, the crew belongs to the Cinematographer. The Cinematographer will insist on his own Gaffer, Key Grip, Camera Operator and assistant camera people. He is right to do this because in the end he will be responsible for how the set runs and what goes on the screen.

A case in point: I started my career in New York in the Seventies. In those days New York crews were rude, abrasive, contentious and rarely not talking. I'll never forget a day when the Director had finished the rehearsal and was talking to the actors on set. Now, I grant you they should have moved from where they were so the crew could start lighting. However, one of the electricians walked up holding a ladder and slammed it down right between the actor and the Director and said, "We're working here."

The actor took exception. The Director was embarrassed, and the Director of Photography caught hell for the rude behavior of the crewmember, a person he did not hire. A good working relationship and the productive short-hand that goes with it affects the relationship between DP and Director. Unfortunately, in the aforementioned incident, the relationship between the Director and DP was never the same again.

What about relationships within the body of the crew? Like with the sound department, for instance. The longest running sibling rivalry (other than that of Cain and Abel) in the history of the universe is the rivalry between sound and camera. This is because sound must have someplace to put their mics and hold their booms that does not throw unwanted shadows around the set. It is a wise and happy crew that can sort out the eternal conflict between these two essential disciplines. Sound, in my opinion, doesn't get the recognition it deserves. Not only is it hard work to hold a boom mic over your head for twelve hours, but the sound department must also work under the worst conditions. Where do they set their equipment so that it won't be in the way? What are they supposed to do about the fact that the Director fell in love with a location right beneath the glide path of the local airport? Whose fault is it that the museum has high walls that make voices boom and echo?

The one deliriously happy sound guy I can vividly remember was a guy I worked with in Italy. We were filming a television remake of *Three Coins in the Fountain* called simply *Coins in the Fountain*. It starred Stephanie Kramer, Shanna Reed and Loni Anderson. We needed to film in Saint Peter's Square but were denied access by the Vatican. Our Director decided the solution was to walk the three girls across the square while we filmed them from atop a truck across the street. This necessitated employing wireless mics.

The next morning at 6 A.M., when Loni was finished in hair and make-up, the Sound Man took her behind a truck to place the microphone. He got down on his knees and taped the transmitter to her inner thigh, ran the wire up across her stomach and nestled the little mic securely between her considerable breasts.

Loni, who was a trooper, never said a word. The sound guy, who must have thought he had died and gone to heaven, looked up at her and said with a sheepish grin, "If you need your batteries changed, let me know."

No one knows for sure what her response was, but I noticed he was the only guy who, as the day progressed, whistled while he worked.

While that story may be amusing, the importance of good production sound is quite serious. If you can't get good sound on your performances when you are shooting, you will have to bring your actors onto an ADR stage at a later date and record their dialogue. It is not easy to match performances weeks later, playing to a machine instead of another actor. Directors don't like it, and actors try to avoid it.

ADR is almost always necessary when filming at the beach. The waves are a huge problem for sound. Unless your whole scene in one continuous shot, the minute you start to cut the scene, the background sound won't match. You will have to strip out all the sound, re-record the dialogue and rebuild your wave sound effects track from scratch.

This may sound strange, but strained relations on set can extend to the caterer and the crew. I have had to change more than one cook and catering company because of conflicts between them and the crew. Conflicts can arise from the simplest things. The crew doesn't like the food or thinks there isn't enough variation of choices. Personalities clash. Long hours shorten tempers.

The granddaddy of all catering debacles happened down Mexico way. The chef was a prickly, short-tempered man who was drunk or getting there most of the day. Things got so strained that I insisted that he take a few days off and return home to Los Angeles. He did. He was home for two days when he got drunk and shot and killed his wife. Needless to say, we never saw him again. The guy they sent to replace him was infinitely more affable — and, thankfully, unarmed.

The long and the short of acquiring a crew is this: Do your homework and meet the people with whom you will be working. If possible, have a small social get together before production begins so they can all get to know one another. And communicate your expectations. You will be surprised. Ninety-five percent of those with whom you work will strive to meet or exceed your expectations. Never underestimate the professional work ethic and the pride that comes along with it. Film people are professionals and make life-long friends.

When I shot in Europe I was warned not to mix an English and a Dutch crew. They won't get along, I was told. In fact, they worked fabulously well side by side, and we had a great time. In Mexico I was warned that the locals would resent "the gringos." This was also not true. In Hawaii I was warned that the locals would clash with the "Haoles" (Hawaiian for "assholes from the mainland"). Except for Harry-in-the-trunk, that turned out to be false as well.

So, like casting, you will go by your gut and the information garnered from others. If once in a blue moon you are wrong, so what? Fix it and move on. There are other films to make.

Set Protocol

The set belongs to the Director and the actors, and the crew to the Cinematographer; but the operation of the set — and how the show is scheduled — falls in the domain of the First Assistant Director. Contractually, the First Assistant Director works for the Director.

That is a much bigger statement than it appears. Any and every good Producer will do his or her own Production Board. The Production Manager will probably do his own Production Board as well. They will do it for broad outlines of the show, the creation of the budget and perhaps even some actor deals. But the First Assistant Director will make the Board on which the film will run. That is the law.

By the time the First A.D. joins the company, several key pieces of the puzzle will be in place, not least of which is the funding; and "the budget is a living breathing document." Once the First is on, the actual shape of the show will be formed. He will have full access to the Director. They will have discussed concept, style, locations, actors, preferences of working, and on and on. The First will carry a great deal of useful input into his Board creation. And once it is gone over with the Director and approved, it is the predominant document for be mounting the film.

When I was a young, wet-behind-the-ears Second Assistant Director, I marveled at how smart and knowledgeable the First Assistants seemed. They knew everything there was to know about the show — where we would film, at what time and with whom. They even knew how many extras (today we say background performers) we would use. They knew where the trucks would be parked, and where and when we would break for lunch.

"Wow," I used to say to myself, "I'll never be that smart. I'll never know that much about this film. How the hell to they do that?"

The answer couldn't have been more obvious. The First has constant and continual access to the Director. They talk the show to death — every scene, every element, every moment. The First Assistant Director will schedule the show in minute detail, even taking into account hours of set operation and the concept of *turnaround,* because he has all the information.

Turnaround is the time between the wrap of the cast and crew for any one particular day and the time they can be called to work the following day. For actors ,turnaround is twelve hours. For cameramen and camera operators it is eleven hours and for the body of the crew — grip, electric, props and sound — it is ten hours. Make-up and hair may have nine-hour turnarounds, or even eight on distant locations.

Scheduling a movie, as we discussed earlier, takes into account a significant number of variables — what location, actors, vehicles, extras, special effects, stunts, and so on are required. Once the A.D. has assembled his version of the board he must get the blessing of the Director. The schedule is then checked by the art department, the Location Manager and the Production Manager to be certain that all the necessary elements will be ready and available when needed.

Then the schedule is *locked.* We're gonna make the movie!

Locking the schedule also tends to settle the budget, at least so far as day-one projections. Within the body of the budget monies will tend to change. More lunch, less wardrobe, unanticipated crew overtime, fewer trucks. Some categories will rise, others will fall. It is the job of the Production Manager, the Production Accountant and, ultimately, the Producer to see that no matter how the monies change within the body of the budget, the bottom-line figure remains the same.

Now comes the technical scout, or tech scout. The term refers to the final surveying of the prospective locations by all the pertinent department heads to determine manpower and equipment needs, as well as other logistical considerations.

Everyone piles into a van. Who will be in the van and where will they sit? The driver will be behind the steering wheel (obviously), and the Director will be in the front seat immediately to his right. Behind the Director, in the first row, will sit the Producer, the Production Manager, and the First Assistant Director. In the second row will sit the Cinematographer, the Production Designer and the Location Manager. In the back will sit the Gaffer and Key Grip.

Why? Is this yet another Hollywood hierarchy-elitist thing? No, it has to do with the flow of information. A great deal of information is generated in the drives to and from prospective locations, and the quickest, most efficient way to disseminate it is through this seating configuration.

It has just been my experience that if everyone continues to focus on the Director, the ride will not disintegrate into sidebar, non-germane conversations.

You arrive at the first location. Everyone piles out and stands around the Director. Let's examine what happens next, in screenplay format:

DIRECTOR

I want to shoot in that direction. I want flowers for the sides of the walkway, and, oh yes, we have to get rid of that sign.

The Production Designer and the Second A.D. make note of this.

DIRECTOR (Cont'd)

(turning to the Cinematographer)
I want to be looking down that walkway for the night shot.

CINEMATOGRAPHER

Good choice.

He turns to the Production Manager.

CINEMATOGRAPHER (Cont'd)

I will need more than my twelve electricians to light that. Probably four or five more guys at night.

The Production Manager and the First Assistant Director take notes. Suddenly, the Location Manager pipes up...

LOCATION MANAGER

Will you be seeing into that parking lot? I was going to put the trucks there.

CINEMATOGRAPHER

I believe you will see them, even at night, if we light the walkway.

The Location Manager looks at the First A.D. Little beads of perspiration form on his brow. His eyes look as if they will bug out of his head. The First Assistant Director turns his back on the Location Manager, not wanting to discuss this right now.

EXT. BASE CAMP — LATER

Back at Base Camp, the Location Manager pins down the Production Manager:

LOCATION MANAGER

I am going to have to get another lot. I am already financially committed to that one, and we will have to hire vans and drivers to get the crew from the trucks to the location.

Thus the budget that has finally laid down and gone to sleep like some great woolly Mammoth will awaken with a roar. No cause for alarm. The budget goes up before it comes down.

Multiply the above scenario for the entire picture, and you will see the significance of the tech scout and its impact on the budget. It's always best to *anticipate* and *communicate*. This leads to the next important meeting — the production meeting.

At the start of the production meeting the Assistant Directors will distribute the shooting schedule. It is a fairly lengthy document that describes every scene in shooting order and all the elements required for the scenes. It will usually be adjusted as an outgrowth of the production meeting.

All department heads must attend.

The Director sits at the head of the table. Next to him is the First Assistant Director. The First will read through every scene, exclusive of dialogue, to be sure everyone is on the same page in terms of the elements needed for that scene and information gleaned from the tech scout.

Let's peek into a production meeting in progress:

The First A.D. is reading the slug lines and descriptions from the script. He says, "Exterior. Wickstone Estate. Day. Present are Lady Random, Sir Winston, the Earl, Herbert and the dogs. Tea set up, including crumpets and scones."

At this point the wardrobe mistress sits up, interjecting, "What is the weather going to be like? Hot or cold, drizzling or sunny?"

The Director jumps in, pleased at the question. "It's England. Let's have it drizzling. I'd like to have two butlers with umbrellas."

Since "two butlers with umbrellas" was not specified in the script probably no one has it in their notes. These added elements are to be noted by wardrobe, Casting, the Production Manager, the Production Accountant, the First Assistant Director and the Key Second Assistant Director. The First A.D. continues, "Special effects, we will need drizzle and maybe some gentle wind."

The special effects man sits up "Roger! Check!"

Onward to the next scene. If: at this point the Production Manager seems to be fidgeting ever-so-slightly, it's because that discussion has added money to be spent from the budget that was not anticipated; but it's okay, he's a smart guy and will offset the expense somewhere.

The scenario will be played out in similar fashion for every scene in the movie and helps explain why production meetings can go on for several hours. But there is no substitute for the production meeting and its basic philosophy that "the devil is in the details." Every little detail of the production must be discussed at that meeting.

You'll note that our meeting didn't run through dialogue. But wasn't there something earlier about a *Croix de Guerre* medal being mentioned in the dialogue? Yes. And, it is the First Assistant Director's job to have flagged it and it up at the Production meeting. In all likelihood the Wardrobe Department did its own breakdown of the scenes and will have already spotted it, but one must NEVER ASSUME!

Now, let me here disabuse you of the notion that because you have just sat through a four hour Production meeting, that all the questions have been answered and you will never have to discuss the particulars of any and every scene ever again. Not and NOT!

Every day, dozens of crew personnel will approach the Director and ask a question that was settled at the Production meeting. On every film I ever worked, at some point the Director said to me, "Why did they just ask that? Didn't we go over that at the production meeting?"

The answer is, "Yes, we did." However, we are dealing with human beings, and even film human beings are imperfect. I have come to learn that these questions are not asked out of laziness or indifference. They are asked out a desire to be certain the Director gets what s/he wants. So be patient with questions when you are directing. Endless questions are the bane of every Director. Everyone asks them: actors, wardrobe, Location Managers, Set Dressers, prop men, and on and on.

At long last it comes, the first day of principal photography, a very exciting day. At approximately 5:30 A.M., the first trucks roll in, including the catering truck. The drivers will position and secure their rigs. The make-up and hair rooms will be opened, supplied with electrical power and lit. The cooks will start preparing breakfast. Someone from the production department will be there, probably the Key Second Assistant Director.

At 6 A.M., make-up and hair and the first actors, will arrive and begin the process of getting made up and coiffed. A Production Assistant or Second-Second Assistant Director will get the actors breakfast from the catering truck. Very often the make-up and hair department will bring in their own coffee. At this time the set dressing crew will arrive to finish dressing the set. The First Assistant Director will arrive.

Between 6:30 and 7:00 A.M. the crew will start to roll in. They will gather at the catering truck for a breakfast burrito or whatever the company is supplying. The point here is that, if the crew call is 7 A.M., that is the time when the crew goes to work. It does not mean that the crew shows up and starts to eat on company time.

At 7 A.M., the Director will enter, and the company will start the day's work. For the first half hour it is likely the Director and D.P. will talk about the first set-up, while the camera department will take their gear, consisting of many heavy cases, off the camera truck and begin to assemble the camera. Grip and electric will gather their gear and, depending on the size and location of the first shot, begin to run electrical cable.

At 7:30 A.M., the First Assistant Director will instruct his Second to bring the actors to the set for rehearsal even if they are not completely finished in make-up and hair. The Director will set up a rehearsal. The crew will watch. This is not idle observation. Every department will be looking for things in the scene for which they will have to contribute. Props will watch what the actor does with hand props. Will they light a cigarette? Will they take a swig of brandy? The Grips will be watching to see if the blocking will necessitate a dolly shot. If so, they will have to set up the rail on which the dolly will move. The Gaffer and his crew will be trying to anticipate where their lights will be placed and how much cable will need to be drawn.

Once the scene is satisfactorily rehearsed, the actors will run through it one more time for *marks*. Marks are pieces of colored tape, each color assigned to a particular actor in the scene, that are placed on the floor and indicate where the actor will stop. This is done for purposes of lighting. Say Actor One is given red tape for his marks. Everywhere that actor goes in the scene and stops, a red piece of tape will be placed on the floor just at the tip of his shoes. By the time the *rehearsal for marks* is completed, it is possible that there will be lots of red, green, yellow and blue tape all over the floor. Marks are placed by the Assistant Cameraman.

At this point the actors will be allowed to return to the make-up trailer to finish getting made up.

Now comes a mad scramble of babbling crewmembers speeding on caffeinated coffee and tripping over each other to set lights, lay dolly track and supply the set with cigarettes and brandy, right? Not if it's done right.

The First Assistant Director will ask for the *Stand-Ins*. As the name implies, a *Stand-In* is someone of the same gender, height, weight and skin tone as the actor. Some shows have half a dozen Stand-Ins, some only two or three. The Stand-Ins will stand on the first mark. This is done for lighting purposes. They will then go, as directed by the D.P., to the other marks until the set is lit.

When the set is first turned over to the D.P., the First A.D. may ask (or the D.P. may volunteer) how long lighting is estimated to take. Let's say 45 minutes. The First will relay that to his Second, who may pass the info on to make-up. During that 45 minutes the make-up and hair artists can finish working on the actors. The actors can have a smoke, study their lines, call their agents or stretch their legs.

Hopefully, if you are lucky enough to have a savvy and cooperative Cinematographer, he will give you a "ten-minute warning." This is a heads-up that the set is about ten minutes away from being ready for filming. At that point the First will let the Second know of the warning, or he may simply say: "Round 'em up."

This is the signal for the actors to get off the phone, throw away the cigarette, go to the bathroom and get back in the make-up chair for "touch-ups."

"Bring 'em in," says the D.P. when he is down to setting the last two or three lights.

Once the D.P. has turned the set back over to the Assistant Director, the other departments should be through with their work and vacate the set. That means the lighting is done, the dolly track has been laid, the props or set dressings have been correctly placed, and the sound department has enough information to position their mics so they will not cast unwanted shadows.

The Stand-Ins step off the set, and the actors enter. There is another rehearsal. This one is to be sure everything is exactly the way everyone expects it to be — a "dress rehearsal," if you will. This is the time for last-minute corrections. The brandy snifter is too full. It sloshes when the actor walks. The boom casts a shadow when the actor is on his second mark. The actor's key light is slightly off. The Dolly Grip needs the rehearsal for estimating how fast he will have to go. And all of this is accomplished without everyone engaged in private conversations. Remember your Sunday School admonition? *Silence is golden.* The First Assistant Director should have to ask for "quiet" only once.

So all is ready. Now is the big moment, right? Ah, if only it were that simple. Now enters what I call "the Wrecking Crew."

Was-ist-das, you ask. The Wrecking Crew, my friends, are the unholy triumvirate of Make-Up Artists, Hairdressers and wardrobe people who guard their charges like the precious gems they are.

The Make-Up Artist will push his or her way onto the set, take a powder puff to the lead actor's forehead or apply lip gloss to the actress, and hand all of them a mirror so they can be certain they like the way they look. The Hairdresser will fuss with a stray strand of hair, and the wardrobe people will straighten collars and brush away lint. After what will seem like hours (but is only a few minutes), someone in the back of the stage will sing out: "Tick-tock" — a reference to time going by with no actual filming. At this point the key Make-Up Artist will say loudly "Well, it's not your face up there, is it?"

A word of caution: One of the unhappy realities of life on a film set is, Actors, Make-Up Artists, Hairdressers and Costumers come in to work at 6 A.M. and they bond. Get on the Make-Up Artist at that moment and you invite the actor to decide he needs to return to his make-up trailer for additional touching up. You get my drift? The Wrecking Crew is called the Wrecking Crew because they have the potential to completely destroy any rhythm to your set. Hear this well: They are not wrong; they are doing their jobs, and you would do well to accommodate them.

It is a wise Assistant Director who at that moment says to the Make-Up

Artists, "That's all right, Darling, take all the time you need." That might send the hair on the back of the Director's neck to a standing position, but it is also a signal to the actress that you respect that she needs to look good. The real subliminal message, however, is to the Make-Up Artist: From that point on, any time spent not filming is her responsibility.

She will finish quickly, and they will all retreat to their chairs like ghostly apparitions.

Now. Now. Now you are ready to shoot. "Break a leg," they say in show-biz lingo. But don't actually do that. Nobody's leg needs to get broken.

Your big day commences. Some Directors and actors only like to do a few *takes* some like to do many. The scene was comprised of several *set-ups,* or camera positions over-the-shoulder shots, a two-shot (meaning two people onscreen in a medium close-up), and close-ups or *singles.* All of this is known as *coverage,* or covering the scene from all angles and including every person.

But the long and the short of it is you come to the last set-up of that particular scene. In most instances, like on episodic television and low-budget Independent films, time is critical and you may do several scenes in a single day. Therefore, while the D.P. lights for the last piece of coverage for one scene, the Director may be next door rehearsing the next scene.

When the Director returns to finish the first scene, the First Assistant Director will instruct his Second to "Keep the actors nearby." If after that rehearsal the actors disperse to the four winds it can take twenty minutes to re-gather them. The instant the first scene is finished, the First Assistant Director will announce, "Okay guys, we're in the Living Room and Actor One, Two and Three will work."

The point of all this choreography is to establish a rhythm and a momentum for the set. You will be amazed how much work can be accomplished with a good crew, high morale and a fluid set rhythm.

Mercifully, you have come to the lunch hour — six hours after the main body of the crew was called. Remember the actors and Wrecking Crew will have been provided a "rolling or walking breakfast" by the set P.A. or Second Assistant Director.

My advice, as previously stated, would be for the P.A.s to get lunch for the actors off the catering truck and place it in their motor homes. Next will come the crew. Production eats last. This is not a bias against production. It is a holdover from a long tradition when meal breaks and turnaround did not exist in the contract for Assistant Directors. If the caterer runs out of food, there was no contractual obligation to feed production, and, theoretically, they could slip away from the set and get something to eat from a restaurant or fast food joint.

You have regrouped, continued filming and developed a set rhythm.

Good for you. Once you have developed a rhythm and a rapport with cast and crew, work gets easier and less stressful. Hopefully, a sense of camaraderie will have developed.

Around four o'clock the famous *valley of fatigue* can start to rear its ugly head. Low sugar, the sluggishness of a good lunch, and general fatigue can start to slow the pace of filming. This is where craft services will become a significant part of your daily life. Snacks, in whatever form they take, will help to reenergize the cast and crew. I have been on shows where two hours after lunch they are serving chicken wings, Swedish meatballs and cocktail franks.

Unnecessary, you say? Perhaps. It also doesn't need to be that lavish. It can be warm soup or a bowl of chili in cold weather, or a simple slice of pizza. The point is, as I have already said: "The Army runs on its stomach."

Something else begins to occur between four and five o'clock. The Second Assistant Director finds a way to slink off and start to rough in the call sheet for the next day. Most First Assistant Directors don't like to see their assistants doing paperwork on the set. They want them standing at attention, within their eyesight, ready to jump to whatever task is assigned. When there is a break in filming the First and Second will get together and finalize the next day's call sheet. The First will check it with the Director to be certain nothing *bumps* for him, and then turn it over to the Production Manager. The First A.D. and the Production Manager will sign it and seek the final approval of the Producer. Once all of that is done, it will be transmitted to the production office, where it will be emailed to everyone or printed on paper and distributed at the wrap. I always prefer a paper copy because I keep it on set with me in a shirt pocket. I refer to it constantly.

If yours is a studio picture, you will probably be required to phone in a five o'clock report to the studio production department. A five o'clock report is really nothing more than a day's progress report. Something like, "We will finish at seven and have gotten the day's work done."

However, if, after calling in that summary, something changes and you go later or don't complete the day's work, you have to call back and let the studio know. Communicate. Communicate. Communicate.

There is nothing worse than a studio executive getting a call from his boss wanting to know why you filmed until midnight and didn't finish the day's work when the executive has just told his bosses that everything went perfectly. Death. Death. Death. Better an artful explanation of why things changed than a nasty surprise.

You finish the day's work. Everyone has their call time for the next day. There will be one last document required — the production report. The production report is the official and legal documentation of your production.

Legal because the studio's or your accounting department will pay the crew based on the hours listed on the production report. That is why it must be totally accurate. The crew will still fill out time cards, but the times must match. If they don't, the Production Manager must get together with that crewmember and resolve the discrepancy. The Production Manager cannot just change a crewmember's time card. That is illegal.

From the production report, the accounting department is also able to create the *hot costs*. This is the document that summarizes several accounts to give you the sense of the bigger picture. Crew overtime, numbers of extras, number of meals or whether there was a second meal, and some rough costs of set dressing may all be part of your hot costs.

There you have it. Your first day of filming is behind you. People are still speaking to one another, no blood has been spilled, and you've gotten some darned good performances.

You might just pull this puppy off yet.

Elements of Production

Films cost a lot of money. Most of it goes to salaries, exotic locations and lots of expensive equipment. But guess what? That's not all. Much of your money will be a contingent cost of your production elements. In a nutshell this means that not all your costs are obvious and directly related to your props.

Guns

Let's start with guns. Yes, they're only props; maybe they fire blanks, but for heaven's sake, they're not real. You know that. Your cast and crew knows that. You've even hired an Armorer (someone whose sole responsibility is to handle, maintain and teach the safe usage of such weapons) just to be extra safe.

What you haven't done is isolate yourself and your shoot from the outside world of non-film people. Huh? Stay with me; this is so important.

Take, for example, a mugging scene in an alley. One man holds a rubber — but very real-looking — gun on another man. There are bright lights, dolly track, a large film camera and a substantial amount of crew. Obviously a film shoot, right? Not so fast.

This was exactly the scenario on a student film shoot near the USC campus, where nothing could possibly go wrong. Except at three in the afternoon a Little Old Lady walked by the alley and completely failed to make the nexus between all the filming activity around her and the fact that it was not a real mugging. She called the cops — the L.A. Cops. Just for the record, let me say that when the L.A.P.D. gets a call about a mugging in progress involving a gun, they come flying. Believe it or not, they do not say to themselves, "Oh, must be those crazy little USC film students doing a mugging scene in an alley near their school." No. They take it extremely seriously. The worst possible thing an actor, film student or studio executive can do is turn toward the police officer and try to explain that the gun he is pointing back at them isn't real. The police will tell you — after they've shot you — that "We don't see the person, only the weapon." It is a recipe for disaster. Just remember this: *Always Drop the Weapon!*

Now take that scenario and plunk it down in the middle of Times Square at night. Add *squib hits* on the person getting shot (squibs are little capsules filled with red dye to simulate blood that burst when activated by an electrical charge wired into the capsule) and you could have a super-disaster.

In order to be safe, the elements of your scene with the guns requires the following elements:

(a) Multiple police officers
(b) Standby ambulance
(c) Standby paramedics
(d) Fire Marshall
(e) Fire truck
(f) Water truck
(g) Additional crowd control personnel

With the exception of the Police, who might be provided free of cost (New York is a great place to shoot), all the other men and material will be costs resulting from the weaponry. Take away the guns and you will be left with police, crowd control personnel, and a lot more money in your budget.

My point is that if all you think about are the weapon rentals, you will have underestimated the costs of the scene. Any good First Assistant Director or Production Manager should have anticipated those costs — as well as the call from the Producer asking why that one scene is so damned expensive.

Some years ago down in Texas on *Dallas: The Early Years* we filmed a major action sequence in an oil field. The scene called for a fight between sharecroppers and the Klu Klux Klan. It resulted in a massive fire that engulfed the entire oil field. There were explosions, bulldozers pulling the legs out from beneath oil rigs to make them topple, and lots of trained horses whose exposure to fake fire was untested — an expensive enough sequence by television standards. On top of that, we had to add the ancillary or non-direct costs to the scene, and they were significant:

(a) A dozen off-duty police officers who, unlike in New York City, had to be paid for their time. Double-time pay, in fact.
(b) Three ambulances

(c) A dozen paramedics

(d) Six fire trucks

(e) A dozen firemen

(f) 2 Fire Battalion Captains

(g) Three water trucks

(h) And because we were thirty miles from the nearest hospital, a Medivac helicopter.

Talk about pricey. It was the perfect example of unanticipated costs of a scene when it was being written. And, by the way, all the above personnel had to be fed lunch and dinner, and reimbursed for their gas mileage.

When it was budgeted, we knew it would be an expensive night, but no one realized we would be required to have the Medivac helicopter, a $10,000 surprise. Remember me? I'm the guy who said there are no good surprises in production.

Guns in film come with another cost, a psychological one. They are stressful. So many things can go wrong when filming with guns.

I was moved up to be Gordon Park's Assistant Director during the filming of a movie called *Super Cops*. It was shot entirely on location in the Bedford-Stuyvesant section of Brooklyn. It told the story of two out-of-control narcotics agents named Greenburg and Hantz. Their nicknames on the streets were Batman and Robin. In one scene they followed two suspects into an abandoned tenement to arrest them. They had their prop guns drawn, as did the four uniformed police *extras* with them.

We had real police officers working with us. In addition, we had notified the local precinct of what we were doing. When it came time to do the scene, we called again and said we were starting to film. All was well — until we rolled cameras. The villain's car came screeching around the corner and slid to a stop in front of the building. They ran in. Our heroes, all six of them came running down the street brandishing their guns.

Suddenly, behind them, came two real undercover Detectives in an unmarked car thinking they were assisting their brother officers in a real confrontation. My heart jumped up into my throat. I called, "Cut, cut, cut." But it was too late. The undercover cops rushed into the building. I waited for what I knew would be real gunshots.

Only by the grace of God was disaster averted when one of the actors did a very quick mental head count and realized something was wrong. He immediately called "Cut" inside the hallway.

At first the real cops were angry, then embarrassed, then apologetic. We had done everything by the book — had police with us, permits from the city, and ongoing communication with the local precinct — and still came perilously close to tragedy. It was a horrific example of Murphy's Law. And it is not the only one.

On the series *Hotel* I worked with a really nice young man named John Derek Hexum. He was big, blond and good-looking — a young Arnold Schwarzenegger. He was only twenty-seven years old. Several months after I worked with him he was on another show. His scene involved a gun that fired blanks. In that instance it was only a quarter load. For whatever reason, he was allowed to keep the gun between scenes. He was sitting off-stage waiting for the lighting for the next scene to be finished when for reasons known only to himself, he put the gun to his temple and pulled the trigger. I suspect he was just fooling around. John Derek Hexum died. His unfortunate and tragic death changed procedure at USC. We no longer use blanks at all, for any reason, on any project. Stupid things like this happen.

And yet our closest call did not involve guns. It involved a young man and a ski mask. I was seated at my desk one Monday morning when a man called and said, "What the hell are you guys doing down there? You almost got my son shot!"

I was shocked to say the least and pressed the man for details. One of our students had gotten permission to film at night in a small convenience store. The scene called for a robber in a ski mask to enter and pretend to have a gun in his pocket in an amateurish attempt to rob the place. The store windows were frosted, and no one could see in. In a further attempt to be responsible, the students printed a small hand-lettered sign on a piece of white paper saying a prop weapon was in use and taped it on the window outside. The actor was warned repeatedly not to put on the ski mask until he entered.

The actor waited outside for his cue to approach. The Director called "Action." The actor lowered the ski mask into place and started to enter. At that precise moment a motorist driving by saw the kid in the ski mask and called 911. The cavalry came running.

We had on film two very big uniformed officers holding shotguns. One of them said right into camera, "If we had seen you go into the store, we would have shot you."

No more little hand-written signs taped to windows. The cops never saw it, never thought to look for it and were not obliged to do so. Our very talented and hard-working Stage Supervisor, Stephen Goepel, designed very large, very bright red and yellow signs that proclaim: "USC film shoot in progress. Prop weapons in use." They are routinely given out to students who place them at any point of set access. In addition, paid police officers are required on any student film shoot that goes off-campus with weapons.

Call it nature, but student films tend to break down along gender lines.

Males mistake guns and violence for real drama. Females create drama and call it drama. I've seen it a thousand times. It is the girls who write the gratuitous sex and nudity scenes, a subject I will get to soon; but the boys prefer the guns. I suspect it has to do with how each gender perceives power.

This tendency towards violence carries into the mainstream of the industry. It helps explain why there is so much violent content in films and on TV today. In my humble opinion, guns, violence, and action in general should arise from the organic nature of the character and the necessity of the plot, and not be foisted upon the audience indiscriminately.

There ... I've said it.

Stunts

Generally speaking, they are acts of such complexity and danger that you would not risk your actor doing them. The film business is rife with stories of macho actors getting hurt because they did not want to turn the scene over to a stunt person, lest someone think them less manly. But stunt work is serious business. It runs the gamut from fight scenes to wire work, high falls to motorcycles, car stunts to fire, and many, many near-misses. Every time you see a car run through a busy street market and people jumping out of the way, you are looking at the coordinated efforts of several stunt people under the aegis of a Stunt Coordinator. I have done scenes where Stunt Men have set themselves on fire, something your lead Actor should not do. This is not as humane as it sounds.

There are two reasons to employ stunt personnel. First, a wounded actor slows down production and screws up continuity. He isn't trained in this highly specialized area. But the second reason is what I call "getting more cluck for your buck." An actor is doing a fight scene. He is big, good-looking, and physically fit. But unless he is expert at close combat, he tends to anticipate the punch and flinch or hesitate. You can handle this one of two ways. You can photo or stunt-double the actor with a Stunt Man who is expert in this kind of action — someone who will even take the blow if the other actor over-acts — or you can have the Stunt Man work with the Asctor to make him more comfortable and look more realistic. Either way it is money well spent.

On *Knots Landing* I had a jerk of a Director who constantly needled one of our actors about not being macho enough. One night at the beach the scene called for that actor to run down a steep hill into the parking lot. I hired a Stunt Man for the run down the hill. The Director insisted the actor do it himself. We argued. I was just at the point of saying, "That's it! A Stunt Double or we're not doing the shot," when the actor took me aside and begged,

"Please, Joe, I can do it. Let me just shut this asshole up." Against my better judgment I acquiesced, and you can fill in the dots. Three quarters of the way down the hill the actor lost his balance, came down headfirst and slammed his chin against the concrete lip of the parking lot. Eighteen stitches later we were through for the night, and I had a lot of explaining to do at the home office.

By the way, this was the same jerk who, at a later date, turned water hoses on some homeless people on a downtown street because he didn't want them in the shot. The police were outraged and shut him down. Arrogant, egotistical bullies like that have no place in professional filmmaking.

Stunt Men and Women do a whole lot more than merely keep pretty people looking pretty. They literally risk their lives, sometimes with catastrophic results. I was filming on a Friday night at a San Fernando diner location called Cadillac Jacks on *Malibu Shores* when a forty-two-year-old Stunt Man named Paul Dallas died on another show in a high fall off a building across an open field from us. His body hit the air bag, but his head struck the sidewalk.

Many years ago, on a television pilot for Fox, we had a scene in which the actor caught fire after a car crash. The car burned, and the actor was to come running out of the car and roll around in the street. Obviously we hired an experienced Stunt Man to do the fire gag. He wrapped himself in all sorts of protective clothing and doused himself with fire-retardant gel. There was only one problem. Because of the fire and his face being covered we could not hear him if something went wrong. It meant we had only his body language as a clue if he got in trouble. The action called for a lot of the same gestures — arms flailing, stumbling about — that would occur if the gag went wrong. It was extremely difficult to know whether to cut the shot because he was being burned or whether he was merely acting.

There was a second fire safety Stunt Man standing by with a fire extinguisher and a pail of sand. Unbeknownst to us, there was a prearranged signal between Stunt Man and Safety Officer that would indicate the shot needed to be stopped. I remember watching the guy burn — my mind screaming, "Why doesn't he stop the shot?!" — only to discover that the shot worked perfectly. The Stunt Man came away with not so much as a blister. I admire real professionals who know what they are doing.

I shudder to think what could have happened if the Director I mentioned previously had talked the actor into doing his own fire stunt. The fact is, I would not have allowed it; but the point is, neither should you. If your film calls for stunt work, spend the money on professionals. It is money well spent, and it will end up on the screen looking perfect. Plus, you will be able to go to sleep at night knowing that you didn't senselessly injure a fellow human being.

Very often, if the stunts are more complicated than merely a fight scene or a near miss, in addition to the basic SAG pay rate, the Stunt Man may negotiate a per stunt, or per take, fee. A case in point: *A New Leaf* was a film starring Elaine May and Walter Mathau. We shot it in Penobscot, Maine. In one scene Walter and Elaine end up clinging to a rock in the middle of a raging rapid. Walter lets go and is swept over the falls. It took days, and some of the most creative grip work I have ever seen, to construct the camera platform at the apex of the rapids just as it plunged fifty feet into a pool. It was clearly a stunt that Walter was not going to do. We sought and found a tall, good-looking park ranger. He looked like Jimmy Stewart. He was soft-spoken and fearless.

Wisely, he had enough respect for Mother Nature that he insisted on being thoroughly protected. His legs were wrapped in thick rubber pads. He had layers of clothing on top of the padding to diminish the thermal effects of the frigid water. He had boots for his feet and thick gloves for his hands.

We agreed to pay him $1,500 per take, a lot of money for a stunt in those days. He went over the falls flawlessly twice. But each time something went a little askew. The camera missed focus; the operator missed the shot by just a little. He had to go a third time.

He did it and struck a jutting rock. He survived, but when we pulled him out of the water and unwrapped his padding, the rock had sliced through the pad down to the last inch. One more inch and he might have lost his leg, or worse, his life.

In the technologically sophisticated world of today, a shot like that would probably be accomplished on a Green Screen stage. It would be a lot cheaper and a whole lot safer.

Nudity

When I stop to think that in the world in which I grew up you could not say the word "pregnant" on television, I know we have come a long way, baby. In today's world, so many actresses and actors have appeared nude or nearly nude that it is almost a non-subject anymore. Except that taste and appropriateness are still on issue.

Every year at the University of Southern California, when I do my safety seminars, some incoming student will raise his or her hand and ask, thinking they are being terribly avant-garde, "Do you allow nudity in films?"

To which I reply, tongue-in-cheek, "Allow it ... we encourage it." Everybody laughs; then I go on to say, " But only under the strictest compliance with the rules of the Screen Actors Guild." This past year was no exception.

They asked, I replied, they laughed. Only this time the Dean was in the audience.

When they all laughed, I looked at the Dean. She was not laughing.

I no longer say that.

All kidding aside, taste and appropriateness are subjective, but so are the personal sensibilities of performers, male and female. As a Producer and/or Director, you must always be sensitive to the feelings of your actors. The subject of nudity begins at the casting session. A script may be written in one way but shot in another. Therefore, it is essential that the Director, Producer or Casting Director let the auditioning performers know what will be required of them should they get the role. It is perfectly legitimate for an actor or actress to say, "Gee, I love the role but I am uncomfortable with taking off my clothes onscreen."

You have two choices. Reassure the performer that in spite of what is written, there will be no actual nudity required, or you can push on and keep casting. What you cannot do is state that there will be no nudity and then insist on the set that there will be some. Under the guidelines of the Screen Actors Guild, an actor or actresses can change their minds right up to the moment of filming, and no one has the right to attempt to pressure or coerce them into doing a nude scene.

Remember movie magic? Very often what is seen on the screen is not what is happening on the set. Onscreen you may only get a glimpse of a breast or buttock, but on the set that actress is completely nude. In my experience, there are not a lot of actresses who want to spend the day naked, being ogled by 20 grips and electricians.

I was the Second Assistant Director on a Patty Duke–James Farantino movie titled *Me, Natalie*. Fred Coe was the Director. Michael Hertzberg, a terrific guy and an outstanding First Assistant Director, was the First. Michael became a big Producer in Hollywood, and he and I have remained friends. On this day we were shooting a love scene between the two stars. Patty, rightfully, insisted the set be cleared of all non-essential personnel. When it came time for the first take, the only people present were the Director, the Cinematographer, the First Assistant Camerawoman and the Script Supervisor.

Patty proceeded to get undressed and lay on the bed. She looked up at the rafters. All along the scaffolding she noticed a dozen eyeballs staring down at her. The Grips and Electricians, barred from the set, had climbed to the rafters and hid behind the velour curtains. They would not be denied.

Patty freaked out and screamed blue murder. That was followed by what sounded like a stampede of exiting crewmembers. Patty would only do the scene if female guards stood on the scaffolding. I told you that things were very different in those days. Today almost anything goes; but the key word is *almost*.

A student at USC a couple of years ago talked an up-and-coming actress into appearing nude in her thesis film. There was quite a bit of implied sexual activity as well. The actress was willing and more than a little fearless. Fortunately, our student Director had the actress sign an extremely explicit nudity release. It was so graphic in its detail it was difficult to read. It very carefully described every body part that could be filmed, what angle it could be filmed at, and what it was doing at the time of filming.

When I first saw the agreement I thought it was overkill and even wondered if its true intent was to make me blush, something that is not easy to do. Well, as luck would have it, when the Director showed her cut to the actress they disagreed on how it was edited. The actress really didn't have much room to argue, however, since she had no right of editorial content. Time went by and the actress got a manager. The manager got the actress a part in a network movie and believed it was the beginning of her upward climb. Then the student film surfaced.

The manager was livid. He threatened to sue the school, the Director and anyone else he came in contact with. He claimed the film was little more than soft-core pornography that would ruin his client's burgeoning career. The only thing that kept the case from going to court was the student's meticulously written nudity release. At USC we draw a sharp distinction between nudity and actual sex on camera. While nudity is allowed, as are implied sex acts, no real or actual sex is permitted. There are moral, ethical and, even, medical reasons for this.

The subject of nudity in films, particularly student films or low-budget independents, could go on for pages. It generally breaks down along gender lines, and it can spin off into directions never intended.

First let's discuss the gender lines. Despite what many would say, boys are uncomfortable with nudity and try to minimize it in their student films. The girls are much more explicit and willing to push the envelope. Boys seem to feel if they envision nudity someone will say they are just being salacious, a bunch of drooling frat boys looking for a cheap thrill — not true artists. The girls have no such self-doubt. They seem not to fear being judged and will write some very explicit stuff. I can't count the number of nude lesbian shower scenes we have done via female student directors. The girls never flinch. They can also come to my office and ask some really difficult-to-discuss questions. The one I remember most vividly was: How explicit could a scene involving female masturbation be? At that point she proceeded to talk about explicit parts of the female anatomy. I wanted to do something else for a living.

At this juncture, I would like to set the record straight about what the USC School of Cinematic Arts will and will not allow. We strive to nurture student art and avoid censorship, but we do have boundaries.

First and foremost, we are not a guerrilla filmmaking school. We do not allow our students to sneak around in the dead of night shooting surreptitiously from the rear of vans. We pride ourselves on mimicking every aspect of the professional filmmaking world. We do not permit pornography, and we are not a performance-art school.

What is performance art? An example: A young woman at NYU brought a male and a female into the class. They proceeded to have sexual intercourse on the desk, and she filmed it. As you might imagine, it caused quite a stir and raised serious questions about the judgment of those involved.

A man from the *New York Times* called me, asking about this event. "What would USC do," he wanted to know. "Not that," I replied. They could have simulated sex, pretended to do it, faked it, given the impression thereof, but not have actually done it. Along the same lines, if a scene called for someone to be shot to death, we wouldn't allow someone to actually kill an actor. Film is smoke and mirrors, make believe, pretend. He-lloooo!

At the School of Cinematic Arts we pride ourselves on not censoring students. There is, however, one significant exception. We have an ironclad rule that there may be no genital-to-genital or mouth-to-genital touching. In this era of rampant STDs and HIV/AIDS, that is a major health concern. At USC, health and safety do trump a student's "freedom of expression."

In fact, safety trumps everything at the School of Cinematic Arts. We have a moral and ethical responsibility to return our students, the actors who work with us, and the public-at-large to their families intact.

I have strayed pretty far from "nudity generally breaks down along gender lines." I won't belabor the point.

My second point is that nudity can spin off into unintended directions. Several years ago we did a student thesis project called *Streakers*. You can do the math. It involved five young men running naked across campus. However, we are just one of nineteen schools that make up the University of Southern California. Other schools are not quite as liberated. When those five young men ran naked by the USC swimming pool at night, the Director of Sports and Recreation just about had a nervous breakdown. He screamed bloody murder and it took us more than a year to get back the swimming pool as a filming location. Oops.

I guess the correlation to the outside world is this: People not involved in your film may not be as forgiving about naked people romping around their beaches, parks neighborhoods or hotel lobbies. Think past your film into the real world and act accordingly. This, by the way, is how the concept of *closed set* came into being.

One last point before I leave this subject. The Director must always be in control of the set. This story doesn't involve nudity, but intimacy. A young woman director was doing a short film in which a man and woman begin to make love. She cast for several days. She had a couple of *call-backs* (returns for another look) and finally narrowed her choices to one guy and one girl. She wanted to be sure they had the right chemistry with each other, so she called them back and replayed the scene. During the scene emotions got carried away. The actors, "lost in the moment," went too far. The girl had her hands all over the guy. When the audition was over, nothing was said. They all went their separate ways. However, over the course of the next few hours the actress began to feel betrayed both by her own behavior and the lack of control exercised by the director. Worse, she worried that somehow her boyfriend would find out. She called the Screen Actors Guild and complained.

Guess what? She was right.

When actors perform they are turning over their lives, literally and creatively, to the Director. In this instance, when the purpose of the scene had been realized, the young director should have stopped the performance. Actors, by instinct and training will not stop the scene themselves. They wait for words like "Cut" or "Stop" or "Scene" or "get your goddamn hands off of me."

This notion that the director must control the scene is not limited to romance or nudity. It applies to stunt work, work with vehicles, animals and special effects, fire, water and on and on.

Minors

No, not those guys with lights on their helmets, but people under the age of eighteen.

On July 23, 1982, the notorious *Twilight Zone* tragedy occurred. It cost the life of actor Vic Morrow and two Vietnamese children, ages six and eight. It was horrific, unnecessary and illegal. Minor children in the State of California are not allowed to be working at two or three o'clock in the morning, much less participating in dangerous stunt and pyrotechnic work. California, which has always had stringent child protection laws, redoubled its efforts and focus after *Twilight Zone*.

At USC we comply one hundred percent with California's child welfare rules. We have a permit to employ minors, and we insist that each and every project that involves a minor child be correctly staffed and all paperwork correctly filed. Every project employing a minor must fill out and have signed a "Hazardous Shooting" form. The students must bring a copy of the studio teacher's (a type of welfare worker) credentials to the physical production office, where we keep it on file. The work papers of the minors must be filed with our office. Use of minors must be recorded on a production report or some other class-appropriate document.

What is the difference between a studio teacher and a welfare worker? They are one and the same, but with two very different responsibilities. The welfare of the minor child is always their first priority. In this regard they have enormous power on set. They can pull the minor off the set and even shut a production down if the danger is sufficiently egregious. The welfare board can levy heavy fines and even suspend a studio's permit to employ minors.

Some years ago, some film students placed a ten-year-old boy in a bath-tub full of water and strung Christmas lights around his shoulders. The parents were standing right there. They never objected to what could have been a life-threatening circumstance. It was the welfare worker who halted the film-ing, removed the child from the water and refused to let the show continue. That is not only their job, it is their obligation.

The other thing the studio teacher does is teach. Children taken out of school for the purpose of filming must continue their education. Every age has different hours of permissible work. That is why the studio teacher's union publishes a *Blue Book*, the compendium of every rule and regulation pertaining to the employment of minors in the state of California.

By the way, just like with worker's comp, all fifty states have fifty different rules about hiring minors. In New Jersey, for example, there are no studio teachers or welfare workers but all minors must be accompanied to work by a parent or legal guardian. Paramedics will not treat children under the age of eighteen until consent is granted from an adult guardian. Clearly, California is the most concerned because of the amount of child work in Hollywood, and the long, dark shadow of *The Twilight Zone* disaster.

Studio teachers are credentialed differently than regular teachers. That is why you either want to get somebody from the union or see their credentials with your own eyes. Two years ago we had a really serious incident involving a minor child. A student thesis project was filming on one of our several soundstages. They employed an eight-year-old boy and hired someone they believed to be a credentialed studio teacher.

On the day of filming one of the Producers, an assertive young lady, approached the man and asked to see his card. The man produced it but seemed annoyed that she had asked. This aroused her suspicions, and she demanded to see his driver's license to verify that he was who he said he was. He said he needed to get his license from his car. He left and never returned. When we did a thorough check, it turned out the card was a total forgery. In other words, someone of unknown background and purpose was placed in charge of an eight-year-old child. When I think of it now, I still shudder. I am eternally grateful for the diligence of that young, up-and-coming Producer, who listened and applied what we try to teach.

By far the most difficult theme to navigate is child molestation. Think we don't have students who want to go down that path? Think again. An undergraduate Junior thought he was being terribly *edgy* (a weasel's word I really dislike) when he handed me a script that included a scene where a nine-year-old boy finds himself in a seedy hotel room with a sexual predator. In the scene the boy is clad only in his underwear. The adult male approaches him, stands him on a bed and begins to lower his underpants. Bad enough?

Here comes the shocker.

The child's mother was okay with the scene as written.

I was stunned. I couldn't believe it, so I called the mom. Instinct, and years of experience, convinced me to record our conversation. I informed the woman at the start of the conversation that I was recording every word for legal reasons. She was okay with my taping our call. I asked if she understood the specifics of the scene. She assured me she did. I asked whether she had explained it to her son. She said she had. She went on to say that her son knew it was only make-believe, and she had no reservations about him being nude in the scene.

I was appalled but didn't challenge her parenting perceptions. I did, however, re-record the conversation and place it on my desktop computer, where it sat for a year and a half. I was convinced she had a screw loose and that one day I would hear from her outraged ex-husband. He never called.

Still not reassured, I called the student into my office and told him exactly how I intended he shoot the scene.

"You can take one shot of the child standing on the bed in his underwear. You can have one shot of the adult male standing fully clothed in the doorway. And you can have one shot from behind the adult toward the bed, but his body must be blocking the child. In other words, in that shot the kid won't even be on the set." Movies are about smoke and mirrors, and perceptions.

The student frowned and left my office. Not convinced he would comply, on the day of filming I went to the location. I called the student, the mother, the child, the adult male actor and the welfare worker into a closed set meeting. I told the welfare worker he was to close down the show if the student Director deviated from the shots I had outlined.

The student grew indignant and asserted: "You are interfering with my vision." To which I replied, "Let me tell you about your vision. You do anything different than what I have stated, and the vision you will have next, will be you attending UCLA next semester."

He shot it as I had dictated. It is extremely rare for me to intercede in the concept of a student film. The point of the story is to show why the presence of welfare workers is essential on set. Someone has to be watching out for the children. Filmmakers too often get caught up in their vision to use wise judgment. Parents have such strong dreams of child stardom and early retirement that they can also be poor judges of appropriateness and safety.

Animals

The USC School of Cinematic Arts has a motto: "Nothing Dies for Film." Happily — and coincidentally — it is also the motto of the American Humane Society, with whom we have a strong relationship. Every year they provide us with thousands of dollars worth of their materials, and their executive director, Karen Rosa, comes and speaks at our safety seminars. They publish guidelines for the safe use of every living creature, or, as they say, "Everything from ants to elephants." It is a wonderful organization that does everything it can to protect both the animals and the filmmaker's vision.

One of the more shocking surprises that awaited me when I took over as Director of Physical Production at USC was the number of students who were willing to harm living creatures. I don't mean setting up dog fights or running over pigeons. I mean simpler things like flushing gold fish down a toilet, leaving a pet rat in a dumpster to fend for itself or filming a live scorpion in a ring of fire.

To my way of thinking, the way a society treats its animals speaks volumes about the kind of society it is. Compassion and filmmaking are not mutually exclusive. Your humanity is worth more than all the films you will ever make.

Jorge Luis Borges wrote: "Along this path so many great minds have lost their way, that a mere detective might surely lose his." Don't lose your way. Treat all living creatures with respect and dignity. It's just a movie, and there are always multiple ways to get a convincing shot.

This includes ants, spiders and ladybugs, all creatures I have filmed. I am proud to say in every instance they were returned to their natural habitats intact. In the case of the ladybugs, I learned an interesting lesson. It is actually possible to return nine hundred and ninety out of a thousand ladybugs to their point of origin.

Come on, Joe, get serious.

A true story. A student wanted ten ladybugs for a scene she was doing in a botanical garden. The curator was okay with the ten, but when he learned they could only be purchased in lots of a thousand, he balked. That many ladybugs in one place could do serious damage to his flora and fauna. Up stepped the American Humane Society. It turns out there is a gel you can smear on a popsicle stick whose scent will draw ladybugs to it. Who knew? The student was able to get her shot, and all but a mere handful of the ladybugs were returned to the place they were bought.

Back to the scorpion and the ring of fire. A student wanted to do a shot where, to disprove an urban myth, a live scorpion is placed in a ring of fire. The story goes that a scorpion trapped by flame will, after three unsuccessful attempts to escape, sting itself to death — in other words, commit suicide.

In pre-production the student was told, in no uncertain terms, that a live scorpion was not to be placed near real fire. For the shot where the scorpion enters the flame she could use a rubber look-a-like.

The student, in her arrogance (and defiance), chose to place the real creature in the real fire. She was brought up on misconduct charges. Her footage was confiscated. She failed the class and was required to perform ten hours of community service. The community service took the form of accompanying American Humane Society representatives to film sets where they oversaw the proper treatment of the animals being filmed. Her two Producers were required to do community service as well. One of them had an epiphany and volunteered as a rep on other films; one returned home to her native country thinking all Americans are crazy. Unfortunately, the Director remained un-chastened. I believe it is her loss.

On the other end of the spectrum stands "the horse."

I remember this girl because of the shock of orange hair that defined her personality. She raised her hand at the safety seminar and asked if she could use her own horse in a film she wanted to make. The action had someone riding the horse into a barn. I indicated she could but suggested she contact the American Humane Society as a precaution. Even the sweetest horse, perfectly comfortable with you, can react strongly when confronted with lights, equipment and the general hub-bub of production.

To her credit, she contacted the American Humane Society. They put her in touch with a horse wrangler. Just before she was due to begin, she came to my office for a safety sign-off. All students using weapons, stunts, cars, fire, minors, nudity or animals fill out a *Hazardous Shooting Form* and have it signed by their professors and myself. She seemed to have all her ducks in a row. Then, for no other reason than habit, I asked her how the horse was going to enter the barn. I meant in terms of speed — walking, trotting, galloping?

Her answer? "Oh," she said with a straight face, "it crashes through the window."

I suppose she had been inspired by the film *True Lies* in which Arnold Schwarzenegger rides a horse onto a hotel elevator and escapes by crashing through the glass.

I was so taken aback I didn't know where to begin. Talk about "the devil is in the details." This is a very complicated stunt. Professionally, such a thing could take months of training. And the glass? I asked her, "Was there to be glass in the window?"

"Oh" yes," she said, "candy glass."

Let me just stop here and say, that for some reason film students think "candy glass" is the cure for everything. However, it is still possible to get cut by candy glass. Not as severely as real glass, but it can injure. Plus, it bounces and ricochets and can easily get in your eyes.

I asked a lot more questions: "How big is the window? Could both man and beast make it through? Would half the wall come down with them? Did she have the resources and knowledge to replace a window and frame? Could she do it five times if need be? Could the horse?"

Needless to say, the shot went away. However, it did point out another truism of physical production: "You can't ask too many questions, only too few." I'm going to write that one down for Chairman Joe.

Here's another one:

"Success in film school is measured by a peculiar yardstick." Or, put another way: "Progress is made in inches, not miles."

Recently a young man came to my office to discuss his rather ambitious project. He had done a thorough job of preparing and was very proud of the fact. He had cars, fire, stunts and minors in his film. He had all the right paperwork and needed personnel. But what he was the most proud of was the turtle in his shot.

He had contacted the American Humane Society and learned the correct procedure for procuring, caring for, maintaining and returning his star turtle. He was really pleased with himself. It was very cute. It was as if his ability to correctly handle that small creature was the real measure of himself as a professional filmmaker. I was proud of him as well.

When students have successfully navigated the compassionate waters of animals in film, they are entitled to place in the credits the statement: "No animals were harmed in the making of this film." They may also state, "This film was made under the auspices of The American Humane Society," or simply, "American Humane Society." It may seem like a small thing, but when our student films go out beyond school boundaries it sends an almost subliminal message to the industry that graduates of the USC School of Cinematic Arts are ready to hit the ground running. They are prepared as professionals to join the motion picture industry.

And, as any baseball fan will tell you, "A tie goes to the runner."

Good Money vs. Bad Money

One of the endless debates in the world of filmmaking is the conflict between *good money* and *bad money*. In its simplest form, *good* money is money that goes up on the screen — a first class actor, a spectacular location, fabulous costumes, some piece of equipment that makes an almost unachievable shot possible. Therefore, the opposite — money that does not end up on the screen — is *bad*.

However, if we've learned anything along the winding road of production, it is this: Nothing is simple. A wise friend of mine, a terrific First Assistant Director, once observed, "On paper, a film is made in black and white; but on the set, a film is made in the *grays*."

Computers work in ones and zeros to come to mathematical conclusions. You can think of ones and zeros as on or off; up or down; black or white. As you prepare, you do everything you can to thwart Murphy. But remember, I said film lives in the grays. Here's what I mean.

The grays are those unforeseen (and impossible to anticipate) events that no amount of mathematical equation or precise plotting could have anticipated. These most typically occur as a result of interaction between human beings. That's quite a mouthful. Perhaps an example might be better.

I shot a western at the J.W. Eaves Ranch an hour east of Santa Fe, New Mexico. Mister Eaves had made a bloody fortune transporting nuclear fissionable materials to Los Alamos Atomic Labs during the Second World War. He invested part of that money in a Western film ranch. It had a long main street, several side streets, a blacksmith shop, a general store, horse barns and the all-important saloon. The show I was working on was called *Independence*, and it starred Mathew Perry's father, a terrific guy named John Bennett Perry.

Every morning we had to dress three hundred extras, drive two hundred head of cattle from their holding pens to our set, and organize a fairly large shooting crew. It took a highly skilled Assistant Director to organize and propel this circus. His name was Cliff, and he was the best at ramrodding a project of this scope that I have ever worked with.

Enter the grays — Cliff had a personality that could start a war between Switzerland and Israel. The cowboys on the show disliked him with such fervor that at night when the rest of us were nestled into the bar at the hotel, he had to wander off to another part of town for fear of suffering bodily harm.

He took an intense dislike to our female lead. The feeling was mutual. He developed a nickname for her. He would refer to her as "Tondalaya." I don't know what it really means, but he used it as a pejorative for female anatomy. Worse, she knew what it meant coming out of his mouth.

We were staging the climax to a bar fight outside the saloon. Stuntmen would be throwing themselves through breakaway glass, horses would break loose and run off, costumed extras would scurry out of harm's way, and our female lead would enter at the aftermath.

Cliff rehearsed the action several times. When all was set to go, he called for our actress. She did not reach the set within the time frame Cliff thought she should. With his back to the porch, Cliff asked loudly, "Where the hell is Tondalaya?" As it turned out, she was right behind him and not even slightly amused.

"I'm right here, asshole," she announced in a voice that could have been heard in Albuquerque. "But for the rest of the day I'm going to be in my trailer." And with that she turned and stormed off.

I remember thinking at that moment, I wonder if there is a liquor store within fifty miles of here, because it's going to take a case of wine and buckets of flowers to fix this one. Mercifully, she only pouted and fumed for half an hour, then came back to the set.

The point here is simply that no amount of slick computer mathematics or Murphy-blocking efforts could have foreseen that encounter. I could never have pinned it down in black or white. It was *gray*.

Their relationship never got better, but the pace of filmmaking did. I actually received an award for "Best Western Drama" from the Cowboy Hall of Fame. Go figure.

This means that if you only count pages and your number of actors, you could come up with some approximation of how long it would take to accomplish it. But unless you know the temperament of the actors, the disposition of the Director, the difficulty of the location, and the quality of the crew, you don't really know much about making your day. I mentioned earlier the working style difference between Julie Harris and Joan Van Ark, both highly professional performers. Julie would get to her performance on the first or second take, Joan on the tenth or twelfth. Both looked great on the screen, they just had different needs in order to get their performance there.

Many years ago I did a show in New York where the actors had this game of refusing to be the first to leave the make-up trailer. It was an egomaniac thing. This childish game went on for days until the Director threatened to fire the whole lot of them.

My point is that none of those quirks and delays could have been foreseen on the pages of the script or the colored strips of the Board. Experience alone is the only real measure of how to schedule.

Another example of the *grays*: We were doing a show in our one-hour episodic class where an actress finds herself in limbo, literally. It was an all-white set. The scene, during which she discovers her status as "not-quite-dead," was about four pages long, and was to be shot on one of our sound stages (we have seven). However, in parts of the scene she goes back and forth in time. In order to show the time transitions, several moments were shot on a green screen stage. As far as the computer was concerned, the scene, because of the page count, would only take half a day.

The computer was incorrect.

Only working out the details of the scene revealed that the sequence would be shot twice, on two different stages, miles apart on different days. Clearly not a half day's work. Only working out the details with the Director, Production Designer, Cinematographer and First Assistant Director could produce an accurate schedule.

In terms of *good* or *bad* money, it means nothing is as clear-cut as you would like on set. Many of the decisions you make must be on instinct. Some will utilize information at hand, others will be based on second-hand information. The painful part is that sometimes you will be right and sometimes you will be wrong. Don't be too hard on yourself— if it's wrong, your superiors will be there to do that for you. It's a sad truth that often he who makes the decisions stands alone.

I do have examples of making the right decision but still earning a negative outcome. In order to see one, we will have to look beyond the film business. Back in the late sixties, in a small town in Northern California, there was a rock concert known as Altamont. For those of you too young to remember Altamont, it was a Rolling Stones concert marred by violence in which a young black man was stabbed to death by a group of Hell's Angels. Not wanting a repeat of this tragedy, the local sheriff went to the town council requesting an additional $50,000 for the next year's event. He wanted to hire additional security. They agreed. He did. The concert went off smoothly, whereupon the city elders fired the sheriff for wasting their money. Stupid, you say? It's what I call "the Firehouse Effect."

A firehouse, is built, maintained, peopled, stocked with big expensive red trucks, and for the most part, it sits idle. But oh baby, when that bell rings, when your house is on fire, they sure as hell better be there. In other words, the firehouse is not created to be busy 100 percent of the time, only that one percent when it is critically important.

We were filming right down the block from the CBS Radford Studios in Studio City, California, on a television series called *Married: The First Year.* Linda Hamilton was one of the stars; this was pre–*Terminator.* The scene was short. There was no dialogue. All that was required was for Linda to drive up and stop in front of an apartment house, get out and go inside. For reasons of focus, missed camera marks and Linda not hitting her mark perfectly, we were on our seventh take. No one noticed that Linda had taken her shoes off during the shot. On the seventh take she pulled up, got out and managed to step on the only piece of broken glass on the entire strcct. She yelped and her foot bled.

Fortunately, we had a studio nurse with us. She cleaned and bandaged Linda's cut, and Linda, ever the trooper, kept right on working. Had we not had the nurse with us, our only alternative would have been to put Linda in a car and take her to the hospital. In Los Angeles, when someone, even an actress in production, goes to the emergency room, you lose them for three to four hours. And losing a primary performer in the middle of the shooting day is an obstacle from which it is difficult to recover.

In other words, the nurse was our firehouse. Under most normal circumstances we would have paid her to just sit and read a book or finish her knitting. But when we needed her, she was worth her weight in gold. She saved us half a day of production.

Bad money is money that does not show up on the screen. Here is a for instance: walkie-talkies. They are cheap to rent and bloody expensive to replace. At USC we can rent *walkies* for twelve dollars for ten days. Wow! That's the cheapest rental in the movie business. However, the replacement cost of those little beauties is five-hundred-and-seventy-five-dollars a piece. Yikes! The students routinely leave them on lunch counters, bus benches, somebody else's car, or lend them to a friend and then forget which friend.

A couple of years ago I was green-lighting a thesis project for a young lady who seemed very buttoned up. When I got to my spiel about walkie-talkies being cheap to rent and expensive to replace, she stopped me, "Joe ... dear," she began in her most condescending voice, "don't worry, I've got it handled." Uh huh.

She lost three of them. The replacement cost was $1,725.00. Lost walkie-talkies equals bad, bad, bad, bad money. She would have been better off using the money for a wrap party. That was seventeen hundred dollars just thrown away.

Here's a quiz. Is this *good* or *bad* money?

You are filming in the desserts of Southern California. First of all, they are snake-infested, spider-infested, rocky and sometimes occupied by cacti bearing sharp quills. Your crew would be well advised to wear boots and long pants, not shorts and flip-flops. It is hard work and, for most of the day, extremely hot. However, as night approaches the temperature plummets. Suddenly, the young energetic crew that has been schlepping equipment over rugged terrain all day begins to get cold and lose energy.

You, the ever-wise Producer, tell one of your minions to drive down to the roadhouse and buy $200 worth of piping hot chili. It was not planned for, nor is it in the budget, but you will make it available to the crew while they work.

Now, the question: Why? Who the hell is going to see the money you spent for chili on the screen? The answer is everyone. They just won't see it as chili. What will happen is, that a newly energized crew, warmed up and feeling well cared for, will have higher morale. Their productivity will rise. Their vigor will be restored. That will show up in the work on the screen. That's *good* money!

You passed the quiz. You're getting good at this.

It's time for the test. Three scenarios good or bad money? Remember, the only questions is, will the money spent end up onscreen?

1. A fight scene among four teenage actors is not particularly violent — more shoving than hitting. Do you hire a stunt man, or is that a waste of money?

2. You are filming in the Mexican desert. For most of the film you have used seventeen horses onscreen. They come seven to a trailer. The trailers are expensive. The Director says he will only need fourteen horses the next day. Do you listen to the Director or do you hire the other three horses and the expensive trailer for the next day anyway? Sound familiar?

(Obviously a trick question.)

3. You need a drive-by shot of a truck passing the camera going from left to right. It is an eighteen-wheeler on the open highway. Do you hire Highway Patrol Officers to be with you for such a simple shot?

While you ponder your choices, let me tell you a story. It isn't exactly about *good* or *bad* money. It's just ... well ... judge for yourself.

We were going to film in a school hallway, a long school hallway. When we scouted it, the Director said, "I will only see down this hallway."

I asked, "Since we are going to have to rig and pre-light the hallway anyway, why not rig the entire hallway?"

"Oh no," said the Director. "I'll never see that way. It will just be a waste of time and money."

We spent three days rigging and lighting half the hallway. The reason it took so long was that the lights had to be hidden behind the ceiling beams so they wouldn't be seen in the shot. Then the cable had to be run along the narrow space where ceiling met wall, also to be hidden from the camera. During that time I asked again and again whether we wouldn't be well advised to rig the whole way down. Each time I was reassured it was not necessary.

Sure enough, we were filming in the hallway when the Director turned to me and said, "I just realized. I have one shot I need in the part of the hallway you haven't lit."

I stifled my urge to strangle him. I was just pondering whether to remind him that he was a moron when an electrician standing on a ladder nearby piped up: "Hey, Mo, how about I give'em one a these?" And he turned his 10K light around and shined it down the hallway.

"It's perfect!" the Director cried "Let's shoot."

Was I happy? No. This electrician had just shown me that we had spent three days and tons of money carefully lighting something that could have been lit by two or three big lights simply pointed down the hallway. Bad money! What can I say? It's a strange business.

And "yes," I know. What was I doing believing the Director? What can I say, some people never learn.

Time is up. What have you decided on your test questions? Here's my take on it.

Answer 1: On *Malibu Shores* there was a scene that required our four young leads to get into a shoving match. They were all good kids and eager to play the scene. It wasn't particularly dangerous or violent, so safety was not the issue. What *was* the issue was that two of the kids were athletic and two were not. I decided to hire a stunt man to work with them.

In exactly one half-hour the stunt man got these kids to relax, take a push, fall over a couch and rebound as if it was the most natural event of their lives. We got the shot on the second take. Was the money on the screen? You bet. It was more than *good* money. It was essential. It was what I call "getting more cluck for your buck."

Answer 2: Bear with me here. I know I've told you this story in regards to Jamie-the-wunderkind.

I was hired to be Earl Bellamy Senior's First Assistant Director on a made-for-TV movie called *Desperate Women*. It was to be shot in Mexico. Unfortunately, the movie wasn't nearly as good as the title. It was, however, a chance to work with a terrific director. We shot sixty miles south of Mexicali at a place called Laguna Salada. It was late June, early July. It was easily the hottest place on the face of the earth. It was so hot, in fact, that the electricians needed gloves to handle the lights. It was so hot that water was meaningless — only Gatorade, and lots of it, could keep you hydrated. We wore water-drenched scarves around our necks and wrists to keep from passing out.

The box canyons were their own hell. They trapped the heat. And, worst of all, there were countless rattlesnakes, sidewinders, adders and scorpions the size of mayonnaise jars. In this garden paradise (sarcasm noted), we needed seventeen horses that we begged, borrowed, and bought from local ranchers. They had to be loaded onto trucks and driven to the location each day. They traveled seven to a truck.

One day Earl came to me and said, "Joe, we won't see back down the canyon tomorrow. Therefore I will only need fourteen horses for the shot."

I was filling out the call sheet for the next day. By instinct, I had decided to add a few extra horses just in case, and one extra trailer.

My Second Assistant said to me, "Joe, they'll have a fit back at the office if you order all those horses. Earl said he wouldn't need them."

It was true. Earl had said that, and Earl was extremely knowledgeable and prepared. Why spend the money on extra horses and another trailer? I removed three horses from the call sheet, as well as their trailer.

The next day — right smack dab in the middle of the shot — when it was too late to do anything about it, Earl came to me and said, "Joe, I've changed my mind. I have one shot looking back down the canyon. I will need those horses after all." Gulp and gasp!

I want to make this point: There is such a thing as Director's prerogative. It means more than just some wild-eyed idea conjured up in the dead of night by an unprepared Director. It means that a Director can change his mind, and your job is to be able to accommodate him. Yes, the home office was happy we hadn't spent the money; but I had let my director down. I was his assistant.

Answer 3: What about the simple shot of the eighteen-wheeler traveling left to right on the highway? I hired four Highway Patrol Officers. I'll make this one easy. It's *good* money. Better than good money, it's *great* money. The answer is simple. Film crews are a distraction. At freeway speeds a distraction can be the difference between victory and disaster. Those officers will slow traffic, guide motorists and keep your truck driver and crew safe.

Here's the truth of the matter. Like with so much of the entertainment business, whether something is *good money* or *bad money* is subjective. You will make many correct decisions and a few you will wish you could make again. As my stories have illustrated, sometimes you will get hung out to dry by well-meaning (and not-so-well-meaning) directors. You just have to hope that you are right more than you are wrong.

One thing is for sure, no matter which way the dice tumble, there will always be someone to second-guess your decision. It is just another version of "sliding down the razor blade of life." Slide on!

Practical Locations
vs. Stage Work

In its simplest form, a *practical location* is a set that already exists — a restaurant, a house, a museum. It doesn't have to be an interior or a building. If you want to film Yankee Stadium, that is a practical location. Obviously, you can't afford to build it. However, if you just want to film a small portion of it, you might shoot somewhere else and pretend, or make it look like Yankee Stadium. What if it's the dead of winter in New York and you need the Stadium in summertime? Just because it looks like it's outside doesn't mean it has to really *be* outside. It's movie magic.

On the television series *Dallas*, the outside of Southfork and the swimming pool were built on a sound stage at MGM.

Still, if you wish to film the Chancellery in Berlin, you are going to have to go to Berlin and film it. Building it would be too expensive. It's all about the look you need and what you can — and connot — fake.

For argument's sake, let's say you need a portion of Grand Central Station in New York — not the rotunda, but the areas where the track entrances are. In the basement of the Doheny Library on the USC campus is an area that could very easily double for the track entrances at Grand Central. In fact, our students have filmed it as such — more than a dozen times. All it takes is some signage (track 14, track 9), a few extras dressed as businessmen with briefcases, a skycap with a rolling luggage cart, and off-screen sounds of a conductor calling "All aboard!" and voila, it's Grand Central Station.

By now, if I have done my job right, you are really confused. That is exactly the point. There is no one definition of practical location other than to say it is *not a set on a sound stage.*

The most compelling reason not to build but to travel to the actual location is *authenticity*. No matter how hard you try, and no matter how dedicated and talented are your Scenic Artists, the real thing will always look better than a recreated one. I exclude from that statement modernizing or restoring a location that has fallen into disrepair.

Another reason for wanting to *go practical* is unlimited camera angles. If it is the real thing you don't have to crop or cheat your angles to avoid showing the artifice.

Lighting? Let God do the work. It is easier to film in natural sunlight than to create it. Then there's, manpower and equipment. Think you got it? Good. Now let me throw something else into the mix.

The word *practical* has another meaning in the film business. It pertains to lighting. Many Cinematographers prefer the look of a *practical* house, restaurant or hallway. It is easier, faster, cheaper and, in most cases, better looking to use the lights already in the location to light the set than it is to run cable, fasten spreaders (bars that expand between beams from which lights may be hung) and place lights.

I did a series in New York many years ago for a woman named Jay Presson Allen. She was a fabulous writer; she wrote *Prince of the City*, and *Just Tell Me What You Want*, and was one of the creators of the hit series *Family*. She was a tough old bird. We hired a Russian Cinematographer named Misha. He was the spitting image of Sascha, the Russian bartender in Rick's Café in *Casablanca*. He was tall and lanky, with a narrow angular face.

Misha was an artist who suffered for his art. For him, getting stuck on an American prime-time television series must have been like being relegated to a gulag in his native country.

Misha loved practical light. Consequently, every interior was lit by table lamps, chandeliers and candles, even in daytime. It was a great look but technically incorrect.

Jay would come into the dailies, take one look at the scene and bark, "It's broad daylight. Why is every light on in the house?"

"Well, yes," I would say, trying to alibi our way out of it. "It's a great look, though. You know, suspended disbelief."

"But it's wrong," she would wail. "It's lights out."

Misha would come out of the dailies mumbling, "These foo-king Ameri-canns. They have no foo-king soul." Of course, Misha, who had selective translation issues, went right on lighting every light in the house in his own practical way.

Jay bitched about it so much that eventually the network started sending me notes, like, "Great scene. Why are the lights on?"

The day I had to tell Misha there was to be no more practical lighting in daytime, he wept.

Another thing to remember about practical locations is that, "you must control your environment, and to control it, you must own it." If you wish to film in Grand Central Station at rush hour, you will need to have control of the entire facility. Just a small piece will never do. That is a big challenge.

The concept of controlling your environment rears its ugly head most often when doing *car work* on public streets or roads. This is because in car work, staging is everything. By *staging*, I don't mean the choreography of the scene; I mean how it will be done. Where are your trucks? Where is your crew standing while rigging the car? Are they cleaning the windows or headlights, or placing the actors inside? Who will hold traffic while you position the vehicle in a lane? Who and how will someone cue the actor? How will other drivers know what you are doing? What happens when you cut the shot?

The answers to these questions are simple when you come down to it. You will have secured permission from the appropriate controlling authority and hired several motorcycle officers to be with you and hold traffic at bay. Thus, *you will control your environment.*

Can you just stroll into a practical location and start filming? If you are lucky, yes. In reality, it rarely happens that way. The answer lies in your script.

Rarely is the location you choose perfect for your shot. Something will have to be added to the room, the hallway, the tunnel, whatever it is. This is usually cheaper, assuming you aren't paying some astronomical site rental, than building a set.

Let's talk about building a set. There are reasons not to build, and many more reasons to build. What are the cons and pros?

In the con-department, stage rentals can be very pricey, especially if you are waiting to hear whether your pilot episode will be picked up and, if it is, when it will actually go back into production.

If you are on location and decide to build your sets, you will have to establish a mill or place where your sets will be built. You will have to purchase equipment, big and small, and hopefully find a sufficient number of craftsmen to accomplish the Production Designer's or Art Director's vision.

Let's, for argument's sake, say you are making a studio film. What are the advantages of building on a sound stage? There are many. Assuming you live and work in L.A., it will keep you close to home. You can film during the day, even if your scene calls for night. You have air conditioning in the summer and heat in the winter. Your restroom facilities will be nearby and well maintained. Your cast and crew will be able to sleep in their own beds. You, as an executive on the film, can leave your office and in a very short time be on your set. This is important if there are script changes or different interpretations of a scene between director and actor that require your mediation. But by far and away the best reason to build on a sound stage is: You can pull wall pieces.

Most sets are constructed in such a away that company grips are able to remove designated walls. They are also able to replace them. They then require only some touch-up paint to make them look the way they did before they were removed.

Pulling walls is a great advantage. Imagine the same scene played in two sites — practically and on a sound stage. Imagine that the scene involves three people in a living room. One of the actors gets up and walks to a wet bar for a drink.

On the practical location the actors, crew, lights and camera equipment will all be crammed into the size of the actual room. Since on a practical location you will not have the ceiling height of a sound stage, all the lights will be on the floor, adding to the heat, clutter and confusion of the set. When the actor gets up to go to the bar, if the Director wants to dolly with him, it will only further complicate the choreography of men and material in a relatively small space.

Now picture that living room set and those actors on a sound stage where one of the walls has been removed. You can light "from up high," meaning you can hang lights from the overhead grid. With the wall out of the way, everyone has room to work. Having room to breathe makes a difference in the mental acuity of both cast and crew. You have more room to set up and accomplish an amazing dolly move.

Most importantly, shooting on a sound stage really means shooting with the absence of off-screen noise. Most sound stages are soundproof— no honking horns, no descending airplanes, no police sirens. They are called *sound stages* because they afford perfect sound. The only sound that a sound stage can't baffle is the low rumble of heavy trucks that comes up through the floor. Not having to wait for sound distractions saves you time and money.

There is one more reason to film on a sound stage. Once your set is lit overhead, you need only flip a switch to be eighty percent lit for your scene. That is one of the reasons (there are others) that episodic shows build their permanent sets on a sound stage. A permanent set is one that is central to the show and likely to be used on every episode. A police station on a police show, Southfork on *Dallas*, the six cul-de-sac interiors of *Knots Landing*. A permanent set is different from a *casual* set. A causal set is one built specifically for that one episode and never utilized again. What you can and can't do for sets is ultimately a function of your budget. Thus, a word about episodic television, pattern budgets and standing sets.

A pattern budget is a map of expected costs. It is your *pattern*. A show gets picked up for twenty-two episodes. How much will each episode cost? It is impossible to know because the scripts have not been written. But the production entity needs to know how much to designate (or borrow) in order to fulfill the contract. Will each episode cost two million? Will it cost three million? Whatever the number, it will then be multiplied by twenty-two to come up with a final cost. Of course, every episode won't cost the same. Some shows will cost more, some less. However, at the end of the season the total amount spent will equal the amount approved. In other words, a series pattern of three million per episode will result in a sixty-six-million-dollar loan. If episode one costs four million, then episodes two and three might have to cost two million to make it up. You ever wonder why some episodes are full of exciting explosions and others are lots of talking heads or boring recaps of previous episodes? You have to make the explosions up somewhere. However you get it, at the end of the year you had better not have spent more than sixty-six million dollars.

Part of establishing the pattern budget is determining how many days will be shot on the stage and how many will be *shot out* or off the studio lot. *Knots Landing* was a four-day-in, three-day-out show. *Hotel* was a six-day-in and one-day-out shoot.

Generally speaking, work on sound stages is more cost effective because you need not carry as many drivers. Your camera, grip, electric and prop trucks will be settled outside the stage, and most of the equipment positioned inside for ease of access. On a six-month show those costs can be significant, particularly on a union show where you are also paying fringe benefits (meaning health and pension benefits).

On a low- or medium-budget film, whether to *build* or go *practical* is another one of those painful decisions that you the Producer will have to make. But here is one last reason why you should consider building your sets: *cover sets.*

A cover set is a standing set where you can film in case of inclement weather. A cover set is not a duplicate of another set. It is an alternative to exterior filming a place to which you can retreat in case of bad weather or if an actor doesn't show up. Hey, it never rains in sunny California, right?

I was once directing an episode of *Knots Landing* in late July. It rained, off and on, for seven days. The cul-de-sac on which the show was filmed was located one block above the Knollwood Country Club in Granada Hills, some thirty miles from our stages at MGM in Culver City. On this particular morning I had a scene that was to play in the middle of the street. The sky was dark, and thunder was rolling across the valley.

At ten-thirty I called my boss and said, "Eddie, I am fast approaching the crossroads. If I am moving inside, I have to do it now; otherwise it will take our trucks an hour and a half, they have to unload, break for lunch and we will not get a shot before 3 P.M. We will never make our day."

Eddie pondered our options for a moment, then said, "Stay put, Joe. Ride it out. There's a fifty-fifty chance of clearing in the afternoon."

We waited. My heart was in my throat contemplating losing a day's work in the middle of an episodic series. But one hour later, at exactly 11:30 A.M., the sky cleared and we went to work. By noon we were fighting bright blue skies.

When I ran into Eddie a few days later, he said to me, "What were you worried about?"

I smiled and said, "I wasn't worried. I was just testing whether you still had your Producer chops."

He laughed.

Wait a minute, Joe, I hear you say. Let me get this straight. On a film, you would build a cover set and hold it through the entire shoot in case it rains? Wouldn't that be very expensive? Yes it would, but not as expensive as not shooting. Remember you have contracts with actors that for the most part are not "run-of-the-picture." A cover set isn't always a set built on a sound stage, but it is somewhere to shoot.

Let's revisit *The English Lady*. It was to be shot in Germany and England. It would have been prohibitively expensive to build cover sets in both countries. So, in Germany we looked for practical interiors that we could use as cover sets.

The First Assistant Director looked for interiors that we would, for reasons of architecture and authenticity, film in to represent the Motherland. We had three days scheduled for a restaurant called the K Dam Bar. It was decided to contract for three *hold* days for that location. It would serve as cover had it rained while we were scheduled to shoot on the Berlin street. When we were in England we would build a standing set of various apartments at Shepperton Studios, just in case.

The long and the short of it is this: A cover set may be a practical one, a set built at a nearby location, or one constructed on a sound stage. Just so long as you're covered. If you don't cover your own ass — and those of your actors and crew — who will?

Production Insurance

Probably the least sexy but most important element of physical production is insurance. It will generally run around 2 percent of your all-in budget. But do shop around.

There are many types of film insurance. I will list them and try to explain them. There are Production and Cast; Liability; Property; Stunt; Automotive; Worker's Comp; Errors and Omission (E & O); and War Insurance.

Production and Cast Insurance

Okay, you've found a one-of-a-kind script. You have hired a brilliant director. You have cast the perfect ensemble of performers. You are all set to go. Then your lead actor twists his ankle. Your female lead gets a bad cold, and your director's plane gets stuck in a snowstorm in Minneapolis.

What are you going to do? Cast insurance. Prior to the commencement of principal photography you will want your director and as many cast members as you are willing to pay for to be seen by an Insurance doctor. An insurance doctor is someone of the medical profession who will examine your cast and director and certify them fit to work. If one of them falls ill or is in some way incapacitated so that they cannot report for work, you are covered for your financial losses by your production insurance policy. A word of caution here. Your deductible will not be cheap. You will have to weigh the cost of the deductible against the projected loss of a day's work.

Many years ago, when I worked at Lorimar Productions, there was a doctor, not affiliated with the company, to whom we would send our performers to get checked out for insurance coverage. To say his standards were lax is like saying trees grow in the forest. The joke was that if you could make it up the stairs to his office, you qualified for insurance. All you needed was a pulse and a reasonable facsimile of breathing; the breathing was optional.

Now let me give you a nightmare scenario that has happened more often than I would like to admit. Your show is going out of town. You don't want to be constantly sending back to town for your raw stock (your unexposed film). You decide to buy a large amount and take it with you. You shoot for a day, send your film to the lab and discover there is a flaw in the raw stock. Everything you shot the first day is unusable. Not only are you out the money for the first day, you have to re-shoot, and it completely screws up your schedule. You call the raw stock company. They very graciously offer to replace that batch of film with a new one. However, the lost production costs are your problem. What to do? Production insurance. Yes, there is a high deductible, but it is better than footing the entire bill yourself. In fact, on a tight budget your insurance could be the difference between making the movie you envisioned and losing it to the bonding company (completion guarantor).

Liability Insurance

You are running lots and lots of electrical cable. Because you and your crew are responsible filmmakers, you have covered most of the cable with rubber mats. But a little old lady crossing your set has managed to find the one spot where the cable is only taped down (and not very well at that). She trips. She may be hurt, but not so severely that she can't hobble to her lawyer. Guess who gets sued? She may have a case. Depending on the negotiating skills of her attorney, she might be in line to collect just enough money to mess up your post-production budget. But you have liability insurance — the financial antidote to "Murphy." Yes, things go wrong. Stuff happens. Accidents happen. Again, the deductible, challenging though it may be, is preferable to the alternative.

Film companies, big and small, are targets. To most people the equation goes film company = money = liability insurance = substantial payout = early retirement in the Florida sun. Think I'm kidding?

I have a good friend named Jonathan Sanger. Jon is a terrific Producer. He produced the highly acclaimed *Elephant Man*, as well as *Mission Impossible 3* and *The Producers*. Some years ago he was leaving the 20th Century–Fox lot at rush hour. Traffic outside the studio was bumper-to-bumper. Jon momentarily took his foot off the brake. His car rolled forward at about one mile an hour and struck a woman's car in the rear. The woman got out of her car. She was obviously okay, and there was no damage to either car. But as she stood there she noticed Jon's car was angled as if it had just left the Fox lot, and a light went on in her head. Studio = Producer = nice car = big Producer = easy money = new face lift.

She sued him. For what, you ask. After all, there was no damage to the woman or her car. How about "loss of spousal cohabitation." What?! Are you kidding?

That's right. For some reason, because he had tapped her bumper, she could no longer have sexual relations with her husband. I remember asking Jon, "Where exactly did you hit her and how hard?" The case did get thrown out because it was idiotically without merit. But with crazy juries these days, it could have gone either way.

Film companies are targets. They are universally perceived as "deep pockets." Make sure nobody else's hand is in your production pocket.

Property Insurance

"Break it, and if you fix it, you can go back. Disrespect it, and it is no longer a money issue." Remember Chairman Joe? He warned you. Film companies, by their flamboyant nature, invite a certain overreaching on the part of location suppliers. "Sure, we'll paint, we'll paint it for you. Sure, we'll seed the lawn and you can keep it. If we scratch it, we fix it; if we break it, we'll replace it." Is it any wonder that periodically someone submits a bill for damages that is out of line with reality?

Three years ago we did a project at school that shot in a modest home in the San Fernando Valley. It consisted of three people seated in a living room having a discussion. When the show was over I was sent a bill for damages in the amount of twenty-five thousand dollars. There was purportedly damage to the floor, damage to the walls and damage to the ceiling.

I recall saying to the homeowner, "The only way these guys could have done this much damage is if one of them had tossed a hand grenade into your living room." In the end, he settled for about five grand. The grip stands had damaged his hardwood floor, and we did make it right.

A more interesting property damage situation occurred last year. One of our shows was shooting in a mortuary in Inglewood, California. A light fell over and scratched a coffin valued at ten thousand dollars. The mortuary manager called me and said, "Fixing it is not an option. You will have to buy it because we can't sell it as new."

Now, in spite of the axiom that, "academia is where Elephants go to die," we had no use for a ten-thousand-dollar coffin, but we sure as hell owned one now. We ended up donating it back to the funeral home with the understanding it would be donated to a family that could not afford to buy it. It was a creative solution to an unusual problem, if I do say so myself.

Property insurance, as the name implies, protects the film company from outrageous claims, and reassures legitimate site rental houses and equipment purveyors that they will be made whole for loss and damage. It is a must-have for any film.

Stunt Work

Almost always dangerous, stunt work is perfect for unintended consequences. As an Assistant Director, I hated stunt work. I don't mean a staged fight scene.

There comes a moment in stunt work that is similar to that moment for an airline pilot who has passed the point where he can abort the flight. What happens next is solely in the hands of God.

My most frightening moment doing a stunt sequence happened on the streets of Brooklyn at 2:00 in the morning on *Super Cops*. The scene called for my actor to drive at a high rate of speed along Fourth Avenue, blowing through lights. The shot covered about five short city blocks. The car was driven by a very experienced stunt driver. We had security controlling all ten points of entry from side-streets, five on each side blocking cross-traffic from both directions. We controlled our environment.

We rolled cameras and I cued the stunt driver. He took off like a bat out of hell. He came screaming down the avenue in excess of eighty miles per hour. And just as he roared through the light of the first cross street, a drunk stumbled out of a bar onto the street. He had somehow eluded our security net and was sitting in his car with the engine running. Paying no attention to the fact that his traffic light was red, he started forward into the intersection.

I saw him and almost vomited in fright.

It was too late to slow the stunt car. Had I yelled "cut" into the walkie-talkie I might have startled the driver who was concentrating on keeping his car from going airborne over every pothole. It was an awful moment.

And then the hand of God intervened.

The drunk opened his door, fell out and walked to the rear of his car, where he proceeded to piss on his bumper.

I can still see that moment: our car flying through the intersection past the urinating drunk who, to this day, has no idea how close he came to buying the farm.

Many insurance companies will insist on an added rider because of the added risk of stunt work. That rider will be about money and will add to the overall cost of your budget. Shop around and shop carefully. The devil is in the details. But don't underestimate the importance and the prevalence of stunt insurance. Stuntmen are people and need to be protected — sometimes from themselves.

They are a rare breed to be sure, and for the most part fearless. I have met some I like a lot and others I want nothing to do with. I was filming at a location called "Cadillac Jacks" in the San Fernando Valley the night a young Stunt Man named Paul Dallas died in a high fall from the roof of a power plant three hundred yards away across an open field. His body hit the air bag but his head struck the ground.

One of the greatest Stuntmen was the world-renowned Dar Robinson. Dar died doing a simple motorcycle drive-by on an Arizona highway during filming of *Million Dollar Mystery*. He lost control of his bike and went over the side of a cliff. There was no ambulance to take him to the hospital, and by the time they placed him on a helicopter, it was too late. His wife sued the production company but ultimately lost in a jury trial.

I encourage you to search the internet for Dar Robinson and see some of the amazing stunts he performed.

Automotive Insurance

The value of auto insurance to a film company should go without saying. Cars are expensive, and Murphy happens. As Director of Physical Production at USC's School of Cinematic Arts, I have decided not to insure vehicles of any kind for any reason.

Most of the stories I can tell you deal with students getting into trouble with vehicles. Trying to get film students to understand how not to put themselves, their actors, their crewmates and the general public at risk is like asking an elephant to fly.

By the way, something we have learned the hard way here at school is that when you go out to rent a grip truck and you take their insurance, be sure to read the fine print on the second page. Item Six will basically say that the insurance does not cover the roof of the truck. As it turns out, the tops of grip trucks rip and peel back very easily. In one year we spent over $13,000 replacing, repairing and re-supplying tops to grip trucks.

Let's see ... One got torn off by low-hanging braches outside the Greek Theater in Los Angeles; one student misjudged the ceiling height at Cerritos City Hall's underground parking garage; and one slammed it into an Arco sign at a gas station.

However, the reason you don't want to be transporting actors or crewmembers is that you will be putting your personal liability insurance into play.

Another thing you learn as you go about truck insurance shopping is the word "mechanical." Let me put it this way. I had a student doing a thesis project in Nebraska. He could have shot it in California; but no, it had to be Nebraska. Apparently, cornfields in Nebraska look different from cornfields in California. At least that's what he insisted. I asked him how he was going to get the equipment to his location. "I will rent a truck and drive it," he informed me, with all the certainty of one who doesn't have a clue. Here, not surprisingly, Chairman Joe has a theory to share: "The less the students knows, the surer of it they are."

"You should air freight it up," came the voice of years of practical reason. "It's faster and safer, and you will be able to insure it," I said, as if to myself.

"Too expensive," he assured me. "But don't worry, I've got it handled."

Over the course of the next week I begged him not to drive but to ship. Each time I was met with the same response.

"This will be more cost efficient. You worry too much."

"Okay," I finally relented when I realized he was going to do whatever he wanted anyway. "Just make sure it has an automatic transmission," I added.

"Why" asked Mister Know Everything Show Biz. "I drive stick shift."

And he did — for about sixteen hours the first day out. Never mind that we are on a twelve-hour workday.

After sixteen hours he grew weary and wisely turned the driving duties over to his assistant, a young lady who did not know a thing about manual transmissions. The young lady, ever the trooper, said to herself, "How hard can it be? Weeze makin' a moo-vee." She then attempted to take the rest of the 400-mile journey in second gear. A heavy truck going up steep hills in second gear? It's an oxymoron.

Yes, she blew up the engine. I mean dead.

Whereupon the first student decided that they should rent another truck, off-load the first and keep moving. After all, "The show must go on." And "they was makin' a moo-vee."

They got to their location and commenced to film. However, the company that had rented them the truck began to wonder where it was and when they would be seeing it again. They called to ask that very question. The answer: "I'm really tired. I am going to fly back to L.A. and figure it out." That might have been an adequate answer from the student filmmaker's point of view but it was at decidedly opposite perspective from the truck rental company's perspective. They said, "Give us our truck back, and it had better be in the same good condition as when you picked it up."

Enter the concept of "mechanical insurance." The insurance that covers stripped gears and blown engines. Well, uh, Mister Show Biz hadn't thought to purchase it.

The end result of this fiasco was that we flew our fabulous Stage Manager, Stephen Goepel, to the location. He drove another truck back to L.A. in order to return the gear our student filmmaker had left behind when he returned.

As far as I know, the first truck, the one with the blown engine, stills lives where it stopped, and the student and the truck company are embroiled in a $40,000 lawsuit.

And you want to know why we don't deal with automobile insurance on a student level?

Worker's Comp

Worker's Comp, as the name implies, is about being compensated for your injuries should you be injured on the job. At the USC School of Cinematic Arts anyone who volunteers on a student project is covered. Anyone who is being paid must provide proof of their own health insurance.

What happens when the show originates in one state but shoots in another, and the local hires are also volunteering? The answer, like those of child labor laws, varies from state to state: fifty states, fifty variations of worker's comp. Do your homework in every state.

As a Producer, anytime someone is even slightly injured you will want it recorded on the production report. What if the injury is so slight that the person keeps working? The simplest example is someone who cuts his or her finger while filming. No big deal, right? Throw a little iodine on the cut, wrap it in a band-aid, and keep on working. Only two days later the finger becomes infected. The worker, no longer on the show, seeks medical attention. It is likely to be seen as a legitimate worker's comp issue. But you have not bothered to note the event on the production report. What should have been an open and shut medical reimbursement now drags on for weeks and requires lots of forms. That's not a super big deal. But you've got movies to make, not tons of new forms to fill out. Once in a while it is okay to do things the easy way.

Listen to your Production God, Chairman Joe: "Let easy be easy."

Errors and Omissions (E & O) Insurance

E&O insurance is expensive but crucial because human beings, being the flawed people that we are, make mistakes. We forget or neglect to get appropriate signatures, rights and clearances. We omit things. We inadvertently leave the production vulnerable to legal challenges.

I spent all my adult life believing that the Hollywood sign and the Golden Gate Bridge were in the public domain — that anyone could film them at any time.

I was wrong.

Both of these American icons have been legally positioned so that anyone wanting to film their likeness in a commercial venture must pay to do so.

Suppose I had filmed my entire film on and around the Hollywood sign. And one day, just as my picture is about to be distributed, I get a letter that basically says: "Uh, excuse us. You owe us tons of dollars or we will sue you."

Now what? I no longer have two nickels to rub together. Do I just sink under the weight of my own ignorance, or do I have a safety net? If I have E & O insurance I do. Nevermind that it was expensive and hard to get, it is the difference between going forward and sinking like a stone, a very stupid stone.

Remember the Medivac helicopter I was required to have on standby while shooting *Dallas: The Early Years?*" The one whose sole purpose was to airlift someone to a hospital if something went wrong on my burning oil field sequence? It was pricey, and probably not necessary — and would have been a Godsend had anyone gotten hurt.

E & O insurance is your Medivac helicopter.

By the way, one of the little known but highly valuable advantages to being a film student at the USC School of Cinematic Arts is that each and every project is protected by E & O insurance. Students happen.

War Insurance

War insurance? Please! Who in their right mind would buy war insurance? The correct answer is no one. Except back in the seventies, the State of Israel was trying to attract film dollars to their economy. They offered "war insurance." Basically, it went that if any crewmember, most of whom were reservists in the Israeli army, or any military equipment on loan were re-distributed or recalled in the event of war, the production's costs incurred by such a disruption would be reimbursed by the Israeli government.

The good news for you is that you don't need it and probably couldn't find anybody to sell it to you now if you did. I mention it only in a shallow attempt to impress you with how much I know about Producing.

The Myth of
Cinematic Immunity

Ever drive down a street and see a group of otherwise normal middle-aged men standing in the middle of the street gazing at a house. You are watching the very essence of cinematic immunity. The odds-on bet is that they are scouting a location with their director and cinematographer. They are trying to get the right angle of the shot and discussing what equipment they will need to achieve it. At that moment the notion that they are standing in the bus lane has no place in their mental ergs. They are in the protected cocoon of *cinematic immunity*—a delusional state that allows grown men and women to believe the significance of their film somehow re-orders the structure of the natural universe. It is an unfathomable condition unless you've seen it and dealt with it up close.

I once worked with a director who routinely walked in front of moving cars as he crossed from one side of the street to the other. On his third near miss I asked him if he did that all the time. His answer was, "Why would I do that all the time? I could get killed."

"Then why do you do it now?" I asked incredulously. He looked at me as if I had just asked the dumbest question he had ever heard.

"Because now," he said straight-faced, "I'm making a movie."

I rest my case.

Even I cannot escape the sorry truth that I once fell victim to its siren's song. I was a Second Assistant Director working on a film in New York's Greenwich Village. We were just about to roll camera when the Director yelled, "Hold the traffic." Without a second's hesitation I dashed into the street and held up my arms in an attempt to halt a rapidly approaching truck.

It screamed to a halt inches from my face.

Stupid.

I don't know how many of you remember or have ever seen the classic

184

North by Northwest, starring Cary Grant. In it Cary finds himself at a four-way intersection in the middle of nowhere. The horizon stretches for miles in every direction. A truck, an eighteen-wheeler, comes toward him. He steps in front of it and raises his arms. The truck slides to a stop just inches from his nose. I don't know what the logo on Cary's truck said, but I'll always remember that mine said, "Frank's Towing Service."

Later that day, after work, the First AD and I stopped for a beer. "What were you thinking about, stepping in front of that truck like that?" he asked.

"I dunno," I replied. "The Director said stop the traffic and I did."

"Did it ever occur to you the truck might not have obeyed the Director, and we would not be sitting here enjoying this fine brew together?"

"Yes," I admitted sheepishly, "afterwards."

"Don't do that again," he warned, "otherwise I gotta do all the paper-work."

I never did it again. But you would be amazed at how many otherwise intelligent people fall prey to its perfume.

I mentioned earlier, in another context, about a student doing a thesis film titled

Streakers. Non-film people don't understand the concept of *cinematic immunity*. They don't get swept up in its unalterable brilliance. They just run over you or get offended. This past week a student came to me to sign off on a location agreement. They were going to film in another part of the university. Since you can only hit yourself with the claw end of the hammer so many times, I asked the student producer what they intended to do at that location.

Take a wild guess.

They were going to run twelve naked men and women through the halls and classrooms of that building.

"Anybody bother to mention that to the head of that facility?" I asked, already knowing the answer.

"They gave us permission," the student said.

"For the location, yes," I reasoned. "Did anybody mention the twelve naked people to them?"

"Uhhhhh..." was the reply.

"Right," I said "Get your director on the line."

"You mentioned the nudity?" I asked on the phone.

"Uhhhhh..." stammer, stutter and so forth.

You get my drift. I refused to sign their form and warned them not to do it. They will probably do it anyway, and then they will be some other school's problem because they won't be attending USC.

The point is that *cinematic immunity* is not some universal truth that allows any filmmaker to ignore the rules and regulations, or the basic structures of life.

Get past yourself.

Post-Production

Post-Production is more than editing. This chapter is written for the aspiring filmmaker who hasn't spent sufficient time learning the post process. To you goes a wary eye. In today's technologically advanced world it is possible to digitally shoot an SxS card on your EX3 camera, insert it into your computer and start editing your film immediately. But remember me, the Old Dog of Filmmaking, the guy who thinks Production Boards should still be done by hand? Don't rush it.

Editing is not the start of the Oklahoma Land Rush. It is the fine wine of filmmaking and should be savored. Let me start this chapter by declaring unequivocally that I revere post-production. To sum it up: If you only know a little about post, you don't know about it at all.

It is amazing what happens in the editing room. You can alter the style, the structure, the pace and even the story of your film. You can alter performances, even build some where they didn't exist. It is incredible what you can do in the editing process. In fact, it is the bookend of your film.

There are Directors who prefer to take a long time and those that like the speed of the electronic age. There is Hal Ashby or Elaine May, who could take a year rummaging through a million feet of film, or Larry Elikann, who cut the *Menendez Brothers* mini-series in four days. I am passionately neutral as to which is correct, but I believe it should not be rushed.

Editing is subjective, just like everything else. It is as fascinating and complex as writing. However, in some circumstances delivery dates or play dates may force your hand. These are references to contractual obligations to your network or distributor.

On my first job as a Production Assistant, at a commercial production house in New York (Video Productions, Inc.), I would spend my evening hours in the projection booth watching all the dailies. One day the projectionist said to me, "Watch enough dailies and you will learn how to make movies." I think what he meant was, look at other people's films and you will learn variations in style and technique. As to your film, that is strictly visceral.

However you get to it, you have made your final cut. Now what? Now music, ADR, sound effects, foley, walla, mixing, color correction, titles. Editing is only one element of post.

Let's take them one by one starting with music. It is impossible to overstate the importance of music (and silence) in your film. There are several kinds. One type is incidental and source. This comes from a radio, off-screen instrument or some other real-world source — what you might call ambient music. There are also recognizable songs, recordings or vocals. And then there is music composed, arranged and recorded specifically for your film. This latter has the added burden of supporting — and not interfering with — your movie. I saw a film some years ago whose score was so intrusive that it made concentrating on the movie itself impossible.

You can have the best music score in the world and play it too loud or too low, or worse — at the wrong time. That is why careful attention should be paid to *music spotting*. Music spotting is studying the film specifically for where to place music cues when the film is mixed. Then there are re-enactment films like *American Hot Wax* or the more recent *Cadillac Records*, whose soundtrack is rife with recognizable recordings by known artists.

Can you say "publishing rights," "synchronization rights," "needle-drop rights," "royalties" and everybody's favorite word, "favored nations"? Music rights and clearances can be so complex that most (if not all) studios have their own music clearance departments. When young filmmakers come to me about wanting to use non-original pieces of music, I send them where I would send you: the American Society of Composers, Authors and Performers (or ASCAP). While I would defer to them for specifics, in general there are two rights you need to clear to use someone else's music.

- *Synchronization License:* This is the right to synchronize music with visual images. Usually the publisher will hold this right; but in any event, it belongs to the copyright owner of the music. You can find out this information by using ASCAP's Clearance Express Services. Songs that are not represented by ASCAP can usually be found through the National Music Publishers' Association. Most of this information can be found on the Internet.

- *Master Use License:* The second license needed is the right to reproduce a specific recording of a song. You would think that this would be the same thing as synchronization rights. But as I tell my students, "The devil is in the details." Both rights are needed. You clear this right through the record label who owns the specific recording you want to use. You can get contact information through ASCAP's Film/TV Department.

It is important to realize that even if you get the rights to both synchronization and use, you still have to get separate permission to place the song on your soundtrack album. Yes, music can be complicated. These rights are called soundtrack rights, and both the publisher and the record label may hold these together. You can never ask too many questions. It is likely that each right will come with its own fee.

A book could be written about what determines licensing fees. There are many factors, but this will get you started. Ask yourself the following: How will the music be used? What is the duration and number of times the music will be used? Where will the film be shown? Remember that there are no hard and fast rules here. All fees are negotiable. No two publishers or record labels charge the same amount.

Students working on films not intended for release or that are only shown within an educational environment may not need permission or can often negotiate reduced fees. I have known famous musicians to grant student use for free just because the student asked. Of course, it never hurts to tell the musician how much you love their music and how it inspires you and how you own every single album they ever made. Even wealthy artists need a little ego stroking.

Independent filmmakers planning to show their films only at festivals can often negotiate a reduced fee called a festival use license. Once the film has been sold for theatrical release, the fees often increase based on the potential for greater box office. It is wise to negotiate this increased fee in advance. When you negotiate for possible performances in different types of media (such as cable or the Internet) this is known as a step deal.

When requesting music rights, submit a synopsis of the story and the overall budget. Provide as much detail as possible how you want to use the song. Will it be a main title or closing credit piece? Will it be prominently featured as the main focus of the viewers' attention or merely background? How many times will the song is used? How long will it play? And where within the film will it be heard?

Be sure to state where your film will be screened: at school; at festivals in Japan; at Sundance, and so forth. Be sure to contract how the fee will increase in the event of additional performances in all types of media. And, again, don't forget to ask about the soundtrack rights at the same time.

So I hear you saying, "Joe, music is a pain. Why don't I just steal it. The world's a big place, who will find out?"

You should know that U.S. and foreign copyright law allows a music publisher or musician to sue you for using their property without consent. Considering that you will want to work professionally in our industry, not clearing rights in advance does not make friends. And if your movie catches the eye of someone big, and you do not have the rights nor a working relationship with copyright holders, distributors will not be able to show your film. You will eventually get caught, and if you pull a studio or distributor into a lawsuit, your reputation will be tarnished.

In many cases it is just easier to deal with original music. "Okay, Joe," you say, "How do I find a composer?"

Music that is composed originally for your film is called a score. Working with a composer to create original music can be one of the most rewarding parts of filmmaking. One way for young filmmakers to find musical talent is to check out your local university's music school. Chances are you will find a young musician eager to write music simply for the experience, bragging rights, and to build up his resume. It is also likely that he will give you all rights to the music for free or at a limited rate. You can also approach ASCAP. They maintain lists of film composers at every level of experience and cost.

Professional composers know the business and this can be good and less-good. It is true that you "get what you pay for." A professional is just that — a real talent who, assuming you can afford him, will give you a top-rate score. A professional is usually paid an up-front fee for writing and recording a score. These fees are negotiable based on your budget, the amount of music requested, and the composer's fame. No two film fees are ever the same. Professionals also understand ownership.

You must spell out ownership in a composer agreement. This is also known as the "publisher share" of music. It will either be the production company or the composer. Obviously, the more money you pay the composer, the more rights he will give away. You can always call ASCAP to ask more about these things.

Other rights to keep in mind are called broad rights: these include rights like worldwide synchronization; worldwide free, pay, cable and subscription television rights; in-context and out-of-context television advertising and film trailer use, including promos on other film videos; theater distribution outside the United States; and all future technology rights whether now known or not.

Music is so critical to your film that its creation (and the time and effort it takes to get rights) is absolutely worth your time.

One of the great pleasures of producing occurs after you have cut your film, worked with your composer, perhaps listened to a piano/tape demo of your score and are settled in at a recording session. Here, if you are lucky, there is only you, the Director, the Music Producer and the Engineers. You will sit on an oversized sofa, eating lox and bagels, sipping coffee, and watching an orchestra of musicians assemble in the studio beneath a giant screen that runs your film. You sit with your legs up, hands behind your head and immerse yourself in the incredible talent of the musicians and the emotional sweep of your score. No one will ask you whether you want the green car or the blue one, whether her hair is too frilly, or whether the practical lights on the table should be turned up higher.

A Music Contractor will deal with the paperwork, start cards and time sheets of the players. It always struck me as fairly remarkable that some of the most incredible musicians would work on a film score during the day and spend their nights with a philharmonic orchestra. You wouldn't know most of their names, yet they are as talented as anyone who worked on your film. They will probably all belong to the American Federation of Music (AF of M), a union as strong and dedicated to the well-being of their members as the Screen Actors Guild.

Let's back up a minute and discuss production sound. This is the sound recorded concurrent with the picture or filming. It is your dialogue. Production sound is also those other sounds caught at the same time as speech: car horns, crashing waves, descending airplanes, fire engine sirens and background chatter, like in a busy bar or crowded restaurant.

Back to the infamous "two people strolling and talking along the beach." Remember I said you could just bet that the waves would break at exactly the wrong time, drowning out or crowding the actors' words.

"How will you fix it?"

What you are going to do is strip away the sound track and start over. You are going to get the actors onto an ADR stage. ADR stands for automated dialogue replacement. An ADR stage consists of a small screen, headsets for the actor, an adjacent control room where the new dialogue is recorded, and a lectern upon which the performers may place their script of dialogue to be re-recorded.

Many Directors and many actors dislike ADR. It is not easy getting back to the original performance in the cold sterility of the ADR stage, and some actors get distracted by the physical process. Just as the scene rolls to where the actor is to begin speaking there are three beeps. The actor hears "beep, beep, beep," and is then expected to begin speaking. The idea is that the dialogue will match perfectly the mouth movements seen on the screen. Yeah, well, good luck with that.

You now have the objective of replacing the original dialogue with the same performance intensity and the mechanical obligation to match it perfectly. That's not so easy, my friends. But okay, you get through the first part. The actress is sent on her way, and in comes her male counterpart. She may have been brilliant with the "beep, beep, beep," but he is a disaster. And worse, he gets progressively more frustrated with each take. It is also very difficult for some performers to play to the screen and not another performer. My point here (as it will be throughout post-production) is that you have no reasonable way to project how long it will take to ADR a scene.

You re-record the dialogue. Now you have to put the "waves" back in. You can do it before you get to the mixing stage, or you can "build the track" and take the scene to the mixing stage as one piece.

Two things about the wave sounds: They need to match the visual of the actual waves, and they need to rise or fall at the correct spot (i.e., not over the dialogue). If the waves were crashing on the shore, your sound track should reflect that. In that case, the waves' sounds must duck below the spoken words.

So you manage to get the waves back in at just the right time and just the right level. Is that it? Maybe not. What about the seagulls that were riding the wind currents overhead? Okay, so you feather in some bird sounds. How about children at play? Your actors passed them as they talked. What about people or activities that you didn't see but are part of the ambiance of being at the beach — the off-screen volleyball game, the kids throwing a football?

The scene you will have re-built will be vibrant and real and ready to go to the mixing stage. You also have the option of taking all the sound elements to the mixing stage and building your sound track there. In other words, you don't have to make the final decision about the sound for your beach scene until you can play it in continuity. This is my personal preference, even though it pushes the cost of the mixing stage out of the ADR account and into the mixing account.

Once you ADR the scenes that require it, you are ready to move on to the *spotting* sessions. That doesn't mean what it sounds like it means. A spotting session is where you decide where to place your music cues and your sound effects. It is very precise and requires being able to *rock and roll* the film forwards and back. You probably won't want the most important moment of dialogue, the music and the passing fire engine hitting the exact same cue. This is usually accomplished in a small movie theater built expressly for this purpose. You may find that while you have only one or two music editors in the session, you may have five or six sound effects editors present. For that reason the two sessions are generally separated.

One of the things you notice while spotting is a peculiar lack of certain sounds — Footsteps when your actor made that long walk in his apartment hallway, the crowded restaurant scene in which there is absolutely no sound of clinking glasses or dishes being placed down or picked up. The scene is flat. That is where the concept of *foley* comes into play.

Foley

A foley stage is usually a small stage in which you can play like a child and make great noises. Crunching corn flakes to simulate walking on gravel. Running your fingernails against the hardwood floor to emulate a cat skittering across the floor. It's rather fun to participate and see in action.

Once built, your foley track will also go to the mixing stage. I just mentioned the noiseless restaurant scene. What about those people seated at other tables who looked like they were talking, but we heard none of them? Were they really just mouthing their conversations through the whole scene? Yes they were. Extras (or background performers) bring quality to your picture. If you think they aren't worth the money, try holding a credible, real-looking, ten-minute conversation during which neither you nor your partner actually utter a word.

Now we need to hear their background chatter to complete the scene. Enter the wonderful and wacky world of....

Walla

Walla is created verbal sound.

One of the great things for me was always to sit in on the walla sessions. It consisted of a dozen highly creative, slightly crazy men and women walking in a circle speaking up to an overhead mic pretending to be a boiler room marketing operation in Chicago or a bookie joint in Brooklyn. They could switch, with a snap of the fingers, to a stuffy old bank in England — or women gossiping in a beauty parlor changing to an upscale boutique in the blink of an eye. In the case of our restaurant scene, you will hear a dozen conversations, none of which will be intelligible enough that you could pick out specific words. That takes a talent all its own. The walla track also goes to the mixing stage.

Two important elements I have yet to mention are *wild lines* and *room tone*. A wild line is one not synched to the picture — an off-camera line, important to the scene but not requiring ADR. For instance, the actor looks over to the lunch counter and says, "Check, please."

An off-screen voice says, "Coming right up, Hon."

You may have seen the waitress earlier in the scene but the line wasn't pertinent then. It is now. Everyone will stand very still and not speak while the Recordist records several readings of the actress saying the line.

At the end of filming a scene the Recordist will request that everyone stand very still and remain silent for a few minutes while he does nothing more than record the sound of the very quiet room.

Why in the world would he do that?

Because room tone is to film what primer is to paint, what padding is to carpet, what ambient light is to illumination. The bottom line is, you will need it. You will have it, and you will be glad that somebody recorded it.

Wild lines and *room tone* go to the mixing stage. The mixing stage — huzzah, huzzah — at long last.

I would imagine, although I am really guessing here, the term *mixing* refers to the mixing of all these aforementioned elements. In a perfect world there will only be three mixing engineers — one for *dialogue, music* and *sound effects* — present on your stage. There should be a Post-Production Supervisor, who has overseen all the processes, the Producer and possibly the Director.

I said early on that film is not a democracy.

Ever hear, "Too many cooks spoil the broth?" Someone must make the final decision. Someone must be in charge. In production it is the Director. On the mixing stage it is the Producer or the Director.

Allow me a moment to digress.

There is a saying that "A camel is a horse made by committee." Remember all those people with a producer credit. What did I say? The only thing worse than them thinking they were actually producing would be for all of them to be in the same room at the same time. I was thinking of the mixing stage when I said it. Mixing a film is torturous enough without a room full of jabbering magpies espousing their opinions on every frame of your picture. There is a saying: "Opinions are like assholes ... everyone's got one." You don't need or want them gassing up your mixing session.

So the process commences. But even here, with all the prior work that has been done, there is still work to be accomplished on the dialogue track. A sibilant "s" (hissing sound), an electronic crackle, or too much treble or bass must all be smoothed out before completing the sound track.

You sit back and watch a fascinating ballet of dueling artists creating a choreography of sound elements that are combined to be invisible and yet compelling additions to the visuals of your film. When it is over, no one element will stick out. You will be watching and hearing a completely created world, your film universe.

Speaking of your own film universe, David Jacobs once told me there was no geography in film sound. I questioned him. "What do you mean, David?" He referenced two sequences we shot on *Knots Landing*. In the first, we watched as a team of heavily armed SWAT officers climbed over a stone wall into a back yard. Such an occurrence in real life would have sounded like a herd of elephants going over the wall. In our show, it was completely silent, because that is what the scene required. Two scenes later, Sid and Karen Fairgate are sitting in their kitchen, and they can hear Kenny and Ginger, two houses away, arguing. This was not true to real life, but it was what the story required.

Here comes a major quote from Chairman Joe: "The audience will never know what you might have shown them. They will only know what they see. Therefore, tell them the most interesting story you can and see that it is well-mounted."

Mercifully, we are coming to the close of this chapter. However, I have to admit I have left some things out — the most glaring of which is visual effects. It is a world unto itself, and I fail to include it here because it deserves its own book. I will only observe that on many big studio pictures the credits for visual effects can equal or surpass those for the main body of the crew. The credits on *Avatar* went on forever and were justly deserved. Don't be so foolish as to try and budget visual effects yourself. Get someone or some company that is really knowledgeable and work closely with them.

Other things I could comment on at length include color correction, main and end titles, and DVD creation. These all take time and cost money. Remember the guys who just wanted a top sheet? Now you have an inkling of why I disdain that.

Someone is asking, "Joe, why do you disparage post-production by calling it the 'black hole' of filmmaking? You hold it in such high regard."

Let me come full circle. I meant to call it "The Black Hole of Possibility." Through all the fifteen thousand films I have overseen during my stint at USC, I have said to the kids, "The bad surprises happen in production. The good surprises happen in post-production."

Some surprises go like this: "I went to pick up my actor this morning and he was in jail;" "I went to get the actress, and she had had a fight with her boyfriend and drove back to L.A. without telling anyone;" "We only have the location until six o'clock, and it is now ten after four." Those are bad production surprises.

Post-surprises go like this "Wow, I love that piece of music; let's go back and put it in the earlier scene — we can reprise it here." "I really want those more expensive end titles because they are so thematically symbiotic with the concept of the film." "Look, I was able to cut two opposing scenes together and make a better performance than I thought possible."

Production has the contingency account. Post does not. All good post-production Supervisors will overestimate their budget if they are wise enough and experienced enough not to trap themselves with hard numbers.

Unlike pre-production and physical production, post-production is comprised mainly of individuals who come together for a relatively short period of time and do not have the same vested interest in the project as those who have spent months toiling in its trenches. Can you really say with absolute certainty that those twenty musicians you hired for two scoring sessions will absolutely get it done in that amount of time? Are you positive the people you want for your walla group will be available when you want them? Are you willing to bet your professional reputation that the mix will take exactly three twelve-hour days? The answer to all of the above is a resounding "No." And if by some lapse of judgment the answer is "Yes," I have someone named Murphy I would like to introduce you to.

Way to go, kid. You have made your film and lived to tell about it.

Marketing

There are entire books on marketing, so I won't spend much time expounding on it. But I will tell you a story. I was the First Assistant Director on a film called *American Hot Wax*. It was the story of Cleveland disc jockey Alan Freed, an icon in the world of rock music whose career was cut short by his involvement in the payola scandals of the early sixties. The story culminated at a rock and roll show at the Paramount Theater in Brooklyn, New York. Freed would die broke and alone in 1965.

I was hired because of all the people who worked on the project, I was the only one who had actually been to a rock and roll show at the Brooklyn Paramount. I was eleven years old. My poor father (he hated rock and roll) took me. One of the acts we saw there, Screaming Jay Hawkins, actually performed in the film. The Director put together a whole crew of singers to recreate the era — street musicians who practiced a-cappella and were forever searching for a place that had an echo. He and producer Art Linson were able to attract such artists as Chuck Berry, Jerry Lee Lewis, Dion and the Belmonts, and Jay and the Americans. We filmed at the Wiltern Theater in Los Angeles. The Brooklyn Paramount was long gone by then. In fact, it became the administrative office of Long Island University (LIU).

It was a terrific little film, full of youthful energy and great performances. We were all very proud of it. Paramount, in its infinite wisdom, decided to open the film on Easter weekend in an eleven-hundred-seat theater in Westwood and schedule a midnight showing. The thinking was that long lines at midnight would spell "The film to see, the hot ticket!"

Unfortunately, on that very same weekend other films with big-name stars premiered. One theater had a movie starring Robert Redford, another had Al Pacino, and a third featured Dustin Hoffman. The end result of so much competition meant there were no long lines at midnight. In fact, we never came close to filling the eleven-hundred-seat theater. After one week the midnight show was cancelled, sending the opposite message to the public.

197

After three weeks the picture was pulled from the theaters. There the story would end, except *American Hot Wax* found its way onto cable and ran for twenty years. It made its money back and more.

God bless shelf life!

My point here is only this. To the degree you can stay involved in the marketing of your film, it is in your best interest to do so. Don't get me wrong, I have no illusions that studios are going to defer to your judgment about how to sell a movie, but it is an area of the business with which you should become familiar. How your film is sold is as significant as how it was made. What's the point of all that blood, sweat and tears if in the end no one is going to see what you have created? It's a short point, but it's everything.

And I kept my word. Short chapter.

Epilogue

When I was a kid I spent my summers in a small town in New England, in Connecticut to be exact. Five miles out of town, hidden in the wooded hills, was a summer camp called Buck's Rock Work Camp. It was world renowned and attended by kids from 30 different countries. The owner had an absolutely ingenious plan. He charged families thousands of dollars for *camp*, and the kids worked their tails off building and refurbishing his facilities. They built the bunkhouses, the mess hall, an arts and crafts shop, and a theater. Those who didn't work the construction gang worked the maintenance detail picking up garbage, mowing the lawns and tending the many flowerbeds. There was some sports, and swimming in an honest-to-goodness watering hole. Some scam, huh? No — because the kids loved it!

At the end of summer they would gather on the train platform and wait for the train to take them back to New York City, from whence they would disperse around the world. As they waited, their emotions roiled; the amount of weeping, embracing and rending of garments was something worthy of a Shakespearean play. I used to marvel at how intense their feelings were after a summer of labor.

Many years later I got into the film business and went on location. It was then I understood. Lo and behold, at the end of a film, the amount of hugging, weeping and long good-byes was reminiscent of those summer platform farewells.

Perhaps you understand me; if not, all I can say is that forty to eighty people thrown together in common labor, working fifteen-hour days in the heat of summer or cold of winter, falling in and out of love, is a friendship forged in one word bonding.

The bond that is created is intense, and with a tip of the cap to the last line in *The Usual Suspects*, "just like that ... it's gone."

The sense of loss, of disorientation, of conclusion, can be overwhelming. I remember coming back from my first distant location unable to sleep or eat, gripped by an unceasing restlessness. Melancholy overtook me, and I had a genuine case of "the blues." I liken the feeling to running on a diving board only to discover you have overextended its protective flooring and there is no water in the pool. You are suspended in midair with no cushion to soften your fall.

The good news is: the feeling only lasts a few weeks. If you experience it, and many of you will, know that it is normal and will pass.

The thing about being in a group with a common purpose is that you will travel, work, eat and play with people who you might never interface with in your real life. I went to the track with Walter Matthau, and the pro bowl with one of the co-stars of *Jake and the Fatman*. I've had fabulous discussions about foreign affairs with Jay Presson Allen, and wonderful talks about Latin jazz with the drivers on *Seventh Heaven*. I learned about brain implants from Harvey Laidman, and was turned on to the writings of Jorge Luis Borges by Jon Sanger.

These relationships glow warm long after the circus has moved on. That and getting paid to go to places I might otherwise never have seen are two of the greatest satisfactions of my career.

I hope it will be yours.

So you have survived your first film. You have learned a great deal. People have surpassed your wildest expectations and broken your heart with ineptness and inefficiency.

What will you do?

You will pick yourself up and start all over again. There is no better remedy for the post-production blues than you pre-producing your next film.

This time you will have a sense of what to do, who to avoid and what to never take for granted. You will know what actor you wish to work with again and who you hope to never see. You will have met crewmembers for whom you have great affection and those you have come to loathe. You will have interfaced with purveyors who were helpful and some who were not. All of this information must be stored in your mental ergs because you will be accessing it in the future.

Speaking about your future, one question that will remain with you your entire life is: "Who do you want to be in film?" Will you be honest, efficient and compassionate in your dealings with people and companies? Will you be an opportunist who will step over anyone and everyone to achieve your goal? It is not an idle question.

I have known men and women in the industry who spent most of their adult life lying, cheating and stealing. Most have fallen by the wayside and been forgotten. Integrity and filmmaking are not mutually exclusive. In fact, I believe they are essential components of creativity. I have known people who have achieved great things and maintained their honor. We still think fondly of them now.

In the film business you will be confronted by many temptations, from women on location to purveyors eager to curry your favor. I have gone out of my way to never succumb to either.

When I produced *Knots Landing* I was offered cars, food and cash to work with certain companies or individuals. I declined all of it. I was concerned that even the appearance of impropriety would compromise my reputation with my peers. I would return gifts, refuse offers and even go so far as to tell the caterer not to send steaks to my office. My reputation was my sacred honor; it was all I really had.

I am proud to say that my honesty was never questioned. My loyalty to my team was never in doubt. I even once turned down an offer to receive a percentage of any underage on a project I produced because I wanted no doubt that all my decisions were in the best interest of the film and not my personal finances.

The two best things ever said about me were, "Joe really cares," and "Joe is a real professional."

My wish for each of you is that, in the end, people will say the same when they mention your name. It will always be about who you are and who you want to be.

So get started. You've got films to make.

Appendix A:
The English Lady

First 24 pages

Screenplay by David Jacobs

Based upon the novel by William Harrington

THE ENGLISH LADY

FADE IN:

INT. CHANCELLERY BALLROOM, BERLIN, 1933 - NIGHT

A state ball. Between courses, between announcements, between
musical selections. House lights off: candles the only
illumination. Nicely modulated chatter, tinkly sounds of
crystal and china.

In the near-darkness, we can make out a huge swastika banner
behind the orchestra. Two flags -- a Union Jack and the flag
of Lufthansa -- are lowered into place, one on either side of
the Nazi flag; then a SPOTLIGHT comes on and lights up the
three-flag configuration. The guests APPLAUD.

The Orchestra CONDUCTOR looks toward CAMERA. Someone
enshadowed by the CAMERA nods. The Conductor turns to face
the orchestra, conducts. The MUSIC is the first movement, a
jig, of Gustav Holst's ST. PAUL'S SUITE for strings.

The enshadowed figure who gave the go-ahead turns his profile
into FRAME: ADOLF HITLER looks to a guest for approval.

The guest is LADY NANCY BROOKEFORD, scarcely more than a girl
but elegant and poised, every inch a well-bred English
noblewoman. Recognizing the music, drawn from English folk
tunes, she smiles, nods at the Führer, acknowledging.

Hitler beams. MOVE IN on the orchestra, then past it to the
huge German flag and Union Jack.

FADE to WHITE and

                                        DISSOLVE TO:

EXT. THREE MALLARDS IN FLIGHT

Descending from a cloud-white sky, touching down on the glassy
surface of a pond, cruising toward the dense foliage near the
shore. The birds are visiting ...

EXT. WICKSTONE - ENGLAND [1932] - DAY

...the estate of the Earl of Edham. As the mallards seek the
camouflaged safety of the foliage, whispered VOICES alert us
to SPORTSMEN, waiting in ambush.

MOVING IN toward the voices, we first find an Irish setter,
poised to do his duty, then a portly man of 58, with a big
cigar and a moon-round face, intelligent and witty: WINSTON
CHURCHILL.

                                        (CONTINUED)

CONTINUED:

Because he is ostensibly out shooting, his distinctive cat's-roar voice is reduced to a whisper.

> CHURCHILL
> She's said nothing about it?

With him is SIR HENRY BROOKEFORD, EARL OF EDHAM, 60s, crusty, opinionated, a Tory, clubman, patriot and snob -- English.

> THE EARL
> (too loudly)
> What could she say? If the Prince of
> Wales does not wish Nancy to be the
> Princess of Wales...

The Earl's son, HERBERT, at 30 much stuffier than his stuffy father, implores Sir Henry to keep his voice down.

> HERBERT
> Please, Father...

> CHURCHILL
> I had heard the opposite. I had
> heard that Nancy discouraged His
> Royal Highness.

> THE EARL
> Winston: My daughter is headstrong
> and independent...

A FLUTTER of wings from the pond; Herbert tenses...

> THE EARL
> (continuing)
> ...but she is not stupid.

A duck rises; Herbert takes aim... FIRES.

> HERBERT
> Aha!

He starts to move off, snaps his fingers for the dog.

> THE EARL
> No, Herbert.

> HERBERT
> I'm quite certain...

> THE EARL
> He is more certain.

The Earl is referring to the dog, who, rather than following Herbert, yawns and sits.

(CONTINUED)

CONTINUED: (2)

>   CHURCHILL
>   The King is disappointed. He
>   approved of the romance.

Herbert resumes his posture, his aim.

>   THE EARL
>   So did I.

Another flutter of wings as another mallard takes flight.
Herbert shoots. The dog doesn't budge. The Earl frowns,
looks up at the sky, SEES...

The reprieved mallard flies over the low-rolling hills of the
big country estate. We go with it to...

EXT. WICKSTONE - THE HOUSE - DAY /

Tea time -- no conversation, uneasy. Present are the Earl's
daughter LADY VIOLET, late 20's slender, horsy; her husband,
NATHAN; Herbert's wife, LADY RANDOM, a pinched 30; LADY
CHURCHILL, and ...

NANCY, age 20, the cause of the uneasiness. She looks from
face to face; in each case the eyes are averted just before
Nancy's eyes make contact.

>   NANCY
>   My dog has not died.

Everyone looks at her quizzically.

>   VIOLET
>   Your dog, Nancy?

>   NANCY
>   Yes, Violet. All of you have been
>   looking at me as though my dog has
>   just died. He has not. He is alive
>   and well, hunting with Father,
>   Herbert, and Mr Churchill. Hunting.
>   He will return when they return.

Everyone smiles politely, sadly, admiringly -- as if to say:
Brave girl. Nancy plops a glob of clotted cream on her scone,
looks up to see Lady Random staring at her with tragic
sympathy. She tries again:

>   NANCY
>   (continuing)
>   There was no romance. No love affair.
>   My heart is not broken. I am not
>   even disappointed.

>   LADY RANDOM
>   You might have been Princess of Wales.

>   (CONTINUED)

CONTINUED:

> NANCY
> I did not wish to be Princess of
> Wales.

> LADY VIOLET
> Queen of England.

> NANCY
> Or Queen of England.

> NATHAN
> Of course.

Nancy gives up, heaps strawberry preserves onto the clotted
cream, and bites the scone.

The Earl, Herbert, Churchill, and the dog approach, returning
from their shoot, no fowl in hand. A few AD LIB greetings,
inquiries. Then uncomfortable quiet again.

> THE EARL
> Nancy...
> (she braces)
> I thought perhaps a holiday with the
> Bachfurts in Germany. You enjoyed
> your last visit so much.

So subtly the change is almost imperceptible, Nancy's
expression turns wistful.

> NANCY
> Perhaps that <u>would</u> cheer me up.

Everyone feels better now that she's admitted that she <u>needs</u>
cheering up.

Churchill, however, has caught her act. And Nancy knows it:
as her eyes meets his, he sticks his cigar in his mouth and
studies her, appreciative, amused; she acknowledges with a
tiny tilt of her head -- the same gesture we saw her make to
Hitler in the prologue.

> THE EARL
> But no aeroplanes this time. I
> forbid it!

> NANCY
> Yes, Father.

Another glance at the admiring Churchill; now he's smiling
openly. He knows, as we all do, what the next SHOT will be.

                                                   CUT TO:

EXT. SKY - A BI-PLANE IN FLIGHT - DAY

A wood and canvas bi-plane climbs, dives, loops. It's an open-
cockpit two seater, one seat behind the other-- and something
of a crate.

In the cockpit, Nancy, a bit apprehensive and very excited,
occupies the front seat; behind her is the pilot, her distant
cousin KURT VON BACHFURT. Nancy's hair is tucked into a
leather flying helmet. Kurt is hatless. Otherwise they are
dressed alike in flying clothes, goggles pushed up.

Kurt is 35, handsome, smiling, the image of a daredevil,
German-style -- which means that he is 100% confident as he
risks their lives.

Presently the aerobatics are replaced by simpler maneuvers
until they are flying straight and level.

Because they can't speak over the ROAR of the engine, Kurt
extends his riding crop and taps Nancy on her shoulder.

Nancy turns, SEES that he has taken his hands off the
controls. A momentary horror crosses her face but she does as
Kurt gestures: puts her hands on the control stick and
throttle.

The bi-plane tips and jerks... then gradually straightens.

Her terror quickly dissolves into determination and as Kurt
instructs her, she steers, she climbs. As she gains control
we can SEE her confidence growing. Indeed, what she's
experiencing is more than confidence, more than control; it's
the joy of discovery. She's obviously a beginner, but she's
beginning an adventure she's meant to take.

                                                    CUT TO:

EXT. VON BACHFURT HOME - DAY

A handsome country estate, prosperous, though smaller and
woodsier than Wickstone. An open Mercedes roadster pulls up
fast, stops hard. Nancy and Kurt hop out as Kurt's mother
HILDA comes outside to meet them. Kurt describes Nancy's feat
of flying MOS to Hilda, who covers her mouth in horror.

                                                    CUT TO:

INT. VON BACHFURT HOME - DINING ROOM - NIGHT

A room that makes one grateful that the Germans concentrated
on music instead of interior decorating: even the coffee cups
are Wagnerian.

Two SERVANT GIRLS pour coffee for Nancy and Hilda. Hilda
studies Nancy with the Prince-related expression of sympathy
that drove Nancy nuts at home.

                                              (CONTINUED)

CONTINUED:

The Servant Girls start to retire, pause for a final look at Nancy and a giggled whisper.

Kurt re-enters with a portfolio of prints to show Nancy.

>   KURT
>   Here we are.

He opens the portfolio on the table. The prints are by George Grosz and his contemporaries, expressionistic, darkly humorous -- some quite raunchy.

>   NANCY
>   Oh my... They <u>are</u> extraordinary.

>   HILDA
>   Inappropriate for the eyes of a young
>   girl.

>   KURT
>   Nancy's not a young girl any more,
>   Mama. She broke the heart of the
>   Prince of Wales.

Hilda REACTS as if the subject were taboo. But now that it's been raised, she'd like details.

>   HILDA
>   So handsome a prince! And what an
>   opportunity!

Nancy stops looking at the prints for a moment.

>   NANCY
>   Handsome...
>   (a shrug: not bad)
>   And a prince. But not an
>   opportunity. David wants a mother,
>   not a wife.

>   HILDA
>   Then you are <u>glad</u> he broke off the
>   affair...

>   KURT
>   If the Prince broke it off, it was
>   only because Nancy willed him to.

Kurt studies Nancy as she studies the art. She affects cool detachment, suppressing any reaction that might seem girlish.

>   KURT
>   (continuing)
>   Lady Nancy is a patriot. It was her
>   patriotic duty to allow the Prince to
>   think himself a cad.

>   (CONTINUED)

CONTINUED: (2)

> NANCY
> (REACTS to a print)
> Oh, Kurt: take me here tonight.

FAVORING THE PRINT

A drawing of a decadent Berlin cabaret populated by grotesquely costumed bare-breasted women and rouged men.

> KURT
> It no longer exists. Like all the things I loved in the Republic, it has become obsolete.

> HILDA
> It is decadent. Self-indulgent.

> KURT
> Like me.

With a puff of dismissal, Hilda leaves the room. Kurt pulls his chair closer to Nancy, affects a confidential air.

> KURT
> (continuing)
> So tell me, Nancy. Is it true? About the Prince?

She doesn't know what he means. He indicates a length of two inches with his thumb and index finger. In her determination not to giggle or blush she tries to sound sophisticated, witty.

> NANCY
> I do not dispense such information promiscuously.

> KURT
> (he laughs)
> Of course you don't.

Nancy doesn't like his laughter: it sounds like the laughter of an adult enjoying a precocious child.

> CUT TO:

INT. KURT'S STUDY - NIGHT

Kurt sits on a high stool at a drafting table, smoking his pipe and working under a single lamp on a series of drawings on large sheets of tracing paper. He HEARS a KNOCK, turns to SEE Nancy in the doorway. Although her silk robe is not especially revealing, she looks mysterious and sexy through the smoky darkness.

> (CONTINUED)

CONTINUED:

                         NANCY
          May I?

                         KURT
          Come. See the future.

She crosses to him; he shows her the drawings. They are of
aircraft of the future, aerodynamic, no propellers.

                         KURT
                      (continuing)
          Perhaps the distant future, perhaps
          tomorrow. Depending on politics and
          finance.

He shows her the final drawing, then turns to her. Because of
the height of his stool they are face to face and very close.
An awkward beat, then...

                         NANCY
          I feel that I should tell you...
          that I did not have the opportunity
          to find out.

                         KURT
          Find out?

                         NANCY
          About the Prince.

And very quickly she half-duplicates his earlier hand-gesture:
two inches. Kurt laughs.

                         KURT
          Your choice... or his?

                         NANCY
          Yours.
                      (off his REACTION)
          When I was ten years old you told me
          to save myself for you. As an
          obedient English child, I did as I
          was told.

She says this with humor but she means it, and Kurt knows it.
Nevertheless, he laughs as though it were a joke.

                         KURT
          Good. Good.

                         NANCY
          Do not laugh.

He stops laughing at once. She sustains her glare for a
conspicuously sexual moment, then turns and exits.

                                        CUT TO:

EXT. AIRFIELD - DAY

Kurt stands at the side of the field, watching as the rickety
bi-plane sputters along the field.

Nancy, in the cockpit, concentrates on her first solo flight.
She waves at Kurt as she passes him, then looks straight
ahead, grim, focused, excited. She taxis, increases speed.
In the moment of expectation before she takes off, she draws
in her breath; she holds it until the wheels leave the ground,
then lets it out slowly through pursed lips with a small,
delighted sound -- more than a sigh but less than a laugh --
that expresses her exhilaration as she flies.

The airplane lifts, turns, rises...

                                                    CUT TO:

INT. LIBRARY - WICKSTONE - DAY

Herbert reads in the library -- a bit musty, stuffy. The Earl
enters, brandishing a letter, crosses to the escritoire,
searches through drawers.

                    THE EARL
              From Hilda. Your sister has
              apparently lost her mind!

                    HERBERT
              Going up in aeroplanes?

                    THE EARL
              Driving the damned-fool things. Where
              are the bloody telegraph blanks?

                    HERBERT
              I can't imagine Hilda's permitting it.

                    THE EARL
              Hilda can't imagine that I allow it!
              I do not allow it!
                    (finds the blanks;
                     writes)
              I forbid... No...

He crumples the page, tears another, starts over.

                                                    CUT TO:

EXT. CLOSE ON NANCY IN THE COCKPIT - DAY

She reads...

                    THE EARL (V.O.)
              I categorically forbid you from going
              up in aeroplanes.

                                              (CONTINUED)

CONTINUED:

She crumples the telegram, shoves it into her breast pocket,
lowers her goggles, and turns her attention to the plane she's
about to pilot.

WIDER - TEMPELHOF AIRPORT - DAY

A major facility -- large hangars, paved runways, various
airplanes, including some large trimotors, on the ground.

Kurt watches Nancy. She has clearly graduated from the little
crate plane and the grass airfield. The plane is a powerful
Henschel.

Behind Kurt, in the background, a heavyset man climbs down
from one of the trimotors. HERMANN GÖRING -- not yet the
bloated, ostentatious pervert he will later become-- is still
just an amiable, kinky guy in civilian clothes. His suit
looks expensive but he's gaining weight faster than his tailor
can keep up.

Concluding his inspection, Göring notices Kurt watching
Nancy's takeoff. Göring looks too, SEES the Henschel rising,
clearing the trees beyond the runway, turning back to land --
clearly the maneuver of a student.

Göring hands his checklist to an AIDE, crosses to Kurt.

                    GÖRING
                  (German)
          A student pilot, Bachfurt? In the
          Henschel?

                    KURT
                  (German)
          A special student, Herr Abgeordneter.

Göring watches skeptically as the big plane descends, touches
down, taxis to the ramp, stops.

                    GÖRING
                  (German)
          Capable... very good.

Nancy cuts the engine, climbs down, approaches.

                    GÖRING
                  (continuing; German)
          I showed your designs to Milch. He
          was impressed.

Only when Nancy pulls off her leather flying helmet and
releases her hair does Göring realize that the "special
student" is a woman.

                                        (CONTINUED)

CONTINUED:

>   KURT
>   (German)
>   Herr Abgeordneter, allow me to present
>   my cousin.

>   GÖRING
>   (German)
>   A distant cousin, I hope.

>   KURT
>   (German)
>   Lady Nancy Brookeford. Herr Hermann
>   Göring, president of the Reichstag.

>   NANCY
>   (German)
>   Herr Göring. Yes, quite distant.
>   Our grandfathers were second cousins.

>   GÖRING
>   (German)
>   Fraulein Brookeford...

The name rings a bell: he mulls over...

>   GÖRING
>   (continuing; English)
>   Lady Brookeford. Of course. The
>   fiancé of the Prince of Wales.

>   NANCY
>   We were never engaged. We were
>   friends -- are friends.

>   GÖRING
>   I see.
>   (evaluating her)
>   I am hosting a small party this
>   evening. I should be grateful if you
>   would honor me with your presence.
>   (to Kurt)
>   You will escort Lady Nancy, won't
>   you, Bachfurt?

>   KURT
>   I believe we have an appointment.

>   GÖRING
>   See what you can do. Milch will be
>   there. He wants to discuss your
>   designs.
>   (taking Nancy's hand)
>   Tonight, then.

He bows again, leaves.

                                          (CONTINUED)

CONTINUED: (2)

>   NANCY
>   The dashing Hermann Göring.
>
>   KURT
>   Hero of the Reich. The last
>   commander of Richthofen's Flying
>   Circus.
>
>   NANCY
>   He is turning to fat.
>   (takes his arm)
>   We must dress. I'm terribly excited.
>
>   KURT
>   Your father would have my neck if I
>   took you to Göring's house. Göring
>   is a hedonist.
>
>   NANCY
>   A moment ago he was hero.
>
>   KURT
>   Heroism and hedonism are not mutually
>   exclusive.
>
>   NANCY
>   In any case my father knows nothing
>   of what goes on here in Germany.

Still walking, Nancy removes the telegram from her pocket and
drops it in a waste basket.

>   CUT TO:

INT. RESIDENCE OF THE REICHSTAG PRESIDENT - NIGHT

Large rooms, lit by candles, gracefully furnished in Louis XV.
A small crowd in white tie, a few in field-gray uniforms with
medals. The women are more likely to be mistresses than wives.

Nancy and Kurt hesitate at the door, taking in the show, as
Göring approaches, greets them. Göring's tailor has kept on
top of the man's formal wardrobe: his clothes fit perfectly.
At his throat he wears the Blue Max -- Pour le Mérite.
Perfunctorily shaking hands with Kurt, he takes Nancy by the
arm and leads her into the crowd.

Left on his own, Kurt crosses to the bar for a drink, finds
himself next to a portly, scholarly looking man named MILCH.

>   MILCH
>   Herr Bachfurt.
>
>   KURT
>   Herr Doctor Milch.

>   (CONTINUED)

CONTINUED:

Kurt is attentive but never loses sight of Nancy.

>   MILCH
>   (German)
>   I have seen your designs. Göring
>   thinks highly of them. So do I.

Göring introduces Nancy to several OFFICERS.

>   MILCH
>   (continuing; German)
>   Versatile. Just what we need to
>   rebuild German aviation. We should
>   make an appointment to discuss them.

Kurt marvels at how Nancy maintains her poise: even surrounded
by debauchery she is an aristocrat.

>   KURT
>   (German)
>   Certainly, Herr Doctor.

A heavily rouged, partly drunken TART staggers over to Milch,
takes his arm, flings it over her shoulders as if it were a
fox stole, kisses him on the neck.

The tart staggers off with Milch in tow. Kurt watches Nancy;
she glances his way. He toasts her, drinks.

>   CUT TO:

INT. PARTY - LATER

The air is heavy with cigar smoke. Hair has mussed, ties have
slipped, buttons have popped, feet are unsteady.

Nancy is surrounded by men. When a hand drapes over her
shoulder, she unceremoniously removes it, excuses herself,
rejoins Kurt.

>   NANCY
>   You told me that decadence was dead
>   in Germany.

>   KURT
>   This is not decadence. This is
>   vulgarity.

>   NANCY
>   You are a snob, Kurt. The only
>   difference between the decadent and
>   the vulgar is class.

>   KURT
>   (not denying it)
>   You're handling this well.

>   (CONTINUED)

CONTINUED:

A MOTION PICTURE SCREEN is lowered into place. Guests look
for seats on chairs, couches, and cushions.

                         NANCY
         Am I?

                         KURT
         You don't seem at all shocked.

                         NANCY
         I'm no longer a child. I don't
         readily shock.
                  (in immediate
                   contradiction)
         Oh, Good Lord!

Kurt turns to SEE...

TWO SERVING WOMEN enter carrying trays of fruits and pastries
to the seated guests. They are not only almost naked; their
parts are outlined by many straps.

For a brief moment Nancy gapes open-mouthed and breathless,
like a pubescent girl. Kurt's laugh brings her back, though,
and she recovers her cool reserve.

A SERVANT -- less revealingly clothed -- slides a love seat
into place for them. As they sit...

                         NANCY
                  (continuing)
         Are you a Nazi, Kurt?

                         KURT
                  (how ridiculous)
         I must earn a living. The Nazis are
         on the rise, and committed to
         rebuilding German aviation. Since
         designing aeroplanes is my career,
         their goals coincide with mine.

During Kurt's reply, the lights dim, the projector whirs, the
movie starts. It is silent, black and white, old-style hard-
core, pornography.

                         NANCY
         Good heavens!

Again, a temporary loss of cool; whatever Nancy SEES on screen
shocks her for a moment.

                         NANCY
                  (continuing)
         I had no idea... Do people really...

But then suddenly the film stops, the lights come up, and
there is a great COMMOTION... a BUZZ.

                                        (CONTINUED)

CONTINUED: (2)

Göring extricates his hand from the open neckline of his
bleary-eyed partner's gown, gets to his feet, gives orders to
servants and guests.

                    NANCY
                 (continuing)
            What's happening?

A SERIES OF SHOTS...

Cigars and cigarettes are crushed out.

Drinks are quickly finished, the empty glasses quickly
collected.

Windows are thrown open.

The two near-naked servant girls are hustled from the room.

Göring indicates a few of the farther-gone women guests, the
drunkest and most undressed -- they're hustled out, too.

A couple of military officers watch with contempt.

The windows are closed.

The room is now smokeless, sexless, and immaculate for the
arrival of...

ADOLF HITLER

Dressed in a blue suit and flanked by a PAIR OF BODYGUARDS, he
enters with the restless air of a man paying a duty call to an
affair where he feels out of place.

People rush to greet him, deferential. He is perfunctorily
cordial, anxious to get away as soon as he can -- until he
SEES Nancy, clearly the class act of the room.

Göring takes Nancy's arm, leads her to Hitler.

                    GÖRING
                 (German)
            Mein Führer, allow me the honor of
            presenting Lady Nancy Brookeford,
            daughter of the Earl of Edham.

That Nancy is titled English aristocracy impresses Hitler, an
Anglophile, but it also intimidates him a little: never a
social butterfly, he becomes even stiffer and more formal.

                    HITLER
                 (German)
            An honor and pleasure, Lady Nancy.
            Is this your first visit to Germany?

                                          (CONTINUED)

CONTINUED:

Hitler looks to Göring to translate, but Nancy replies in
German, which obviously pleases the Führer.

> NANCY
> (German)
> I visit this country often, Herr
> Hitler. My family is German. The
> Brookefords are the Bachfurts who
> went to England with George II.

> HITLER
> (German)
> Ah. In that case you understand that
> Germany and England are the most
> natural allies in the world.

> GÖRING
> (German)
> Lady Nancy is a pilot, Mein Führer.

Hitler REACTS: incredulous, perhaps a bit disapproving.
Göring catches this.

> GÖRING
> (continuing; German)
> One of many women throughout the
> world making names for themselves in
> aviation.

> NANCY
> (German)
> I am merely a student.

> GÖRING
> (German)
> Nonsense. I have seen you fly.

Hitler doesn't like the notion of women pilots, but he does
like Nancy, so he decides to ignore the subject.

> HITLER
> (German)
> I am pleased you are in Germany now,
> Lady Nancy. An historic moment is
> upon us. I am happy that a young
> woman of the highest social order in
> England should be here to witness it.

He kisses her hand. Hitler's solemn formality is almost
funny. If she looks at Kurt she'll laugh, so she simply
smiles dumbly back at the Führer.

                                                  CUT TO:

EXT. GERMAN COUNTRYSIDE - NIGHT

Kurt and Nancy head home in Kurt's Mercedes roadster, top
down. Kurt drives fast; Nancy, her head back on the seat,
enjoys the wind in her hair.

                    KURT
          Obviously they didn't think he'd
          come -- he's such a prig.

                    NANCY
          Not what I expected. Clumsier, I
          think.

                    KURT
          But you've made another conquest --
          that was clear.

                    NANCY
          After the Prince, a trifle.

Kurt turns into the tree-lined road to his house.

EXT. BACHFURT HOME - NIGHT

The car drives up, stops. Kurt and Nancy get out, head for the
house.

                    NANCY
          Kurt? Why do you think Göring
          invited me to the party tonight?

                    KURT
          He liked you.

                    NANCY
          It was a peculiar party.

                    KURT
          Perhaps Göring thought he gleaned a
          depraved side to your nature.

She doesn't smile, thinks about it at the front door.

                    KURT
             (continuing)
          Does that offend you?

                    NANCY
          Not at all. There _is_ a depraved side
          to my nature.

She looks squarely, almost challengingly at him. As ever,
whenever she alludes to her sexuality, or to the sexual
potential of their relationship, he cuts her short.

                                    (CONTINUED)

CONTINUED:

> KURT
> (as he opens the door)
> As befits a national treasure.

Like a little girl she stamps a foot -- hating his wit. He
pretends not to notice and they enter.

                                                    CUT TO:

EXT. TEMPELHOF AIRPORT - DAY

Göring, puffing, crosses to Nancy's Henschel. Nancy is
explaining an operating glitch to a MECHANIC.

> GÖRING
> Lady Nancy...

> NANCY
> Herr Göring.

> GÖRING
> Hermann, please. I have something to
> show you.

She climbs down. He takes her arm, folds it under his and
leads her away.

> GÖRING
> (continuing)
> Where is your cousin today?

> NANCY
> Working, I'm afraid.

> GÖRING
> Good. You are an attractive
> diversion but Germany needs Von
> Bachfurt's talents. And yours.

> NANCY
> Oh?

They enter...

INT. HANGAR - DAY

A number of new prototype airplanes being worked on. Nancy
looks at them all with admiration, but Göring takes hold of
her shoulders, points her toward an ungainly but impressively
large aircraft, a Junkers Ju52, painted Lufthansa blue.

> GÖRING
> How would you like to pilot this
> aeroplane?

                                                    (CONTINUED)

CONTINUED:

                              NANCY
                    It is much larger than any I have
                    flown.

He squeezes her shoulders for emphasis...

                              GÖRING
                    But no more difficult to operate.

                              NANCY
                    Why would I want to?

He lifts her chin, turning her face to his.

                              GÖRING
                    Because you love to fly.

He puts his arm around her, lets his fingertips drop to her
breast. Nancy removes his hand with a sidewise glance that
says Are you crazy?

                              NANCY
                    You of all people should know that
                    one who loves to fly loves to fly the
                    fast and maneuverable, not the big
                    and fat.

                              GÖRING
                         (gets it; smiles anyway)
                    To the point, then. Germany wishes
                    an aircraft industry second to none
                    in Europe. But we need help from
                    private sources. In England and
                    America, the public's attention has
                    been drawn to flight by heroic women.

                              NANCY
                    Don't equate me with Amelia Earhart
                    or Beryl Markham, Hermann. I am a
                    novice.

                              GÖRING
                    Everyone in aviation is a novice.
                    You are already celebrated -- the
                    English lady who was almost Queen.
                    Your flying our aircraft will
                    generate international excitement.

                              NANCY
                    And investment.

He nods: yes. She walks around the huge craft, studying it.

                              GÖRING
                    Lufthansa is about to establish a
                    daily Berlin-London flight.
                         (more)

                                              (CONTINUED)

CONTINUED: (2)

>   GÖRING (cont'd)
>   We would like you to pilot a
>   demonstration flight.
>
>   NANCY
>   I couldn't.
>
>   GÖRING
>   We will train you and see to it that
>   you have the support you need.
>
>   NANCY
>   What of your leader? Doesn't Herr
>   Hitler disapprove of women piloting
>   aeroplanes?
>
>   GÖRING
>   German women, yes. He will endorse
>   this idea as soon as he thinks of it.

She is tempted.

>   CUT TO:

INT. A FLAT - DAY

Sparsely but cheerfully furnished, and very sunny. Nancy and
Kurt enter. She is excited.

>   NANCY
>   Well? Just the thing for a newly
>   disinherited English lady, don't you
>   think?
>
>   KURT
>   Perfect! But how will you support
>   yourself?
>
>   NANCY
>   My mother left me a small income.
>   Lufthansa will pay me something. And
>   of course I can always get funds from
>   Göring.
>
>   KURT
>   How?

Nancy raises an eyebrow. Kurt knows it's not entirely a joke
but he laughs anyway.

>   KURT
>   (continuing)
>   It is a wonderful flat, Nancy. But
>   if we are to help celebrate your
>   triumph, I must let you dress.

>   (CONTINUED)

CONTINUED:

He starts to give her an avuncular kiss on the cheek.   She
steps back, so frustrated that she stamps her foot on the
floor like a spoiled child.

                         NANCY
            No!

And she stamps again, harder, for emphasis.   A beat, then
someone downstairs responds -- hits the ceiling with a stick.

                         NANCY
                     (continuing)
            Oh, God.   Germans!

Nancy and Kurt both laugh.   But in mid-laugh she kisses his
mouth -- hard.

                         KURT
            Nancy!

                         NANCY
            What do I have to do?   Climb into one
            of your portfolios of decadent art
            and leap out at you naked?

                         KURT
            You mustn't...

                         NANCY
            Do not tell me what I must or mustn't
            do.   I fly your aeroplanes.   I defy
            my father to stay with you.   I charm
            your Nazis.   I throw myself at you
            and you laugh!

                         KURT
            Europe is coming apart...

                         NANCY
            Europe has nothing to do with us.

                         KURT
            It has everything to do with us.
            When it ruptures, <u>we</u> will rupture!

The clock begins its on-the-hour routine.

                         NANCY
            Rubbish.   I love you.   Do you love me?

Unconsciously, Kurt straightens up, like a soldier.   But the
gesture is so defensive that it is more eloquent than a "yes."
She moves to him, not-quite against him -- their bodies all
but touching.

                                        (CONTINUED)

CONTINUED: (2)

>   NANCY
>   (continuing)
>   I want you. Do you <u>want</u> me?

He doesn't answer the question he doesn't have to. She can feel his desire as she presses her body against his. The suggestion of a smile crosses her face.

>   NANCY
>   (continuing)
>   Obviously, you do.

After six rings the clock stops chiming.

>   KURT
>   We can't be late. I'll be back in
>   thirty minutes.

He exits.

>   NANCY
>   Bloody rubbish.

She stamps her foot. Her neighbor hits the ceiling. She stamps again. Bang! Stamp! Stamp! Stamp!

>   CUT TO:

INT. CHANCELLERY - NIGHT

The party anticipated in the prologue, celebrating the launching of Lufthansa's first flight. It is somewhat earlier in the evening: guests are still mingling. A string orchestra plays light German MUSIC.

Hitler, with Nancy on his arm, performs his hostly duties, such as instructing servants to replenish champagne, even though he himself sips only ice water. Göring accompanies the Führer and Nancy as they mingle.

Hitler's attitude toward Nancy is more than friendly; it is intimate, at least to the degree he is capable of intimacy. He puts his arm around her, talks quietly to her, excluding others -- except for Göring, who remains close, refusing to be excluded.

Kurt is with them, too, a step or two to the side, speaking to Milch, who is very excited.

>   MILCH
>   (German)
>   It is no reflection on your ability,
>   you understand.

>   (CONTINUED)

CONTINUED:

                    KURT
                (German)
          Of course.

                    MILCH
                (German)
          But if you are her copilot it will be
          assumed you are flying the craft.

                    KURT
                (German)
          I will be her navigator. For that
          matter I would be her lapdog.

Hitler returns Nancy. Milch takes her hand. During this
conversation the orchestra stops playing, and the guests take
their seats.

                    MILCH
                (German)
          I am honored that we will be working
          together, Lady Nancy.

                    HITLER
                (German)
          Let us show the world that even a
          fragile [*zerbrechlich*] English lady
          can fly one of our fine new
          aeroplanes.

The lights dim, sending stragglers to their tables, some
stopping to pay respects to the Führer.

                    NANCY
                (whispers to Göring)
          What is "*zerbrechlich*"?

                    GÖRING
          "Fragile."

She smiles at Hitler.

                    HITLER
                (German)
          We will arrange everything. Won't
          we, Milch? Recruit her cousin to
          help. Von Bachfurt. I understand
          he's very good. Arrange it all!

The Führer kisses Nancy's hand and gives her to Göring to
escort back to her table.

Protected by the darkened room, Göring characteristically
guides Nancy's hand someplace she'd rather not have it. As
she removes it...

                                        (CONTINUED)

CONTINUED: (2)

> NANCY
> Please, Hermann. My *Zerbrechlichkeit*.

At this moment Kurt waylays them, takes Nancy to the table.

> KURT
> He is nothing if not persistent.

> NANCY
> At least <u>he</u> is interested.

Behind the orchestra the Union Jacks and Lufthansa flag are lowered into place flanking the swastika.

> NANCY
> (continuing)
> I may go to bed with him.

> KURT
> Göring?

The spotlight shines on the three flags. APPLAUSE.

> NANCY
> Or Hitler. They all want me.

The Conductor gets his signal from Hitler, conducts Holst's ST. PAUL'S SUITE. Nancy recognizes the MUSIC, nods at Hitler.

> NANCY
> (continuing)
> I am about to become a celebrated aviatrix. I do not think virgins are admitted to that exclusive club. And as you will not accommodate me...

> KURT
> There are other choices. You need accept neither the demon nor Faust.

He looks very serious indeed. She looks at him, trying to figure him out.

> CUT TO:

EXT. TEMPELHOF - A JU-52 TRIMOTOR TRANSPORT - DAY

The music continues through as the heavy trimotor, painted Lufthansa blue, takes off on a late-spring day.

INT. COCKPIT

Nancy at the controls, next to a burly COPILOT. She wears flying clothes -- khaki jacket, breeches, boots, but not the leather helmet in this enclosed cockpit.

> (CONTINUED)

Appendix B: Additional Strip Creation for the Board

The following is what a strip looks likes. You may have to redo strips two or three times until you get comfortable doing them. Eventually it will become second nature. The important thing to remember is that the process serves your collective knowledge of the script. It becomes possible, depending on how focused you are, that you can see the scene in your mind's eye simply by looking at the finished strip. Let's continue:

Scene two: Ext. Three Mallards in Flight — D 1

A yellow strip. The numeral "2" in the first box at the top. "D1" in the next. "Loc" for location in the third. "Mos." in the box adjacent to "sound/no sound" and "⅛" next to the box marked "Page count."

Just below the last upper box, in the open area, write the number "2." Turn the strip sideways and write: "Ext. Wickstone Estate."

Place the yellow strip alongside the header board again and go down to the box adjacent to the word "animals." Run a diagonal pencil line up the strip box and write "3 Mallards" along the line.

Turn the strip sideways again and write: "Mallards in flight." Voila! Strip two.

Next: "Ext. Wickstone Estate (1932) — Day 1"

The very first line of description tells us that this is the estate of the Earl of Edham. Since we have supposedly already reduced this scene to its elements, I won't repeat them here.

Place the yellow strip (day exterior) alongside the header board. "3" in the top box. "D 1" in the second. "Loc" in the third. "Snd" in the fourth. "1 ⅝" in the fifth. In the space below the last box write the scene number, which is "3." Turn strip sideways. In open space write: "Ext. Wickstone Estate "

Reposition strip alongside header board. Write the appropriate number

228

alongside each of the characters identified in the scene description — Winston Churchill, Sir Henry Brookeford, the Earl of Edham. Drop down to the box for "animals" and draw a diagonal line. On it write "Irish Setter or Dog."

Alongside the box for "Special Effects" write "guns." Turn strip sideways. Write "Prince of Wales won't marry Nancy."

Now Scene 4 from the script:

EXT. WICKSTONE — THE HOUSE — DAY 1

Tea time.

Present are Lady Violet, Nathan, Lady Random, Lady Churchill and Nancy, age 20.

The Earl, Herbert, Winston and the dog approach. Somewhere in the scene reference is made to a "clotted scone" and "Winston's cigar."

A note here: Mentioning that the character of Nancy is twenty years old is only significant if, at a later date, it is determined that we cast an older actress when Nancy ages in the script. The chances are we would have found a twenty-four, twenty-five, twenty-six-year-old actress who could play Nancy both younger and older. However, I made the distinction on the odd chance that this might change.

Place strip alongside header board. "4" in top box. "D1" in second box. "LOC" in three. "SND" in four. "1⅛" in five. "4" adjacent to "Scene No." Turn strip sideways.

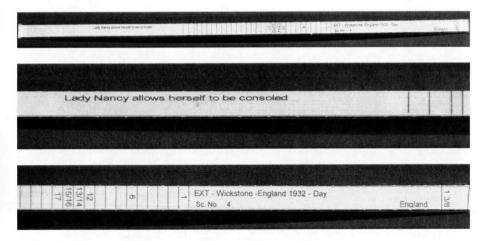

Top: A yellow strip properly labeled for insertion into our Production Board. *Middle:* Close-up showing the bottom portion of the strip depicting an abbreviated description of the scene. *Bottom:* Detail image of the top portion of the strip describing the location, the scene number and the character numbers.

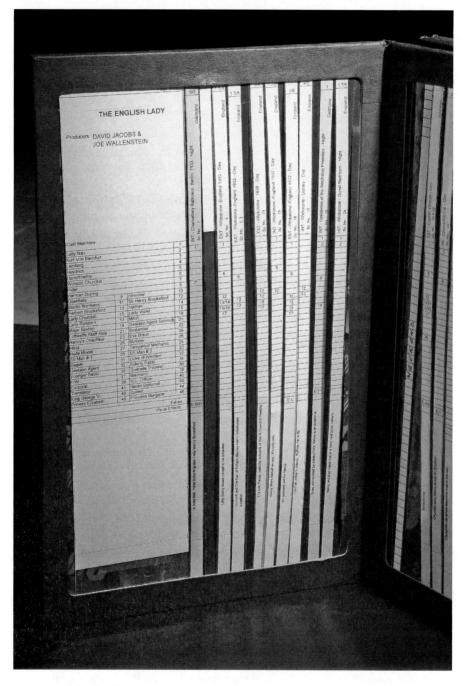

A first assembly of the created stripes on our Production Board.

Place the appropriate cast numbers in the appropriate boxes. Make note of the Irish setter and the guns that would have accompanied our hunters from the previous scene. Turn strip sideways again. Write "Earl forbids Nancy to fly."

The gist of this scene is that everyone assumes that Lady Nan is heartbroken that the Prince of Wales has broken off their wedding engagement. In fact, she is greatly relieved, in spite of the fact that their union would have placed her in line to be Queen of England. Only Winston Churchill catches the twinkle in her eye as she feigns disappointment.

The scene ends with the suggestion she visit her distant cousin Kurt Von Bachfurt in Germany. However, her father absolutely forbids her to take any more flying lessons. It was my choice to summarize the scene with this piece of information because it was a direct transition into the next scene. You could just as correctly have written "Nancy fakes disappointment." Your choice. No right or wrong, only what conveys the most information in the most concise manner.

So there it is. You get it. Keep making strips until you have reached the welcome words "The End. Fade out."

Insert the header board into the production board. Arrange the strips according to the numbers on the very top of the cardboard strip from one to whatever your last number. Step back. Take a good look. You are about to begin the process of scheduling.

Appendix C: Quotes from Chairman Joe

Accuracy is your goal, not expedience.

Accuracy over convenience.

Actors are the leads in the Iditarod that is your film.

The Army runs on its stomach.

The audience will never know what they might have seen, they only know what you show them.

Bad philosophy: Any money for cast, no money for crew.

Bad surprises happen in production, good surprises happen in post production.

Break it and you can fix it, disrespect it and it's gone.

The budget is a living, breathing document, that does not meet its final resting place until just before the "green light."

Fast is not our goal, our goal is accuracy.

A happy crew equals a well-mounted film.

If you only know a little about post production, you don't know it at all.

If your budget is accurate and your film is accomplished on schedule, it is difficult (though not impossible) to be over-budget.

It is easier to shoot than to prep, and prep is everything.

The less they know, the surer of it they are.

Let easy be easy.

Never short-circuit the director's prerogative.

No one ever comes out of the theater humming the dolly shots.

Nothing dies for film.

Perception is reality.

Progress is made in inches not miles.

Safety trumps freedom of expression.

Silence speaks volumes.

Talent is not necessarily a predictor of temperament.

They are not wrong; they are doing their jobs, and you would do well to accommodate them.

You can't ask too many questions, you can only ask too few.

You must control your location and to control it you must own it.

You work just as hard on the films no one has heard of as you do on the hits.

Your budget will go up before it goes down.

Index

DATE DUE

GAYLORD   PRINTED IN U.S.A.